GC REMEMBERS ME

Devotions for Facing
Alzheimer's Disease with Faith

BY PAUL M. HORNBACK

Published by Starry Night Publishing.com
Rochester, New York

Second edition

Copyright 2015 Paul M. Hornback

Paul M. Hornback

DEDICATION

To Sarah,
My devoted wife and best friend for over 38 years. You bring
joy to my life and inspiration for everything I do.

Paul M. Hornback

CONTENTS

INTRODUCTION

This 52 week collection of daily devotions was written for all of God's children who are struggling with the daily demands brought on by Alzheimer's disease. The book is organized in weekly topics to help the Alzheimer's patient deal with their struggles, heartaches, joys, and especially their faith. This collection is an encouraging and uplifting look at how you can deal with a diagnosis of Alzheimer's and continue to live a rich life with faith.

I was diagnosed with early-onset Alzheimer's disease at the youthful age of 55. It happened right in the middle of the most productive years of my life and at the height of my career as a civilian engineer and research analyst for the United States Army. Although the diagnosis was devastating, God still remembered me and provided peace beyond all understanding as I continued life under the His wonderful wings of amazing grace. Soon after my diagnosis, the dream of writing a series of daily devotions for people struggling with Alzheimer's disease began to take hold. In fact, it became a passion! Each day brought a deep desire to write something whether it was just one word, some Scripture, or only random thoughts. This dream took over three years to complete and so much has happened in those precious years. After reviewing my collection of devotions, I have to thank the Lord and the Holy Spirit for helping me write because I simply do not remember writing most of them.

It is my utmost prayer you will be blessed as you read from this collection every day. The Scripture is included with each devotion to make it easier for someone with Alzheimer's disease. All Scripture is quoted from the New International Version Bible ® as it has been my source of reading and memorization for the past twenty years. May God's perfect peace unfold in your life as you read daily from this collection of devotions.

Paul M. Hornback
September 2015

Paul M. Hornback

FOREWORD

More than 5 million Americans are living or have been diagnosed with dementia or Alzheimer's disease. This book offers hope and encouragement as only one who is going through a similar diagnosis can provide. With humor, hope, and unwavering faith, this series of devotions will help both patients and caregivers deepen their faith even though they face an uncertain future.

As Paul's wife, I have shed countless tears and have faced many "Why us?" questions. Through pain and heartbreak, I have questioned God's love as the dearest, most faithful, smartest man I know began to lose his ability to think clearly and remember simple tasks. Paul's faith, however, is unwavering and has been an inspiration to me, to our children, and to our church family. While it may seem overly optimistic and unrealistic to some, I believe his strong statements of faith and contentment with his 'new normal' are real because I see and experience his genuine faith and love for God each and every day, no matter what challenges come our way. He is truly a man after God's own heart and a blessing to everyone he meets. This book can bless you as well. Embrace the 'new normal' in your life and allow your faith to stand firm!

Sarah Hornback
Author's Wife

Paul M. Hornback

Rustyphil © 123RF.com

THE JOURNEY BEGINS

Devotions to help you recognize God's never ending presence in your life as your new journey with Alzheimer's disease unfolds.

Monday: A Journey of Faith

By faith, Abraham when called to go to a place he would later receive as an inheritance, obeyed and went even though he did not know where he was going. Hebrews 11:8

Every journey begins with the seemingly simple decision to start the trip. In most cases we choose the journey and select the path. However, sometimes the journey and the path are selected for us.

Alzheimer's is a journey no one chooses to take on their own. Nonetheless, it is a journey like Abraham's since you have no earthly idea where you are going, what specifically lies ahead, or how long it will last. One thing we do know is God is there and He prepares a perfect path for each of us. All you need do is be obedient, fully trust in His perfect guidance, and relinquish control to Him. Ultimately, God is in control and will lead you through the least difficult path if you let Him.

This is perhaps the hardest part of the journey, letting go and allowing God to have complete control of your situation. Trusting in God is the critical first step. You either go with God, trusting in Him, or you go it alone, ignoring Him.

I choose to walk this journey with Him knowing His guidance will put me on the perfect path. There is no place I'd rather be than right alongside Him as I begin my journey!

Prayer: Father God, we did not choose this journey but we know it is the path laid out before us. We humbly ask for Your guidance, Your comfort, and Your peaceful presence as we fully trust in You! Be with us, calm our fears, and prepare our hearts as we walk through the Alzheimer's valley. Prepare the way for each of us so our journey is not so difficult on those we love so dearly. Amen

Tuesday: A Journey with God

No one will be able to stand up against you all the days of your life. As I was with Moses; so I will be with you; I will never leave you nor forsake you. Joshua 1:5

Joshua faced the difficult task of leading the people of Israel into the Promised Land following the death of their dynamic leader, Moses. Joshua needed reassurance of God's presence so he could be strong and courageous as he crossed the Jordan into the new Promised Land.

When Alzheimer's strikes our lives we also need reassurance God is with us, He hasn't forsaken us, and we can depend on Him when our world begins to change dramatically. Now rest assured He will not leave you and all His promises still hold true no matter what is happening in your life. Just as He was with Moses and Joshua, He remains at your side walking with you through your challenging days.

Each morning I ask His guidance for the day and assurance He will remain by my side. His response comes in so many different ways. Sometimes it is in a spectacular sunrise, a gentle rhythmic rain, a quiet moment of prayer, or a walk outdoors where the majestic beauty of His creation reminds me He is still in complete control. If He can maintain His glorious creation then He can certainly stand by your side and guide you through the difficult days ahead. Therefore, we need not fear anything! Be strong and courageous for God is with you and He will *never* forsake you!

Prayer: Father God, our prayer today is that You will reassure each of us of Your everlasting presence in our lives. Thanks for standing alongside us as we face each new day. Allow each of us to see Your presence in our lives, to take in the majesty of Your creation, and to gain strength for this day's journey. Amen

Wednesday: A Journey of Trust

Trust in the lord with all your heart and lean not on your own understanding. In all your ways acknowledge him and he will set your paths straight. Proverbs 3:5

Trust is a seemingly simple concept when things are going well in your life. In fact, it is pretty easy to trust in God when you really don't need Him to do anything but keep the world turning, the sun rising and setting, and the natural order of things in check.

Our journey through life is amazingly easy. We often think we understand everything, our paths are fairly straight, and leaning on God is taken pretty lightly. Then along comes Alzheimer's and we don't understand what is happening. Now trusting in the Lord isn't just a concept, it is a necessity. Our journey through life has taken a different, unfamiliar path, one filled with uncertainty.

Solomon instructs us not to lean on our own understanding but to trust God and to acknowledge Him in all our ways. Is it possible to acknowledge God in our present state? Absolutely! By acknowledging Him in all our ways and trusting in Him, He has promised to make our paths straight.

I am looking for a straight path through the Alzheimer's valley. It is a journey where I don't want to wander off His perfect path. The valley isn't familiar so I choose to trust, follow, and acknowledge Him throughout my journey.

Prayer: Father God, we don't understand what has happened in our lives or even why it happened. We acknowledge Your presence and we trust in You with our whole heart. Stay with us, guide us, and prepare a straight path for us aligning with Your perfect will for our new journey. Amen

Thursday: A Journey of Hope

For I know the plans I have for you declares the Lord, plans to prosper you and not to harm you, plans to give you hope and a future. Jeremiah 29:11

Hope is a wonderful blessing to have in times of deep despair. It was no different for the children of Israel during their exile from Jerusalem to Babylon at the hand of Nebuchadnezzar. The Lord, through Jeremiah, wrote these words in a letter to the surviving elders, priests, and others who had been carried into exile. These words of hope must have lifted their spirits knowing the Lord God had not forgotten His plans for them.

Similarly, for those of us who have been carried into exile at the hand of Alzheimer's, these words of hope hold true; God's plan for our lives has not been forsaken. This may be a difficult concept to grasp but I have no doubt in God's perfect plan for my life. He remains in complete control, preparing the perfect path, and formulating my future.

I hold firm to His promise the future will be filled with hope and prosperity in ways I have yet to fully understand. All I need do is acknowledge Him and give up complete control of my life. God's hope for your future is a promise even Alzheimer's disease cannot crush!

Prayer: Lord God, you have promised to give us hope and a future and we stand on Your word believing this is true. May Your perfect plan for our lives continue forward even though Alzheimer's attempts to thwart Your precious plan. We trust in You and know our hope comes from You alone. Amen

Friday: A Journey of Peace

And the peace of God which transcends all understanding will guard your hearts and minds in Christ Jesus. Philippians 4:7

The Apostle Paul traveled on numerous missionary journeys during his lifetime. These journeys helped establish the early church. Through his numerous letters to new churches he helped establish, much of the New Testament was penned.

One of Paul's most beloved churches was the church in Philippi. This church held a special place in his heart due to their generosity and love. Paul faced unbelievable hardships during his missionary journeys but throughout his ordeal he carried a peace that transcended all human understanding.

So it is with your unique Alzheimer's journey. You will certainly face situations and hardships you may not have been expecting but don't give up! God will provide a peace that transcends all understanding if you will only ask for it.

Paul's letter to the church in Philippi was written to encourage the Philippians in the face of persecution and difficult circumstances. The key part of today's passage promises God's peace will guard your hearts and minds in Christ Jesus. There is nothing more critical in the midst of Alzheimer's than to have your heart and mind under the protection and peace of Jesus Christ. This is one promise I deeply cherish and thank God for daily!

Prayer: Father God, may the peace that transcends all understanding flow through our lives today in a way that calms our fears and warms our spirit. May Your perfect peace provide protection to our minds and hearts so we might better serve You today. Amen

Saturday: A Guide for the Journey

Who went ahead of you on your journey, in fire by night and in a cloud by day, to search out places for you to camp and to show you the way you should go? Deuteronomy 1:33

The children of Israel were unfamiliar with the desert landscape making navigation difficult if not impossible. If you have ever been in the desert you understand landmarks shift with the blowing sand. As such, finding your way is difficult and unnerving. To provide the Israelites peace, as well as a sense of order while traveling, the Lord Jehovah guided them with a cloud of dust by day and a burning fire by night.

Imagine how difficult it would have been to navigate through the desert without the benefit of God's gracious guide. God went ahead, prepared the way, and provided a physical means to mark the path and a vivid reminder of His presence.

Just like the children of Israel, you can easily get lost in the desert of Alzheimer's without a guide. God goes ahead of you, preparing the way and marking the path. Through His holy word He provides the physical presence you need for each day. When I'm not certain what to do, I seek His word and meditate on it knowing His path will be made clear to me.

Although no cloud by day or fire by night marks the perfect path for me to follow; it is the calming presence of the Holy Spirit and comforting words of the Psalms that give me strength. These are a constant reminder God is ahead of me making my path straight. I'd have it no other way because there is no other way better than His!

Prayer: Lord Jehovah, go before us and prepare the way through our personal deserts. Your way is the only perfect way through the unknown Alzheimer's valley. Help us focus on You so Your perfect path will be made as clear as the cloud by day and the fire by night. Amen

Paul M. Hornback

Sunday: Stillness for the Journey

Be still, and know that I am God; I will be exalted among the nations, I will be exalted in the earth. The Lord Almighty is with us; the God of Jacob is our fortress. Psalms 46:10–11

Have you ever walked outside in the early morning long before the cars start their daily commute, before kids go out to meet the bus or walk to school, or even before the neighbors go out to walk their dogs? Do you remember how quiet it can be at dawn? It is so quiet the sounds normally covered by the hectic pace of life now echo clearly.

If you are still, all sorts of sounds start to surface. Birds announce the morning, crickets call out a greeting, the gentle rustling of leaves fill the air, and if you're lucky, the flutter of a hummingbird's wings softly whisper in your ear. Being still before the Lord provides a similar solitude. I especially love this time in the morning because it provides me proof He is with me and deserves my praise.

This week we focused fully on the new journey we face. Today the focus is on the freshness of being still. It is in the stillness you find God. In the stillness you begin to feel His presence. In the stillness you can praise and exalt Him.

I have found one good thing about living with Alzheimer's disease. I can now more easily be still. No more rushing about to accomplish seemingly important tasks that will be forgotten tomorrow. Now I focus on being still, knowing God, and praising Him. What a blessing it is in the midst of turmoil.

Prayer: Lord Almighty, help us to be still today and know You are God. Let us exalt and praise You with all our heart, mind, and spirit. Amen

Michele Cornelius © 123RF.com

WHO YOU ARE IN CHRIST

Devotions to help you understand Christ is your refuge and your identity even after Alzheimer's disease strikes.

Monday: A New Creation

If anyone is in Christ, he is a new creation. The old has gone and the new has come. 2 Corinthians 5:17

Scripture tells you if you belong to Christ and abide in Him, you are a new creation in Christ. As a new creation, the old ways that held you back are gone. These "old ways" include previous sins, baggage you carry from wounds to your heart, negative thinking, gossiping, and a host of other traits trapping you in a life that is un-Christ-like.

The good news is God promised you can exchange the old for the new, much like trading in an old car for a new one. The old car has dints, dirty seats, a dilapidated engine, a dingy interior, and distressed paint. It has seen better days and the world has left unmistakable marks all over it. Contrast the old car with the new. The new car is pristine with smooth exterior lines, soft clean seats, shiny paint, lovely new gadgets, and the new car smell! The world has yet to touch or leave a mark on the vehicle. This is what it means to be new in Christ, untouched by the world and filled with the newness of a fresh start.

So what does this mean when Alzheimer's strikes? You are still a new creation in Christ; that hasn't changed one bit. In fact, I found some of the "important" baggage I was carrying around no longer seems significant. I can leave it behind. The same holds true for "old" wounds to my heart. They are more easily forgotten. God is using Alzheimer's to cleanse me of the old baggage I was unable to release on my own power. I am becoming a new creation in Christ in spite of Alzheimer's!

Prayer: Lord Christ, we want to be new creations in You, willing to give up the past by letting go of old hurts, setting aside old sins, and becoming completely Yours. Help us become new in You today. Amen

Tuesday: Joy of My Salvation

Restore to me the joy of your salvation and grant me a willing spirit to sustain me. Psalm 51:12

Psalm 51 relates the feelings of David after being confronted by Nathan for his adulterous affair with Bathsheba. King David feels separated from God and is unable to cleanse himself. He cries out for mercy and asks for forgiveness so he might have sweet harmony with his Lord once again.

He asks God to restore his joy and grant him a willing spirit to sustain him. King David wants the separation to end, the sin to be cleansed, and to return to a right relationship with God. God has not left David but is waiting for him to confess his sin, crave His presence again, and seek His counsel.

When I was diagnosed with Alzheimer's I understood King David's yearning for God. I prayed to feel His presence again and to regain my joy. Then I reflected on Psalm 51:12; a Scripture memorized many years ago. I kept repeating it in my mind. I used the words of this passage in my daily prayers. Finally, I realized God had not left me alone to deal with Alzheimer's. I had just been focusing on the wrong thing! I was focused on the disease rather than my relationship with Him.

This is what happened to King David, he became focused on Bathsheba rather than his relationship with God. Once his focus shifted from God to Bathsheba, David got in trouble. Therefore, you must remain focused on God, not on the disease. Then the joy of God's salvation will soak into your soul and sustain you for the difficult days ahead!

Prayer: Father God, restore to us the joy of Your salvation and grant us a willing spirit to maintain our right relationship with You. Help us to focus on You rather than our disease. Sustain us with a joyful spirit throughout the days ahead. Amen

Wednesday: A Steadfast Spirit

Create in me a clean heart, O God, and renew a steadfast spirit within me. Psalm 51:10

Today we continue with Psalm 51 to gain more strength for the days ahead. King David not only needed to restore his right relationship with God, cleanse his sins, and gain forgiveness, but he also needed to renew his spirit. King David realized nothing on earth could provide him strength, steadfastness, and solace so he turned to God for restoration.

Alzheimer's takes its toll on each of us. Like King David, perhaps your spirit needs to be restored as well. There will be good days and not so good days. On the not so good days I cry out like King David and ask God "not to cast me from His presence."

Rest assured God has not left you nor forsaken you! All you need do is call on His holy name and your relationship will be restored through a renewed spirit. He remains by your side constantly comforting you through the presence of the Holy Spirit.

One closing thought on today's Psalm centers on the concept of steadfastness. Not only do I require a renewed spirit but also a refreshed spirit that stays with me continually. God has promised each of us a renewed, refreshed, and everlasting spirit. All that is required is to ask Him! God is always with you. Read His word, converse with Him, and reflect on His majesty every day.

Prayer: Heavenly Father, renew our spirits today and give us strength for the days ahead. Fill our minds with encouraging Scripture that refreshes our souls and reminds us of Your everlasting presence in our lives. Amen

Thursday: God Knows Each of Us

For you created my inmost being; you knit me together in my mother's womb. I praise you because I am fearfully and wonderfully made; your works are wonderful, I know that full well.
Psalm 139:13–14

Once again we turn to the Book of Psalms to hear the words of King David. In this passage David relates how God created us and knew us when we were in our mother's womb. He knitted you together and every part of you is known to Him.

As difficult as it is to comprehend, I believe God knew I would succumb to Alzheimer's disease long before my first symptoms arose. I struggled with this revelation for a long time but God has a unique way of helping me understand.

Today I did a funeral for a stillborn child. Let me say I'm not a minister but our church was between ministers and the family needed someone to do the graveside service. I chose Psalm 139 to speak to their hearts. This passage helped them understand God knew their precious son, Brayden, before he was even born. During the service I reminded them Brayden did not have the opportunity to walk on this earth, to learn about Jesus Christ, and to become a man of God. Then it hit me like a proverbial ton of bricks. Although I have Alzheimer's, I have had the opportunity to live a full life, to learn about Jesus Christ, to serve Him, and to truly know Him. I belong to Christ and He is within me. He knew me from the beginning and His works are wonderfully made! I must remember who I am in Christ and praise Him for His wonderful creation. Having Alzheimer's does not change this precious promise one bit!

Prayer: Lord Jesus, help us today to fully comprehend how each of us are wonderfully made. Thank You for knitting us in the womb, knowing us completely, and for never leaving us. Amen

Friday: Believe He Exists

Without faith it is impossible to please God for anyone who comes to Him must believe he exists and that he rewards those who earnestly seek him. Hebrews 11:6

Have you ever thought about what it takes to please God? Will living a good life, being honorable and just, and doing good deeds suffice? Although these are all indications of righteousness, today's passage from Hebrews suggests it is impossible to please God without exhibiting faith.

We live in a world where we believe in many intangible things like electricity, cold air from air conditioning, hot water from a faucet, and television pictures that come to our home via satellite signals. I take for granted when I need any of these items they will always be ready. When they work I am indifferent and don't express gratitude for their working properly. Thankfully, God doesn't work that way! He takes genuine pleasure when we show faith in Him.

But how do we have faith in God? Simple – like today's Scripture says – believe He exists and He rewards those who earnestly seek Him! I believe with all my heart, soul, strength, and mind God exists and I belong to Him. My earthly father used to tell me faith in God is the one thing no one can take away from you. Only you can choose not to believe and thereby give up your faith in God. I believe my faith is a gift from God and defines who I am in Christ. As my mind begins to fade, God will continue to nurture my faith in ways I may not fully comprehend. Even Alzheimer's cannot destroy faith in God because faith comes from the heart and soul, not from the mind!

Prayer: Father God, help us hold onto our faith. May Your gift of faith remain embedded in our mind, heart, and soul. Amen

Saturday: Stronghold of Life

The Lord is my light and my salvation – whom shall I fear? The Lord is the stronghold of my life – of whom shall I be afraid?
Psalm 27:1

When I was growing up, I was afraid of the dark. Perhaps it was because I could not see if anything was lurking in the darkness waiting to leap out and devour me. The simple solution to calm my fears was to shed some light into the room. Consequently, a flashlight became my stronghold at night. Whenever I felt fear begin to take hold of me, all I needed to do was turn on the flashlight.

So it was for King David; the Lord was his light and his stronghold. Whenever he was afraid, he would call on the name of the Lord and his fear would be vanquished. When I was diagnosed with early-onset Alzheimer's, I was afraid of what was in my future. Then I remembered the Lord is my light and salvation and soon my fear was overcome by the Lord of Light. He is my stronghold in all things. I call upon His holy name and the peace of God which transcends all understanding guards my heart and mind in Christ Jesus.

So, when tragedy strikes remember these three simple things:
- Who you are - A child of the Living God
- Who you belong to - Jesus Christ
- Who has your back - the Lord.

Alzheimer's is far more treacherous than the scary things I thought lay lurking in the dark. However, the Lord is far more powerful than the flashlight I relied on when I was a child!

Prayer: Lord Jesus, You are our stronghold, our light, and our salvation. Thank You for calming our fears, fighting our battles and healing our spirits. Amen

Sunday: Stillness in Knowing God

Be still, and know that I am God; I will be exalted among the nations, I will be exalted in the earth. The Lord Almighty is with us; the God of Jacob is our fortress. Psalms 46:10–11

As I sat looking out my breakfast nook window, I saw a yellow butterfly slowly fluttering around the pink, orange, and crimson daylilies filling my flower beds. It finally selected a large pink lily and sat perfectly still as it sucked up the sweet nectar from the middle of the flower. The sight made me wonder how often I just sit still and spend time soaking up the presence of the Lord. Sadly, I don't do this often enough.

This week we focused on who we are in God. Now it is time to simply be still and bask in His glorious presence. Through faith we know He exists and He is constantly with us. So let us draw near to Him and remember He is the:

- Joy of our salvation
- Ever constant light in our lives
- One who knew us in the womb
- Healer of our hearts
- Crafter of our new creation in Christ
- Refresher of our spirits
- Lord Almighty of our lives!

Rest in the stillness of our Lord Jesus Christ and be refreshed as your spirit is gently renewed today.

Prayer: Lord Almighty, we come today to simply rest in Your presence. Help us be still and reflect on who we are in You. Thank You for Your love and grace in our lives. Amen

Mike Norton © 123RF.com

LEARN TO BE CONTENT

Devotions for helping you find contentment in living a life with Alzheimer's disease.

Monday: The Secret of Contentment

*I have learned the secret of being content in any and every
situation, whether well fed or hungry, whether living in plenty or
want. I can do everything through Him who gives me strength.*
Philippians 4:12–13

Paul learned the secret of being content in whatever situation he
faced. That says a lot for a man who endured suffering, rejection,
resentment, pain, sickness, weariness, frustration, and sorrow as he
spread the gospel and encouraged the early church. I imagine him
beaten, placed in chains, and imprisoned but through it all
maintaining a spiritual sense of joy and contentment few of us ever
experience in life.

How did he do it? What was his secret? Simply put, Paul was
able to do everything and endure anything because Jesus Christ was
his source of strength and solace. This is without a doubt the
unfathomable power of Jesus Christ in your life. Once you
completely commit your life to Him, you are able to be just like the
Apostle Paul, content in all situations as you seek to serve Him.

Am I content in my current state of Alzheimer's? I would have
to shout a resounding yes because Christ has provided an
unexplainable peace in my present situation. Through His power and
spiritual influence I am able to experience contentment as long as I
stay in touch with Him, find new ways to serve Him, and avoid
focusing on this dreadful disease. You see, Alzheimer's cannot steal
my contentment for my contentment comes from Christ!

*Prayer: Lord Jesus, You are our source of strength and
endurance in all things. We humbly thank You for all You do and
pray Your peace will continue to foster a spirit of contentment in our
lives. Amen*

Tuesday: Joy and Peace

May the God of hope fill you with all joy and peace as you trust in Him so that you may overflow with hope by the power of the Holy Spirit. Romans 15:13

Have you ever been around someone filled with joy and peace? I know one such person, Mrs. Nancy. She is a joyous lady who always has a smile and good things to say about life, people, and her circumstances. She is also a gifted seamstress who sews beautiful quilts and wall hangings. Although she has experienced numerous health problems, lost her husband, been through countless surgeries, and lives on a small fixed income, she is always joyous and content. The amazing thing is her joy and peace are contagious to those with whom she comes in contact. Her hope and blessed outlook on life overflow and others are touched by what spills forth from her spirit.

This is what Paul was talking about when he asked God to fill the people of the church at Rome with joy and peace. Paul knew if the Roman church received the gifts of joy and peace, others would see the manifestation of Christ in their lives. Then the people of the church would be content and a spirit of hope would emanate from them. Paul knew contentment flows freely from a spirit filled with joy and peace.

Having Alzheimer's is a difficult situation but it should not impact God's spirit within you. Joy and peace can still be products of your life so you may be content in your current situation. Like Mrs. Nancy, we should all be content and overflow with hope so others can find hope through us!

Prayer: God of Hope, fill us with a spirit of joy and peace so we may be content in our current situations and overflow with hope for others. Amen

Wednesday: Pressing On

But one thing I do: Forgetting what is behind and straining toward what is ahead, I press on toward the goal to win the prize for which God has called me heavenward in Christ Jesus.
Philippians 3:14

Throughout Paul's ministry he focused on what Christ had in store for him in the future, not what occurred in the past. Paul was always oriented toward Christ's goal for his life. He had a spiritual target which provided a sense of satisfaction and contentment in his life. As long as he was moving toward the goal Christ had established, Paul was content in his situation and moved forward toward the goal. Even as Paul was confined in prison and restricted under house arrest for a portion of his ministry, focusing on Christ enabled him to pen many of the New Testament letters to the early church. Paul gained contentment even while confined and constrained in austere circumstances. The joy and peace flowing from these letters stand as a testament today to his contentment in Christ.

When Alzheimer's strikes your life you may feel confined and restricted in ways not evident before your disease was diagnosed. If you continue to focus on the goal Christ has established for your life, like Paul, you can find contentment in your current circumstances. Perhaps you can't do all the things you once did, but there are things you can still do to encourage others and further God's kingdom on earth.

Alzheimer's has made me forget the past but it can't keep me from Christ. I will continue to press on toward the goal to win the prize which God has called me heavenward in Christ Jesus!

Prayer: Father God, help us continue to seek and fulfill Your purpose for our lives through the awesome power of the Holy Spirit. Keep us focused on the goal and not the disease as we serve You with our whole hearts. Amen

Thursday: Godliness and Contentment

But godliness with contentment is great gain. For we brought nothing into the world, and we can take nothing out of it.
1 Timothy 6:6–7

Have you ever received a letter from a trusted friend filled with encouragement during a difficult period in your life? These "love" letters are particularly precious as they provide godly guidance and support to lift your spirits. Paul was such a letter writer; he not only wrote letters of instruction to churches but he also wrote pastoral letters to Timothy and Titus.

Today's Scripture, from one of Paul's pastoral letters to Timothy, deals with godliness and contentment. Paul urged Timothy to focus on God and to learn to be content regardless of the situation. Contentment is something flowing from our spirit not our situation. Paul reminded Timothy he brought nothing into this world and he would take nothing out of it. At first glance the passage appears to deal with possessions but it goes much deeper. Paul starts with godliness which means being like-minded and in-step with Christ. Then he says if we focus on godliness with contentment it is "great gain."

Alzheimer's has had a tremendous impact on my life and how I measure success. Now I realize I brought nothing into this world and I'll take nothing material out of it. The time I spent working to gain "things" means little to me now. It truly wasn't "great gain" in the big scheme of life. What matters most is godliness and a true relationship with Jesus Christ. Fostering my relationship daily will produce contentment which is indeed "great gain" by any measuring stick especially when Alzheimer's is knocking at the door!

Prayer: Father, help us to nurture our relationship with Christ and become more godly people. We desperately need You. Amen

Friday: Bringing Contentment

I am a wall, and my breasts are like towers. Thus I have become in his eyes like one bringing contentment. Song of Songs 8:10

Have you ever given a gift to someone who truly found great pleasure and joy with it for a long time? Conversely, have you ever given a gift, perhaps at great cost to you, and the person probably never treasured or even used it? So it is with God. He has given life to each of us, not to mention countless blessings along the way. If we are genuinely content with what He has provided in our lives then we have pleased God immensely. Contentment not only impacts how we view our circumstances and daily life, but it also impacts our relationship with our heavenly Father. Learning to be content in whatever circumstances we encounter is paramount to pleasing God and maintaining our right relationship with Him.

I must confess, I experience days where I find myself discontent with the realities of living with Alzheimer's disease. However, during these dark days I realize I desperately need to confess my lack of contentment to the Lord and draw near to Him. When I do this, my spirit is refreshed and contentment returns as I focus on Him rather than the disease.

I simply remember He is in control, He knows what lies ahead, and He has prepared the perfect path for me. How can I not be content and trust in Him? My deepest desire is to be like the one depicted in today's Scripture. Then I will become in God's eyes "like one bringing contentment" to His throne!

Prayer: Father God, we want so much to be content in our current situation not just to ease our spirits but to bring joy and pleasure to You. Thank You for all You do in our lives and for the blessings You bestow daily on each of us. Amen

Saturday: Assurance of Being Content

Keep your lives free from the love of money and be content with what you have, because God has said, "Never will I leave you; never will I forsake you." Hebrews 13:5

I remember a financially difficult period in my life when I had three small children, was a partner in a small farm supply business, and was living paycheck to paycheck. I was concerned with how we were going to make it and if the business would survive. I prayed daily for increased sales and hoped for future prosperity. I felt God had forsaken me in this venture. I lost my focus on Christ as well as my contentment in life.

During this financially difficult period, Beverly Newell, my pastor's wife, encouraged me to go on an Emmaus Walk. After much prayer I decided to attend although it meant giving up three precious work days. On that Emmaus Walk my focus returned to Christ, my spirit was renewed, and my relationship with Christ strengthened. God had not left me nor forsaken me during this difficult period. In fact, He had been trying to reach out and reassure me of His everlasting love. Through His faithful servant, Beverly, I was reminded how deeply He cared for me. My contentment was restored even though nothing had changed in our farm supply business. The next week I returned to work with the same issues, financial conditions, and meager salary. However, I was reassured God was with me.

So it is in my current situation with early-onset Alzheimer's disease. Nothing has changed. I still have the disease but I know I'm not alone. God is with me and I can be content knowing He will never forsake me. The same can be true for you as well!

Prayer: Dear Lord, thank You for the assurance You will always be with us and never forsake us no matter what the situation. Help us to be content knowing You are right here with us. Amen

Paul M. Hornback

Sunday: Contentment in Stillness

Be still, and know that I am God; I will be exalted among the nations, I will be exalted in the earth. The Lord Almighty is with us; the God of Jacob is our fortress. Psalms 46:10–11

This week we have focused on being content in our current circumstances. Contentment flows from a soul that has been refreshed through a right relationship with Christ. Now it is time to be still and nurture our relationship with our Lord and Savior Jesus Christ.

He is waiting for each of us to simply slow down, set aside a few moments, and sit still so He can gently touch our souls. It sounds pretty simple doesn't it? All we need do is stop, sit, and seek His presence and He will be there. Some people think being still is really doing nothing, but being still requires a great deal of effort for many of us. We must force ourselves to stop moving about doing mindless tasks, focus our thoughts on our heavenly Father, and quietly listen with our whole hearts and cleared minds. These "stillness" times are precious periods refreshing our souls and bringing contentment back into our lives.

Being still before the Lord is an essential element in the daily life of a content Christian. It reminds us God is with us and loves us beyond measure. His grace engulfs us, and He is our fortress forever. Take time today to be still and know He is God, for your continual contentment in a life filled with Alzheimer's will depend on it!

Prayer: Lord Jesus, help us to be still before You today. Refresh our souls and rejuvenate our spirits as we sit quietly and listen for Your gentle voice. Bring contentment back into our lives. Amen

34

Svetoslav Sokolov © 123RF.com

SHARE THE NEWS

Devotions for helping you understand it is okay to share the news about your diagnosis of Alzheimer's disease.

Monday: Boasting about Weakness

If I must boast, I will boast of the things that show my weakness.
2 Corinthians 11:30

People tend to boast about their salary, the fancy sports car parked in front of their four car garage, the square footage of their enormous home, or the career that has propelled them to the top of the pecking order. These status symbols serve to establish their self-esteem and underline their individual strengths. In today's passage, Paul decides to boast about the things that show his weakness. This is certainly contradictory to how bragging rights are granted in modern society.

As Christians, we must learn to humble ourselves and avoid highlighting our man-made strengths. We should boast about our weaknesses and how Christ's perfect power has given us strength to carry on. To focus on our weaknesses rather than our strengths would serve us poorly in most segments of society.

Since my diagnosis of Alzheimer's I don't brag about the disease. However, I share with others how the disease impacts my life and how Christ's power is made perfect in my illness. It is important to let others know what is going on and how the disease has changed daily life. This doesn't mean complaining about every facet of the disease! Instead, I try to share what God has placed on my heart regarding my daily struggles. This allows God's power to rest upon me and opens the door for others to pray for healing, strength, and grace in my life. God's saints stand ready to pray for each of us so His grace will be sufficient to meet the demands of Alzheimer's!

Prayer: Loving Christ, if we must boast about something, let us boast about our weaknesses rather than our strengths. Thank You for providing us sufficient grace and strength to continue living with Alzheimer's. Amen

Tuesday: Perfect Power

My grace is sufficient for you, for my power is made perfect in weakness. Therefore, I will boast all the more gladly about my weakness so Christ's power will rest on me.
2 Corinthians 12:9

In his letter to the church at Corinth, the Apostle Paul boasts not about possessions or status but focuses on weakness in his life. No one knows precisely what Paul's weakness was with respect to illness, handicap, specific sins, mental condition, or other affliction. It was probably best Paul spoke in general terms rather than being specific because the specific affliction isn't what is important. What is important is the perfect power of Christ to overcome his weakness.

When I was diagnosed with early-onset Alzheimer's disease, I knew I could not rely on my own power to continue in my Christian witness. I desperately needed the power of Christ to rest on me so I could continue to serve Him in whatever capacity He deemed adequate. It is only through Him I am able to write these words. Since my diagnosis of Alzheimer's disease, I truly understand the concept of Paul's weakness and his desire for Christ's power to rest on him.

Do I boast about having Alzheimer's? Not exactly, but I do share with others about how the disease impacts my daily life, how Christ's grace is sufficient for me, and how His power is made perfect in my weakness. One thing is for sure, without Christ's power resting on me, Alzheimer's would be making my life far worse than I care to imagine!

Prayer: Loving Christ, our prayer today is for Your perfect power to rest on us so we may be Your humble servants. Help us to understand Your grace is sufficient for all our needs. Amen

Wednesday: From Weakness to Strength

That is why, for Christ's sake, I delight in weaknesses, in insults, in hardships, in persecutions, in difficulties. For when I am weak, then I am strong. 2 Corinthians 12:10

Paul presses on in his letter to the Corinthians to define his delight in weakness. When Paul is weak, only then is he strong in Christ. Most of us fail to use the power of Christ until we have no other option. We carry out our ministries using only our own power and leaving Christ as a silent partner.

The Apostle Paul recognized his ministry was solely dependent on Christ and Christ had to be in control if it was to be successful. His "thorn in the flesh" kept him humble and helped him recognize his human limitations. As Dirty Harry (Clint Eastwood) once said, "A man's got to know his limitations." Only then can Christ enter our lives and bring perfect power to overcome our limitations. Christ may choose to leave the thorn in the flesh as was the case with Paul; but Christ will compensate and use our weakness to His glory if we humble ourselves and allow Him full reign in our lives.

That is a lot to digest for someone who has Alzheimer's! Since it is a disease I would never wish on anyone, how can I boast about the disease in my life? By simply relying on the fact it is only through my weakness God's perfect power is manifested in my life. Alzheimer's has made me completely dependent on Christ to do anything! He is my Lord and Savior; nothing else matters. What I once thought was strong living pales in comparison to the strength He now provides for me to serve Him. I am humanly weak because of this disease but I am also spiritually strong through Christ's perfect power!

Prayer: Precious Lord, may we boast only about Your power in our lives and how You alone bring us strength for each new day. Amen

Thursday: The Holy Spirit's Power

In the same way, the Spirit helps us in our weakness. We do not know what we ought to pray for, but the Spirit himself intercedes for us with groans that words cannot express. Romans 8:26

In Paul's letter to the church in Rome he explains the basic system of salvation to those who have never before received the teaching of an apostle. In today's passage Paul focuses on the power of the Holy Spirit. He emphasizes how the Spirit helps us in our weakness and even prays for us in ways we may not be able to fully comprehend.

Anyone who suffers with Alzheimer's understands the "weakness" of the disease. There are things you just don't do well anymore. Sharing the news of your illness is one of those things because it takes good communication skills. I remember telling my children about my doctor's preliminary diagnosis. It was the hardest thing I've ever had to do. I remember asking God to help me find the words that would provide assurance He was in complete control. Fortunately, the Holy Spirit was working behind the scenes and interceding for me in groans that words could not express. Perhaps this is why the conversation went so well. Once we decide to surrender the disease to God, He is able to work wonders in our lives that we simply cannot fully comprehend.

That is why it is important to share the news with those close to you. You can be a witness even in your weakness. You may not feel strong enough but the Holy Spirit is already in your corner praying and preparing you for this conversation!

Prayer: Father God, thank You for the Holy Spirit's prayers on our behalf and the strength that flows from Him. Amen

Friday: A Sympathetic Savior

For we do not have a high priest who is unable to sympathize with our weakness, but we have one who has been tempted in every way, just as we are – yet was without sin. Hebrews 4:15

I love today's passage from Hebrews. It helps me understand we serve a Lord who understands what it is like to be human, suffer in life, and struggle with temptation. Jesus understood the heartache of having friends afflicted with all kinds of disease. He healed many but had compassion for all!

I know I have a loving and trusted friend in Jesus. I can share anything with him and know He will listen with compassion and understanding. This helps me share my unique situation with others, especially with close friends and family. By sharing my story, others are able to lift up prayers of healing, encouragement, and compassion on my behalf. These prayers do not fall on deaf ears for our Lord is a sympathetic Savior. He understands all we go through and how it impacts our individual lives and families.

Early-onset Alzheimer's disease is by far the greatest weakness I have ever faced. But one thing I know, I do not face this burden alone! My Savior walks alongside me every day. On days that are more confusing than others, He compassionately carries me until the fogginess fades.

I believe He understands what it's like living with Alzheimer's disease. He knows how the mind becomes confused, the difficulty of concentrating, and how hard it is to carry on a conversation when words no longer flow. He alone fully understands all you experience because of your weakness. Remember, He is with you and will never forsake you!

Prayer: Lord Jesus, thank You for Your compassion, understanding, and encouragement as we confess our weaknesses to You. Amen

Saturday: Serving in Weakness

... he was crucified in weakness, yet he lives by God's power. Likewise, we are weak in him, yet by God's power we will live with him to serve you. 2 Corinthians 13:4

In Paul's second letter to the church in Corinth, he expends a considerable amount of ink boasting about his weakness. He does this so others might understand his human frailties and how Christ's perfect power has allowed him to serve in spite of his weakness. By sharing his weakness, Paul was able to overcome his limitations through the awesome power of Christ. Others were then able to witness the power of Christ in his life.

Serving Christ was the critical characteristic defining the Apostle Paul and explained why he persevered even in weakness. We read in the New Testament of Paul's ministry and stand in awe of how he grew and encouraged the early church in spite of his thorn in the flesh. God's grace was truly sufficient to enable Paul to serve Him faithfully. But what if we did not know about Paul's weakness? How would we understand that God's grace was truly sufficient to enable him to continue serving in spite of his ailment?

Just like Paul, it is important to share with others about your weakness so they see how God's power and grace enable you to serve Him. It is vital you continue serving Christ even though you have Alzheimer's. God still has work you can accomplish for the Kingdom. His grace is truly sufficient and His power is stronger than Alzheimer's disease! Trust Him, boast in Him, and continue to serve Him.

Prayer: Father God, we are weak in Alzheimer's but Your grace is more than sufficient to help us serve You in spite of the disease. Please help us see clearly how we might serve You this day. Amen

Sunday: Stillness in Weakness

Be still, and know that I am God; I will be exalted among the nations, I will be exalted in the earth. The Lord Almighty is with us; the God of Jacob is our fortress. Psalms 46:10–11

This week we have explored the possibility of sharing our "weakness" with others and the good that may come from trusting God with our decision. If you have made the decision to talk with a trusted friend this week about your situation, be still and talk with God about this conversation. If you haven't shared with anyone, be still and ask God who might be a trusted Christian friend with whom you can share. Either way, God is in control of all that has happened or will happen.

It is now time to reflect on this week's devotions. Sit quietly and remember how the Apostle Paul:

- Boasted about his weakness
- Allowed Christ's perfect power to be manifest through his weakness
- Enabled others to see the awesome power of the risen Christ because his weakness was overcome.

As I reflect on this week's devotions, I am reminded all things work to the good for those who trust the Lord and are called according to His purposes. This was certainly true for Paul and it can be for you as well. Alzheimer's may be your weakness but it is not time to surrender to the disease. Instead, it is time to be still and surrender the disease to the Lord. Take time to be still today, allow God's perfect power to rest on you, and prepare yourself to serve Him in wonderfully new ways.

Prayer: Father God, help us to be still today and allow Your power to flow through us so we may serve You in some type of ministry. You know our limitations brought on by Alzheimer's. Show each of us what that ministry might be as we humbly wait for guidance. Amen

Seawhisper © 123RF.com

UNCERTAIN ABOUT THE FUTURE

Devotions to help you learn how to deal with the uncertainty of living with Alzheimer's disease.

Monday: Uncertain of Where Your Hope Lies

Command those who are rich in this present world not to be arrogant nor to put their hope in wealth, which is so uncertain, but to put their hope in God, who richly provides us with everything for our enjoyment. 1Timothy 6:17

It is amazing the things in which we choose to place our hope. In Paul's letter to Timothy, he alludes to the arrogance of rich people who believe wealth will provide security and hope for the future. Paul instructs Timothy to command them to put their hope in God because wealth is so uncertain.

Where is your hope? Before being diagnosed with early-onset Alzheimer's I was a health and exercise nut. I would run 16 to 20 miles a week, walked 2-3 miles every day, exercised daily, and followed a healthy diet. As such, I hoped to have a healthy body and mind. I was so arrogant about the condition of my body, I often looked down on those who did not take care of themselves. I was sure I'd be healthy and live into my 80s.

All of this changed when I had what the doctors thought was a mini-stroke. After 2 years of MRIs, CAT scans, PET scans, blood work, and other medical tests, my neurologist concluded I had early-onset Alzheimer's disease. I realized I had put my hope in the wrong things. Just like the wealthy people Paul talked about in today's passage, my hope was not in God but in something else. It was a rude awakening for me and a necessary wake-up call for my faith. Although I am still uncertain about what the future holds for me physically and mentally, I'm assured God is in complete control. He will richly provide me with everything I need for my enjoyment!

Prayer: Lord Jesus, help us to place our hope only in You as You alone will provide everything we need for our enjoyment. Amen

Tuesday: Uncertain about Fighting the Good Fight

Timothy, my son, I give you this instruction in keeping with the prophecies once made about you, so that by following them you may fight the good fight, holding on to faith and a good conscience. Some have rejected these and so have shipwrecked their faith.
1 Timothy 1:18–19

When I was a young man in college and full of vim and vigor, I did some boxing while in the Navy ROTC program. I was not a gifted boxer by any means but I made up for it with passion and perseverance. I didn't win all my rounds but when I lost, I always put up a good fight and never backed down.

In today's passage Paul was telling Timothy to fight the good fight, to hang on to the prophecies made about him, and follow his faith. If Timothy did this, he would stand worthy of the calling of Christ. He also instructed Timothy to hold firm to his faith and hold others in Ephesus accountable to Christ.

As Christians, do we hold on to our faith and fight the good fight? Do we reject biblical instruction, thereby shipwrecking our faith? As for me, my passion for Christ enables me to fight the good fight and hold on to faith. I know how Alzheimer's can bring havoc into your life. However, I still choose to hang on to my faith and God's promises. How do I fight the good fight? Here are a few things I do in my battle:

- Take my medication and exercise every day
- Participate in clinical trials for Alzheimer's
- Keep my mind active by reading, writing, and thinking
- Stay connected with godly people
- Pray, read God's word, and stay rooted in faith.

Prayer: Heavenly Father, help us fight the good fight and hang on to our faith as we trust in You for strength and courage each day. Amen

Wednesday: Uncertain about Daily Needs

Then the Lord said to Moses, "I will rain down bread from heaven for you. The people are to go out each day and gather enough for that day. In this way I will test them and see whether they will follow my instructions." Exodus 16:4

Most of us have never known real hunger or starvation in our lives. As a young Marine in flight training, I endured survival training during which we had to live off the land for three days. Our training area was the same ground scoured by every flight school class so there wasn't much left to eat. This was the first time I knew what real hunger felt like.

In today's passage, the Israelites grumbled to Moses about their hunger. They thought they'd be better off dying in Egypt where at least they could sit around pots of meat eating all they wanted rather than starve in the desert! God responded by promising them manna from heaven. But there was a caveat: they could only gather enough manna for each day except on the sixth day when they could gather twice as much to cover the Sabbath.

As we face uncertainty because of Alzheimer's, it is important to learn the lesson regarding manna. First, we must focus on today's needs only! We must trust the Lord to provide for tomorrow. Second, we must be thankful for the Lord's daily provisions and the promise of tomorrow's provision. Third, we must trust in the Lord to keep His promises.

Trust in today's passage from Exodus as you deal with the daily demands of dementia. Don't let future uncertainties rob you of today's joy and thankfulness toward God. Otherwise you'll feast on earthly maggots instead of heavenly manna!

Prayer: Lord God, help us to focus on our needs for today and trust You to provide for tomorrow. You are our joy and strength. Amen

Thursday: Uncertain about the Future

When times are good, be happy; but when times are bad, consider: God has made the one as well as the other. Therefore, a man cannot discover anything about the future. Ecclesiastes 7: 14

After I was diagnosed with Early-onset Alzheimer's disease, I researched the disease using the library, internet, and Alzheimer's Association material. There was a wealth of information on the disease and it was difficult to read about what the future holds for someone with Alzheimer's. I finally decided to focus on early to mid-stage information and how to cope with this disease. The approach proved very encouraging because it dealt with my present condition rather than an undetermined future condition. The one recurring theme was there would be good days and bad days in the life of an Alzheimer's patient. I was delighted to know there would at least be some good days to accompany the bad days!

Today's Scripture from Ecclesiastes points out everyone has good and bad times but God made them both. So when times are good, be happy. When times are bad, understand God is still in complete control. This Scripture is an enormous encouragement to me as it helps me realize good days will always be part of my future. During the bad days, it reminds me God is in control of those as well. By focusing on the present, I need not worry about the future because I cannot discover anything about it. Besides, if I worry about the bad days that may arise in the future, I could easily miss the joy of the good days I'm experiencing. Good days should be cherished and lived to the fullest rather than consumed with worry about what might happen in the future.

Prayer: Lord, You are in control of our good days and bad days. Help us to fully enjoy the good days and endure the bad days. Amen

Paul M. Hornback

Friday: No Man Knows the Future

Since no man knows the future, who can tell him what is to come? Ecclesiastes 8:7

As I alluded to in yesterday's devotion, after my diagnosis I researched Alzheimer's disease extensively. Much of the information was disturbing and did not paint a pretty picture of life in the latter stages of Alzheimer's. However, there was one significant study that shed a positive light. It was the Nun Study from 1986 at the University of Minnesota. The study revealed one nun who had shown no outward signs of Alzheimer's but her autopsy indicated her brain was riddled with plaque and tangles associated with the disease.

The significance of this study is Alzheimer's doesn't necessarily impact everyone the same. One sister was able to live her life without anyone suspecting she had Alzheimer's. This startling find encouraged me since it indicates my future isn't written in stone because I have Alzheimer's disease.

According to Ecclesiastes, no one knows the future. Rather than worrying about the future, perhaps we should focus on living a God-centered life, reading the Scriptures, and maintaining a personal relationship with the Lord. These are the important lessons flowing from Ecclesiastes. Even with early-onset Alzheimer's disease, I find comfort in knowing the Lord is still in control of my life. All I need do is trust Him, obey His commands, and not worry about the future.

As Solomon stated so succinctly, everything else is meaningless. Focus on the present, take joy in the good days, and center your life on God. He is good and His love endures forever!

Prayer: Father God, help us live a focused life. We praise You for the good days and lean on You for the not so good days. Amen

Saturday: Hope for the Future

There is surely a future hope for you, and your hope will not be cut off. Proverbs 23:18

I love this passage from Proverbs because it provides hope. I hold on tightly to Scriptures that promise hope and a future for God's children. They provide comfort and assurance God is with us even in the midst of seemingly hopeless situations.

Alzheimer's is a seemingly hopeless situation since the future is clouded with uncertainty about mental capacity and physical abilities. So is it ridiculous to hold on to the promise of hope for the future? I answer this question with a resolute NO! No man knows the future. Only God knows the future! I must live in the present trusting Him to deal decidedly with my future.

Because I have His promise of hope, I chose to participate in an 18 month clinical trial for Alzheimer's disease. In this trial I received an experimental medication every two weeks. This was a Phase III trial so I was assured it was a promising medication since it passed the Phase II trial with reasonable results. But what was more important was I helped to combat the disease for future generations. The trial drug might prove to be beneficial for people with Alzheimer's or it might show no discernable improvement for Alzheimer's patients. Either way, I still assisted in the fight against the disease.

I am providing hope for a future cure by living in the present and participating in a clinical trial. By not fretting about the future, I am able to discern my particular path for the present. Trusting in God for the future and taking positive actions in the present ensures my future hope will not be cut off!

Prayer: Lord, You are surely our hope for the future. Help us take the necessary steps today to ensure a brighter tomorrow. Amen

Sunday: Be Still and Be Certain

Be still, and know that I am God; I will be exalted among the nations, I will be exalted in the earth. The Lord Almighty is with us; the God of Jacob is our fortress. Psalms 46:10–11

This week we focused on trusting the Lord to provide hope for the future rather than worrying about how Alzheimer's disease may affect us later. Now it is time to be still and know God is our fortress, our hope, our provider, and our redeemer. Being still requires a focused effort to set aside everything that steals the quiet necessary to connect with Christ.

I find it much easier to go to a quiet place to pray and reflect. My favorites are the front porch in the early morning or late evening, the dock by our pond in the back yard, or my study where I write. Wherever you choose to go, make sure it is a place where you can have some solitude. Most of the time it is pretty easy to empty my mind of all the concerns and issues of living with Alzheimer's. However, there are times I have to ask the Lord to help ease my churning mind and allow the Holy Spirit to move within me. Other times I can simply read from the Psalms and I'm graced by His peace and presence. I've even sung a hymn allowing the melody to calm my restless spirit.

You may have other ways of calming your soul so you can be still. The method by which you achieve stillness isn't important. What is important is finding stillness and coming before God in a humble manner. He desperately desires quiet time alone with you. He stands ready to calm your spirit and ease your fears. He still loves you and cares about your future and having Alzheimer's doesn't change this fact one bit. Take the time and be still before God today. He is waiting!

Prayer: Father, ease our troubled minds and bring us peace as we rest in Your arms. You are the one true God who gives hope. Amen

Marilyn Barbone © 123RF.com

A THANKFUL SPIRIT

Devotions to help you discover new ways to nurture a thankful spirit in the midst of living with Alzheimer's disease.

Monday: Praying with Thanksgiving

Do not be anxious about anything, but in everything by prayer and petition, with thanksgiving, present your requests to God.
Philippians 4:6

In Paul's letter to the church at Philippi, we find the beautiful words of today's Scripture. The passage directs us not to be anxious about anything and to pray with an attitude of thanksgiving. The NIV Study Bible states anxiety is, "self-centered and counter-productive worry that is not a legitimate care and concern for the spreading of the gospel." It is a succinct definition, from a Christian perspective.

I put to memory this particular passage when I was going through a very difficult time with my daughter. It helped calm my anxieties as I dealt with the situation at hand. I distinctly remember using these words in my prayers and thanking God for safely bringing my daughter home. It was an extremely difficult time for my wife and me but God was faithful in answering our prayers regarding our daughter. Through the comforting words of this Scripture He put our anxieties at bay.

Since this Scripture helped in the past, I prayed it again after being diagnosed with early-onset Alzheimer's. These words provided a gentle reminder not to be anxious about anything (including Alzheimer's) and to petition God with a thankful heart. Each day I try to be thankful in all things as I talk with God. Some days this is a very easy task while other days it is more difficult. However, I generally can find much to be thankful about. Praying prayers of thanksgiving have helped immensely to limit the anxiety accompanying Alzheimer's. Spend time in thankful praise today. It helps!

Prayer: Dear Lord, help hold back our anxieties and give us a truly thankful heart as we pray and petition You this day. Amen

Tuesday: Goodness Breeds Thankfulness

Give thanks to the Lord, for he is good; his love endures forever. Psalms 107: 1

I am an avid gardener who loves to grow all kinds of flowers. I spend hours each day watering, weeding, feeding, and pruning the plants that adorn my gardens. I am rewarded with beautiful blossoms that decorate my lawn and table with incredible color and texture. I love to walk through the flower beds early in the morning as the gardens spring to life. Bees and butterflies happily flit among the flowers. Occasionally I'm blessed by a hummingbird dashing between the blossoms.

In the hot days of August, I generally water the beds in the morning with water from a nearby pond. The plants wait patiently for their morning bath and seem to respond with thankfulness as they gratefully soak in the moisture. As I go about this task, I think how much our heavenly Father is like a master gardener. He feeds us through His word, He nurtures us by the Holy Spirit, prunes us through His discipline, and waters us with the love of His son Jesus Christ. We respond by giving thanks to our heavenly Father for His goodness, grace, love, and mercy. His love for us endures forever and nothing that happens in our lives will ever change His love for us.

Giving thanks is a deep rooted trait all Christians should practice daily. As plants respond to the goodness of the gardener by producing beautiful blossoms, Christians respond to the goodness of God by producing prayer laced with praise and thanksgiving. Alzheimer's may eat away at your brain but I pray it doesn't eat away at your thankful spirit. Why? Because God is good and His love for you endures forever!

Prayer: Heavenly Father, we praise You for Your goodness in our lives and thank You for Your ever enduring love. Amen

Wednesday: Overflowing with Thankfulness

*So then, just as you received Christ Jesus as Lord, continue to
live in him, rooted and built up in him, strengthened in the faith as
you were taught, and overflowing with thankfulness.
Colossians 2:6–7*

Paul laces his letter to the Colossians with an attitude of
thankfulness as he describes the fullness and complete adequacy of
Christ. His letter contains powerful rules for living a holy life filled
with forgiveness and peace. In this passage, Paul reminds the
Colossians to live life firmly rooted in Christ. He closes today's
passage by urging them to be "overflowing with thankfulness."

Have you ever met one who "overflows" with thankfulness? I
met such a lady at a Methodist church my wife and I attended while I
was going through naval flight training. She was a delightful older
lady who welcomed us into the church and expressed sincere
gratitude for our bringing other young couples into their fellowship.
As Sarah and I got to know her, we discovered her gratitude and
grace flowed from a deep rooted relationship with Christ. She helped
establish our young adult Sunday school Class and invited the class
to her home for social events. She was so grateful for all Christ had
done in her life and marriage. She was always ready to share her
testimony, possessions, and heart with others.

I will never forget her kindness and loving spirit. They stand as
a testament of a person overflowing with true thankfulness. As
Christians, we are to overflow with thankfulness no matter what our
situation. Even with Alzheimer's, I have found so much to be
thankful for and I pray this spirit will continue. How about you?

*Prayer: Lord Jesus, help us to overflow with thankfulness in
spite of whatever stage of Alzheimer's we are experiencing. Amen*

Thursday: Giving Thanks in All Circumstances

Be joyful always; pray continually; give thanks in all circumstances, for this is God's will for you in Christ Jesus.
1 Thessalonians 5:16–18

I love the way the Apostle Paul writes his letters. They are always filled with instructions for godly living. In his first letter to the Thessalonians, Paul provides three simple rules for their consideration: always maintain a joyful spirit, be in prayer continually, and give thanks in all circumstances. These three concepts embody how Christians should act in their daily lives. What better set of traits could we hope others see in us than to be joyful, prayerful, and thankful?

Being thankful in all circumstances provides the underpinning for a joyful spirit and provides a perfect heart for purposeful prayer. If we maintain a thankful spirit, then we can overflow with joy and hope so others will know Christ rules our lives. To give thanks in all circumstances does not imply you live in a "Pollyanna" state. It simply means you can be thankful about some aspects of your life no matter what your circumstance.

When I was diagnosed with early-onset Alzheimer's, I was thankful for many things. I was thankful for the early diagnosis so I could get my affairs in order, a good disability retirement plan where I worked, an understanding wife and family who supported my decisions, a clinical trial which showed real promise, and a wonderful relationship with Jesus Christ so I was not alone. Was I "happy" about the diagnosis? Absolutely not! However, I found much to be thankful for in spite of the disease. Maintaining a thankful spirit has made all the difference as I deal with the many life changes brought on by the disease. I hope you can find ways to be thankful too!

Prayer: Heavenly Father, help us to find ways in which we can be thankful for the many blessings You send our way. Amen

Friday: Always Give Thanks

*Speak to one another with psalms, hymns and spiritual songs.
Sing and make music in your heart to the Lord, always giving thanks
to God the Father for everything in the name of our Lord Jesus
Christ. Ephesians 5:19–20*

This week has been filled with incredibly beautiful sunsets here
at the Hornback Homestead. Last night, for the first time in many
years, I sat uninterrupted and watched an entire sunset from start to
finish. It was breathtaking to see the sky change from luxurious light
to soft shades of orange and crimson.

As I watched the sun set slowly over the horizon, I thought of
my father who loved to watch the majestic beauty of a sunset. I
began to thank God for my father who sacrificed so much for my
family and me personally. I thanked God I was raised by a man who
had such a gentle spirit even though he experienced untold horrors
while serving in World War II and the Korean War. Some people
emerge from war bitter and unable to cope with life while others
seem to set it aside and go on living. I thanked God my father was
able to put the wars behind him and go on with life in such a gentle
way.

In the magic moments of a seemingly simple sunset, I found
much to be thankful for in my life. It began with my earthly father
and ended with my heavenly Father. Perhaps that is what the Apostle
Paul was talking about when he said always give thanks to God the
Father for everything. We all have so much to be thankful for in our
lives. Being diagnosed with Alzheimer's doesn't take any of that
away. Maintain a spirit of gratitude in all you do and keep a spiritual
song in your heart! Watch a sunset today and remember to give
thanks to God.

*Prayer: Dear heavenly Father, thank You for the beauty of
sunsets and how they remind us of Your ever present love in our
lives. Help us to maintain a spirit of gratitude. Amen*

Saturday: And Be Thankful

Let the peace of Christ rule in your hearts, since as members of one body you were called to peace. And be thankful. Colossians 3:15

Accepting a diagnosis of early-onset Alzheimer's disease isn't easy. You can let it steal the peace of Christ in your life pretty easily. On the other hand, you can also allow it to deepen your faith and personal relationship with Christ.

I chose the path that deepens my faith and strengthens my relationship with Christ. Of course, you are probably thinking I'm a nut case! Do I really understand all that can happen to me? The answer is a resounding YES! I fully understand what the disease can do to my brain but I really don't dwell on what the future holds. Much can change over the next few years. A cure could be discovered, a promising drug could surface that slows the effects of Alzheimer's, or a miracle could happen as God cures me. All these are possible so I'm not going to dwell on future events that may never happen.

Perhaps that is what Paul was thinking when he wrote his letter to the Colossians while imprisoned in Rome. Did the peace of Christ rule in his heart even though his freedom was limited? Given the tone of his letters written while under house arrest, I'd say Paul had perfect peace. He was grateful for all God had done for him and he reminded his brothers and sisters in Christ to act similarly. Like Paul, I choose to be thankful for all things including Alzheimer's. It just might be another opportunity for God to work a miracle in my life, to bless my family in ways I can't understand, to use me to help find a cure, or to draw me closer to Christ. In any case, I choose to be thankful and praise God! How about you?

Prayer: Lord Jesus, help us to remember to be thankful in all things not just the things that seem to make us momentarily happy. Amen

Sunday: Thankfulness in Stillness

Be still, and know that I am God; I will be exalted among the nations, I will be exalted in the earth. The Lord Almighty is with us; the God of Jacob is our fortress. Psalms 46:10-11

Throughout this week we have focused our thoughts on Scripture laced with thankfulness. Now it is time to be still and reflect on those things for which we are truly thankful. It is funny how God reminds us of what is truly important in our lives. Today, my pastor's sermon was taken from Psalm 46:10 and centered on "being still and knowing that He is God."

Has your week been busy or filled with the frustrations of dealing with Alzheimer's? Have you failed to take time to just be still and know He is God? Being busy seems to be the tempo of life these days. As we try to do more, stress builds up in our lives. Soon we are so busy accomplishing things on our list we push God away. As a result, we become less thankful for the gifts God has placed in our lives. We have little time to acknowledge them and soon our thankful spirit is replaced with selfishness that demands more.

It all happens so innocently. All we need do to stop the chaos is be still and rest in His presence. In this stillness we can reflect on His goodness and grace, read His refreshing word, and open our hearts to Him in prayer. All it takes is a willing and thankful spirit that gently beckons us to pause and be still before the Lord. Do that today and thank Him for all His goodness in your life!

Prayer: Lord Jesus, our lives can get so busy and hectic at times. Help us to slow down and be still before You. Gently remind us to reflect on Your love, grace and mercy in our lives. Amen

Matthew Gibson © 123RF.com

A POSITIVE ATTITUDE

Devotions for helping you maintain a positive attitude as you deal with the daily demands of Alzheimer's disease.

Monday: Positive Thinking

*Finally, brothers, whatever is true, whatever is noble, whatever
is right, whatever is pure, whatever is lovely, whatever is admirable
– if anything is excellent or praiseworthy – think about such things.
Philippians 4:8*

I try to be a positive person no matter what the situation. Of
course, my wife might not wholeheartedly agree with this statement
but I endeavor to think positive thoughts. I attribute my positive
attitude to the writings of Norman Vincent Peale. He asserted if you
think positive thoughts you are more likely to have a positive
attitude filled with hope.

Perhaps this is what the Apostle Paul was trying to get across to
the Philippians in this precious passage from his letter to the church.
Paul wanted the Philippians to concentrate on what was true, noble,
right, pure, lovely, admirable, excellent, or praiseworthy. By
allowing these thoughts to occupy their minds, their speech and
actions would naturally follow their thoughts resulting in a spiritual
life worthy of the gospel.

What do you allow to occupy your mind these days? It's pretty
easy to allow the doom and gloom of Alzheimer's to fill your mind
with all types of negative images. I know because I've been there.
However, if you chose to follow Paul's advice you will certainly
benefit. I know this sounds crazy but there are still positive things
you can find. Life is not over and there are loads of good times left.
Later in his letter, Paul said whatever they learned from him they
were to put into practice so the peace of God would be with them.
His advice is still true today. If we practice positive thinking, the
peace of God will be with us and Alzheimer's can't never take it
away!

Prayer: God, fill our minds with positive thoughts of You. Amen

Tuesday: Positive before God

May the righteous be glad and rejoice before God; may they be happy and joyful. Psalm 68:3

I love the way this Psalm directs us to be glad and rejoice before God. It seems so simple. God asks little of us in the big scheme of things. He holds the universe together, supplies all our needs, blesses us, sacrificed His only Son for us, provides us the opportunity to live with Him for eternity, and a host of innumerable acts of grace. In exchange, God simply wants us to praise Him with a spirit filled with joy and gladness.

Wow, what a great deal! But wait a minute. Does this mean only when things are going my way and I'm on top of my game? Let's look over the Scripture for a minute. I don't see any qualifiers or conditions in this particular passage indicating we are to be glad and rejoice before God *only* when things are going our way. We need to be this way all the time when we come before God.

Even in the midst of dealing with Alzheimer's we are to be glad and rejoice before the Lord. That is a pretty bold request given all Alzheimer's entails! As I alluded to yesterday, life isn't over for us even though we struggle with the disease. There is still lots of living and loving left in our lives. God isn't through with us just yet and the final chapter of our lives hasn't been written. So rejoice and be glad before God today. Praise Him with a joyful spirit and thank Him for all He has done in your life up to this point. Alzheimer's is certainly a challenging condition to say the least. It requires each of us to remain positive and find ways to cope with changing conditions. But God is the key to keeping our spirits joyful!

Prayer: Father God, give us joyful spirits and a reason to rejoice in Your presence today. Amen

Wednesday: Do Not Think Like the Gentiles

*So I tell you this, and insist on it in the Lord, that you must no
longer live as the Gentiles do, in the futility of their thinking. They
are darkened in their understanding and separated from the life of
God because of the ignorance that is in them due to the hardening of
their hearts. Ephesians 4:17–18*

Paul gets uncomfortably direct in his letters to the early church.
Today's two verses are particularly pressing passages in which Paul
insists the early Christians live lives dramatically different from the
Gentiles. Paul wants them to be children of light rather than doers of
darkness.

The same is true as we face the uncertainty of living with
Alzheimer's. Are we to be children of light or doers of darkness?
Children of light keep a positive outlook regardless of the situation.
This reminds me of Corrie ten Boom's attitude while imprisoned in a
Nazi concentration camp.

One particular example of her positive attitude was the
infestation of fleas and horrible conditions in the camp where she
was sent. The fleas bit their bodies causing welts followed by open
sores from all the scratching. The women complained about the fleas
but Corrie found a positive aspect. Because of the fleas, the evil Nazi
guards avoided her barracks and did not hassle them as they did
women in the other barracks.

What a way to look at having a flea infestation! In spite of the
horrid situation Corrie was able to remain positive, encourage others,
and praise God. A positive outlook with a thankful spirit makes us
children of light. Alzheimer's, like an evil guard in the camp, will
have to wreak its havoc elsewhere than here with me!

Prayer: Lord, help us to be children of light this day. Amen

Thursday: Positive Shining Stars

Do everything without complaining or arguing, so that you may become blameless and pure, children of God, without fault in a crooked and depraved generation, in which you shine like stars in the universe as you hold out the word of life – in order that I may boast on the day of Christ that I did not run or labor for nothing.
Philippians 2:14–16

Paul is very direct about how we are to live our lives for Christ. Surely he did not mean we do everything without complaining or arguing! Besides, a bit of negativity never really hurts anyone, does it? Well it certainly must have an impact or Paul would not have put it so precisely.

Have you ever looked at the sky on a cold winter's night and observed the bright shining stars contrasted against an ebony background? Paul implied the blackness of the night sky was the crooked, depraved, and negative generation while the children of God were the bright shining stars. It is a contrast about how our lives are to be so different they drastically stand out against the background of humanity. As God's children, we are to be children of light - pure, blameless, and positive while we live out our daily schedules without complaining or arguing. In so doing, we will stand out from the crowd and our actions will exemplify the presence of Christ in our lives.

Alzheimer's certainly has a way of impacting our daily lives but it doesn't have to make us bitter or complaining people. God can move in each of our lives to bring peace and a positive attitude in spite of our situation. Just like Paul wrote, are we going to be the shining stars or part of the depraved generation? I choose to be a shining star! How about you?

Prayer: Heavenly Father, help us shine so brightly with your love we stand out just like the stars you created. Amen

Friday: Eternal Encouragement

May our Lord Jesus Christ himself and God our Father, who loved us and by his grace gave us eternal encouragement and good hope, encourage your hearts and strengthen you in every good deed and word. 2 Thessalonians 2:16–17

I am often amazed at the seemingly simple things that brighten my spirit. Do you remember the song *My Favorite Things* form the Sound of Music? The novitiate who comes to be a nanny for the Van Trapp family sings this song to the children to tell them of things that brighten her spirit when she is sad. I'm a lot like this lady as it really doesn't take much for me to be encouraged. Here are just a few of my favorite things:

- A handwritten note from a loved one
- An email from a friend
- A walk through the garden in the early morning
- A beautiful sunset or sunrise
- A flock of flying geese
- Reading the Psalms
- Special prayer time with my Lord.

As you can see, it doesn't take much to lift my spirit. Perhaps it is because God's grace gives us eternal encouragement and hope once we become His children. As such, it takes very little to encourage our hearts because the Holy Spirit lives within us. That is why I stay so positive in spite of my disease.

God has a wonderful way of bringing encouragement each day. I stay focused on Him and He promises to take care of the rest. It is pretty simple. Alzheimer's is certainly no picnic but I'm not alone. He is with me and His eternal encouragement is ever present. He sends gentle reminders to strengthen my heart daily. Isn't His grace glorious?

Prayer: Father, thank You for Your eternal encouragement. Amen

Saturday: Always Rejoice

Rejoice in the Lord always. I will say it again: Rejoice!
Philippians 4:4

Once again Paul has a perfect and precise way of stating things that doesn't leave room for questions. Paul says we are to rejoice in the Lord at all times. In fact, he says it twice. Rejoice! Why is this so important and does he really mean <u>always</u>? Rejoicing in the Lord is absolutely critical for our health, mind, and spiritual wellbeing. By rejoicing, our spirits are uplifted and our outlook on life improves. This impacts our mood while helping us maintain a positive frame of mind.

I'll even go out on a limb here by saying a positive outlook and a joyous spirit can help offset the horrible impacts of Alzheimer's. Can I point to scads of statistical data to support this claim? No I can't, but only because there haven't been studies conducted on early-onset patients to determine the impact of medication, positive outlook, and faith. There have been studies for other diseases, like cancer, indicating a positive outlook and a strong faith have a noticeable impact on the affected patients. Why wouldn't this hold true for Alzheimer's patients as well?

Our health and faith are linked together in ways medical science will never be able to explain. Does this mean if we have a strong faith we will never experience a serious illness? No, it doesn't! It simply means our chances of surviving and living an abundant life in spite of a serious illness are certainly higher if we maintain a joyful spirit. That is perhaps in part what Paul meant by the passage, "Rejoice in the Lord always." I don't know about you, but I choose this day to "rejoice" and Alzheimer's disease can't stop me!

Prayer: Lord, help us to rejoice in You for You are our redeemer and our strength. Thank You for Your grace, love, and mercy. Amen

Sunday: Stillness Breeds a Positive Attitude

Be still, and know that I am God; I will be exalted among the nations, I will be exalted in the earth. The Lord Almighty is with us; the God of Jacob is our fortress. Psalms 46:10–11

This week we explored the importance of remaining positive in spite of our situation. Now it is time to be still before the Lord, exalt Him for all He has done, and nurture His presence in our hearts. It is really difficult to foster a strong relationship with Christ if we are busily going about our daily schedules. So often the worries of this life, the deceitfulness of wealth, and the desires for other things steal our time of stillness, choke out the word, and rob our relationship with Christ.

By taking just a few minutes to be still, to read His word, and to talk with our Lord, our spirits are lifted and we can rejoice once again. As "children of light" and "shining stars" we are the sole source of hope for a depraved generation. God wants us to be a light for others who may be going through the same thing we are but with one exception. They may not know the love of Christ in their lives. We become a beacon of hope as they see the positive impact of Christ in us.

We can only shine the light of Christ if we are still before Him every day. The stillness recharges our batteries making our light shine even brighter. He is always with us and His eternal encouragement resides in our hearts through the Holy Spirit. Take time today to quietly reflect on your relationship with Him, mediate on His word, and rejoice in Him. He patiently waits for this precious time with you alone; no distractions, no pressing schedules, and no other priorities. Just be still and exalt Him today. Your positive spirit depends upon it!

Prayer: Lord, quiet our restless spirits and allow us to be still before You today. Fill our hearts with hope and encouragement. Amen

Alta Olsthuizen © 123RF.com

FEAR OF THE UNKNOWN

Devotions to help you fight the fear of the unknown as Alzheimer's disease invades your life.

Monday: Feeding Ravens

Consider the ravens: They do not sow or reap, they have no storeroom or barn; yet God feeds them. And how much more valuable you are than birds! Luke 12:24

Are you afraid of things that might happen or things you can't see? As a child growing up, I used to think monsters lived under my bed. At any moment they could reach from under the mattress, pull me down beneath the bed, and devour me. I lost track of the number of times my father came into the room to reassure me no monsters lurked beneath the bed. Finally, he got the brilliant idea of giving me a flashlight so I could look when fear filled my head. This worked wonders because everyone knows monsters are afraid of the light.

I laugh now when I recall this story. Monsters under the bed preying on little children, get real! But as adults, don't we have similar silly fears? We worry about finances, our children's safety, losing our jobs, or the car breaking down. These events may never happen but we worry just the same.

Today's Scripture reminds us God's provisions are perfect so we need not worry. Facing Alzheimer's can have a similar effect on our worry-wart mechanisms. We may worry what the future holds in terms of declining abilities and mental faculties. Rest assured God's provisions are perfect for those of us with this disease. He will provide what is needed to help us and ease our family's burden. I hold on to this Scripture when I start to worry about future events over which I have no control. If God feeds the ravens, what wonderful necessities will He provide me, one of His most beloved creatures?

Prayer: Dear Lord, help us not to fear what has yet to happen for we are Yours and You love us far more than the ravens. Amen

Tuesday: Fear Not

So do not fear, for I am with you; do not be dismayed, for I am your God. I will strengthen you and help you; I will uphold you with my righteous hand. Isaiah 41:10

Fear is a horrible thing when it gets a foothold in your life. It strangles your thoughts and runs rampant with one fearful thought building upon another. Before long you are a nervous wreck over something completely out of your control.

Nighttime is when I am most susceptible to fear. After going to bed, my mind begins to wander into areas I am able to avoid during the day. I am vulnerable to wayward thoughts about how Alzheimer's disease may impact me later in life. All kinds of scenarios fill my head and sleep eludes me.

To put my fears at bay all I need do is think of Scripture and begin weaving the words into my prayers. Fear is overcome by faith and my heavenly Father reminds me I am His and He is always with me. This is exactly what God was telling Israel through the prophet Isaiah in today's passage. Don't be afraid or dismayed because I am your God, I am with you, I will strengthen you, and I will hold you up.

Holding onto His precious promises, praying these words of strength, and knowing He is with me provides all I need to break the bonds brought on by fear! Alzheimer's can be a fearful and frightening disease. I can't begin to imagine tackling it alone without God by my side. He is my strength, my shield, and my help! How about you?

Prayer: My God, I know You are with me always so when I am afraid or dismayed, I will call on Your name. Thank You for upholding me with Your righteous hand. Amen

Wednesday: Comforted Under God's Wings

He will cover you with his feathers, and under his wings you will find refuge; his faithfulness will be your shield and rampart. You will not fear the terror of night, nor the arrow that flies by day, nor the pestilence that stalks in the darkness, nor the plague that destroys at midday. Psalms 91:4–6

I love to read the Psalms as they provide a glowing testimony to the security and comfort available to those who trust in the Lord. Today's passage is a perfect example of God's promise to protect those who dwell in the shelter of His wings.

As I alluded to yesterday, nighttime seems to be my most troubling time. Even after I fall asleep, my dreams can be fearful and disturbing. These dreams wake me up abruptly and leave me afraid of whatever scenario played out in the dream. It is either the Alzheimer's impacting my brain or the medication causing my mind to produce visions of terror.

When it happens, I find relief by remembering the promises found in today's passage from the Psalms. I envision God's wings covering and sheltering me from anything that might harm me. It is comforting to know He is always shielding me from the terrors of the night. All I need do is call on His holy name and His welcoming wings surround and protect me.

Alzheimer's can be a fearful foe but the loving wings of God shelter those who rest in His shadow. There is absolutely no other place I'd rather be than under His wings of refuge! How about you? Do you need a set of wings to comfort you?

Prayer: Most High and Almighty God, thank You for Your comforting wings surrounding us in times of trouble, terror, or tragedy. You are always with us and when we call on Your name, peace prevails in our lives. You are awesome and amazing! Amen

Thursday: Strength in the Lord

Finally, be strong in the Lord and in his mighty power.
Ephesians 6:10

I love today's passage from Paul's letter to the Ephesians. He asserts we need to be strong in the Lord and rely on his mighty power to be victorious. Our human efforts are inadequate given everything Satan throws our way. We may win some battles on our own effort but Satan is an ever constant threat. He will use everything in his power to bring us down.

Human effort alone cannot stop his constant barrage of arrows aimed at our souls. Going it alone, on our own power, is a fight doomed to failure. However, being strong in the Lord and relying on the awesome power of Christ can make us victorious against Satan.

Having Alzheimer's has made me well aware of Satan's personal efforts to bring me down. In my weakened state, I can easily fall prey to the fears and realities surrounding this dreadful disease. If you choose to fight the Alzheimer's fight alone you will surely fail. However, if you are strong in the Lord and rely on His mighty power, He will lead you through the Alzheimer's battle lines.

I choose to depend on the omnipotence of Christ as He forges through the ranks of fear and uncertainty that lie ahead. He alone knows the weakest spots in the disease. I count on Him to lead me directly to the safe havens so we can forge ahead together. Am I being overly optimistic? No! I'm just relying on the faith that has brought me this far. Alzheimer's can be a ferocious fight but with Christ I can be strong and victorious!

Prayer: Savior Christ, be with us in this fight against Alzheimer's. Help us overcome the fear, uncertainty, and anxieties brought on by disease. Help us to be strong in You. Amen

Friday: Deliverance from Fears

I sought the Lord, and he answered me; he delivered me from all my fears. Psalm 34:4

My wife and I love to go to the beach so we can walk along the shore collecting seashells. No matter what beach we visit, we always seek out the best shelling sites. We ask hotel staff, tourist centers, and local residents where the best shelling spots lie. By doing this we are sure to find spectacular sites laden with all types of shells varying in size and color.

Until we learned the secret of asking and seeking out the best shelling locations, we would just wander aimlessly along the beach in hopes of finding a cache of shells. Some beaches were "shell bountiful" while others were a big disappointment. Now, every beach vacation is rewarded with a plethora of shells we collect and display in jars scattered about our home to remind us of our bountiful harvest and beach vacation.

This is exactly what happened to the Psalmist when he sought out the Lord. The Lord answered him and delivered him from his fears. The same is true when we seek the Lord. He answers our prayers and delivers us from our fears. Alzheimer's has a host of fears associated with it. When I was diagnosed, I asked the Lord to help me and He delivered me from my fear of the future. Was it a one-time event? Honestly, no. I have to call upon His name each time I feel myself falling prey to fear of the future. But there are a few things I know for certain. When I seek Him, He answers me. When I ask for His help, He delivers me from fear. When I sit in His presence, He brings me peace. Talk with Him today and He'll deliver you as well!

Prayer: Lord, You are always there when we seek You. Thank You for delivering us from fear and bringing peace into our lives. Amen

Saturday: The Gift of Peace

I am leaving you with a gift: peace of mind and heart. And the peace I give isn't fragile like the peace the world gives. So don't be troubled or afraid. John 14:27

Is there anything more precious in life than having peace? It seems we do all kinds of activities to gain peace in our lives. Some of the more positive activities we pursue include yoga, tai chi, painting, playing the piano, meditation, reading, and gardening just to name a few. However, there are negative activities as well. These include alcohol, drugs, gambling, illicit sex, and excessive shopping. All these activities are done to gain a brief illusion of peace in order to escape the turmoil of life. Unfortunately, none provide lasting peace. In most cases all we get is a brief escape from a world of worry. When the activity is complete and the "induced high" is gone, the worrisome world crowds back into our troubled lives.

In today's Scripture, Jesus explains to the disciples about the gift He will give them when He leaves. This gift of peace will be a strong and lasting presence that won't slip away. It isn't fragile or short-lived like the peace the world provides. His peace comes from the Holy Spirit dwelling within them. The Counselor He sends will remind them of everything He taught.

This same perfect peace is available through the Holy Spirit for everyone who belongs to Christ. It is a lasting peace even Alzheimer's cannot destroy because it resides in our hearts not our brains. So don't be troubled or afraid because of your disease. Instead, let the gift of the peace of God fill your heart so you will overflow with love, joy, and hope in this troubled world!

Prayer: Holy Spirit, come into our lives and fill us with Your comfort and peace. Let us seek You daily to remind us of the lasting peace that only comes through Jesus Christ our Lord and Savior. Amen

Sunday: Stillness Fights Fear

*Be still, and know that I am God; I will be exalted among the
nations, I will be exalted in the earth. The Lord Almighty is with us;
the God of Jacob is our fortress. Psalms 46:10–11*

Throughout the week we focused on how to overcome fear of
the unknown, the future, and a troubled world. As Christians, our
faith in our heavenly Father helps us overcome the fears that rise up
inside us. Through the Lord's strength and the Holy Spirit, we are
able to overcome fear. Then the perfect peace of God will reign in
our hearts and minds.

Now it is time to be still and exalt our heavenly Father. In the
stillness of this day, the Lord Almighty is with us. His mighty wings
surround our lives, shielding us from the turmoil the world brings to
our door. His mighty power protects us from the terrors of the
darkness and Satan's persistent arrows of the day. God alone
provides perfect protection. He is our mighty fortress which nothing
can penetrate. What do we need to fear? Nothing! All we need do is
to seek out the Lord and He will answer. He is faithful, loving, and
omnipotent. Let us be still and rejoice in His strength.

Let us exalt Him today for He is Lord of all. His love endures
forever. His perfect peace is a precious gift to calm the troubled soul.
Alzheimer's may try to rip through your life like a tornado but He
stands ready to calm the winds, break down the storm, and bring
peacefulness in the midst of chaos. All you need do is seek Him. In
the stillness of this day, will you do just that? Seek Him and He will
deliver you from your fears! Nothing is too hard for Him to
overcome!

*Prayer: Lord of Peace, come into our lives this day. Remind us
of Your perfect presence, perfect peace, and perfect pastures
awaiting each of us if we but call on Your holy name. Amen*

Dean Fikar © 123RF.com

ENCOURAGE OTHERS

Devotions to help you find joy while encouraging others who are struggling with similar trials in their lives.

Paul M. Hornback

Monday: Spurring Each Other On

And let us consider how we may spur one another on toward love and good deeds. Hebrews 10:24

The writer of Hebrews inspires us to do better in our Christian faith. This particular passage from Hebrews encourages us to spur each other on to love and good deeds. When I think of the word *spur*, I think of the boot device used by horse riders. The rider doesn't have to use the spur very often on a well-trained horse. The slap of the reins, a tap of his hand, or even the toe of his boot will encourage the horse to move faster. However, if the horse is tired or contrary, the rider may dig his spurs into the horse's flanks to motivate him to move faster.

Every time I read today's passage I realize we are often like that tired contrary horse. We need someone to spur us on when all we want to do is go back to the barn to eat and relax. Since my diagnosis, I often need to be spurred on to love and good deeds. I have days where all I want to do is stay at home and avoid going out into the world.

Thankfully, my heavenly Father has better plans for me than staying in the barn. Through His urging, I receive a call from a friend who needs a help moving a couch, mowing a yard, or trimming a hedge. Once again I am spurred on to love and good deeds. My reward is good Christian fellowship, an opportunity to get out of the house, and a feeling of doing something good. All this makes me feel useful again and helps break the bonds of Alzheimer's. Now, I don't feel so bad when I have to call a friend and ask for help. I may be the one spurring him on to love and good deeds as well!

Prayer: Heavenly Father, continue to spur us on to love and good deeds so we might continue to serve You and feel useful. Amen

Tuesday: Doing Good

Let us not become weary in doing good, for at the proper time we will reap a harvest if we do not give up. Galatians 6:9

Our church started a food pantry a few years ago. When Susan Phelps started this new outreach ministry, our church members embraced it with enthusiasm. However, after a year of providing food to the needy, the newness of the ministry wore off and the continual drain on people's time and resources took its toll. I suppose people had grown weary of doing good. That is why Susan reminds us of the benefits this ministry provides and how grateful the recipients are for the free food.

Perhaps the Galatians were in a similar situation which is why the Apostle Paul penned these cautionary words. They too may have grown weary of doing good in their community especially under the persecution of the Zealot Jews who did not want them fraternizing with the Gentiles. The Apostle Paul reminded them who they were in Christ and doing good naturally flowed from a heart filled with the Holy Spirit.

There is always good to be done in any community. Acts of kindness and goodness do not have to be monumental affairs. Simple expressions of love and grace abound for anyone willing to put their faith into practice. A call to a sick friend, a note to someone going through a tough time, a visit to a person in the hospital, delivering cookies to someone new in your church, or even babysitting the child of a single mother are simple examples of how you can share the love of Christ. Alzheimer's may take its toll on your life but you can still share God's love with others in need if you don't grow weary of doing good!

Prayer: Lord Jesus, help each of us to continue to do good in Your name in whatever capacity we are able. Amen

Wednesday: Good Is from God

*Dear friend, do not imitate what is evil but what is good.
Anyone who does good is from God. Anyone who does what is evil
has not seen God. 3 John 11*

When I was a boy I joined Boy Scouts and poured my heart into
it. I remember the camping trips, merit badges, summer camp, and
special things we did in Troop 486. One thing remains rooted in my
heart from scouting: do one good deed every day. I can still recall
lying down at night to go to sleep and remembering I had not done
my good deed for the day. I would get out of bed and do something
for my mom so I could fulfill my scout obligation. Soon, doing good
deeds became a habit embedded in my daily routine. Scouting was in
my heart and the good deeds flowed from this true scout's heart.

Perhaps that was what John was trying to get us to understand.
If we belong to God, then "doing good" will naturally flow from
deep within our hearts. John further instructs us not to imitate what
is evil but to imitate what is good. Doing good is an outward
manifestation of Christ with us. Doing evil is an outward
manifestation of Satan residing within our hearts.

Since being diagnosed with Alzheimer's, my prayer is I will
continue to do good. I also pray the disease will not change my heart
or desire to continue to do good. Thus far, this has been the case in
my daily life. By faith in Christ, I know I'll continue to be able to do
good in some capacity. Alzheimer's may impact my brain, but my
heart belongs to Christ. He alone protects the essence of who I am in
Him! He will do the same for you if will only ask Him.

*Prayer: Father God, we humbly ask You enable each of us to
continue to do good as Christ abides in each of our lives. Amen*

Thursday: Good to Your Enemies

But I tell you who hear me: Love your enemies, do good to those who hate you, bless those who curse you, pray for those who mistreat you. Luke 6:27–28

Has anyone hurt you so badly you haven't been able to forget it? Unfortunately, many people, including Christians, have had this happen and they harbor ill feelings toward whomever hurt them. Today's Scripture from Luke reminds us we are to love those who hate, curse, or mistreat us. But Jesus goes even further. He instructs us to pray for and to do good to them.

How could He say that? Doesn't He know how much that person hurt me? How am I expected to do good things for someone like that? Perhaps Jesus knew if I prayed for my enemies and did good things for them, I would no longer harbor a grudge against these people. Praying and doing good for someone always leaves me with a spirit of forgiveness.

After being diagnosed with Alzheimer's, I've found it is much easier to do what Jesus instructed in today's passage. I realize my days on earth are limited and my days of clear thinking are certainly limited as well. I find it harder to get angry at those who curse, hate, or even mistreat me. Time is too short to carry grudges toward others no matter what they have done. Praying for them and doing a kind deed leaves me feeling better and closer to Christ than responding in a spiteful manner.

As Christians, this is exactly how Christ wants us to act. We are to clothe ourselves with compassion, kindness, humility, gentleness, and patience. If we do this, nothing but goodness will flow from us. So do your enemies some good today!

Prayer: Lord, help us to pray for those who hate, curse, or mistreat us. Give us opportunities to do good so You will be glorified. Amen

Friday: Good Similar to Jesus

...how God anointed Jesus of Nazareth with the Holy Spirit and power, and how he went around doing good and healing all who were under the power of the devil, because God was with him.
Acts 10:38

I love the way Luke describes the ministry of Jesus when he says, "He went throughout the land doing good and healing all who were under the power of the devil." It is especially important how Luke places doing good before healing in his description of Jesus' ministry. Perhaps doing good is the first step in living a life orchestrated by God.

Did you catch the secret to how Jesus did this? God anointed Jesus with the Holy Spirit first. I am amazed at the power of the Holy Spirit once He abides within a person. The same thing happened with the disciples. Once the Holy Spirit abided within them, they were able to do good and powerful acts.

The same is true when Alzheimer's strikes. This disease may be a formidable foe but it doesn't diminish the power of the Holy Spirit in one's life. Even with Alzheimer's, we are able to do good and powerful acts if we rely on the Holy Spirit. For instance, today I walked in the park near our home and picked up trash along the path. This act generated kind comments from others walking in the park. These people might not have said a word to me had it not been for my simple act of service.

Every single act of goodness has a way of impacting others in positive and unexpected ways. None of these people knew I had Alzheimer's. To them I was just a normal guy cleaning up a park in which they walked. The Holy Spirit nudged me to do something good and God blessed it in an unexpected way!

Prayer: Holy Spirit, nudge us to do good and be more Christ-like as we live out our lives. Amen

Saturday: Add to Your Faith Goodness

For this very reason, make every effort to add to your faith goodness; and to goodness, knowledge; and to knowledge, self-control; and to self-control, perseverance; and to perseverance, godliness; and to godliness, brotherly kindness; and to brotherly kindness, love. 2 Peter 1:5

In Peter's second letter to Christ's sheep, he instructs the flock on how to stimulate Christian growth, combat false teaching, and encourage watchfulness for the Lord's return. The passage deals with Christian growth with an emphasis on character refinement. It is interesting Peter lists goodness as the first refinement to Christian character. Goodness is a natural by-product of Christ abiding within us. What we do, how we act, and what we say are prime indicators of the depth of goodness within our character.

Our church sponsors a Shop and Swap every year. It is a large yard sale where people in our community can come and get clothing, furniture, dishes, kitchen utensils, and other items at no cost. That's right, everything costs nothing. Our women's group sponsors this event as a way of doing good for the community and to make contact with those who really need Christ in their lives. It is amazing how many lives are touched each year because of this kind act.

Peter said in today's Scripture to make every effort to add to your faith goodness. Perhaps there is something you could give away to someone who needs it. Since my diagnosis of Alzheimer's, I've found most of my material possessions don't mean much anymore. Generosity and kindness are by-products of Christian growth even Alzheimer's can't diminish. So do something good for someone today!

Prayer: Lord Jesus, help us to take our faith to the next level and do something good for someone who needs Your love and grace. Amen

Sunday: Stillness Brings Goodness

*Be still, and know that I am God; I will be exalted among the
nations, I will be exalted in the earth. The Lord Almighty is with us;
the God of Jacob is our fortress. Psalms 46:10–11*

This week we have examined Scriptures containing instruction
on doing good and exhibiting the qualities of goodness. It has been a
wonderful time exploring how:

- To encourage others to do good
- Not to grow weary of doing good
- Doing good is from God
- To do good even to those who hate us
- Jesus went about doing good
- To add to your faith goodness.

Now it is time to be still, reflect on the Scriptures we've read,
and invite the Holy Spirit to move freely in our lives. The key to
doing good is allowing the Holy Spirit free reign in our hearts and
minds. He can begin to change who we are by praying for us, gently
nudging us in the right direction when we wander off course, and
discretely teaching us as we read God's word. The Holy Spirit is a
powerful advocate if we accept His guidance. Taking time to be still
before God allows the Holy Spirit to breathe spiritual oxygen into
our souls.

So much has changed in my spiritual walk since my diagnosis of
Alzheimer's. I have grown closer to Christ and the Holy Spirit has
been freer to move in my life. As I become still, the Holy Spirit
gently reminds me of my Father's abounding grace. As my spirit
changes, then doing good naturally flows from deep within me. Take
time to be still today knowing God is in complete control of
everything in your life.

*Prayer: Father God, let us be still before Your mighty throne
today and allow the Holy Spirit to move in our lives. Amen*

Islam Izhaev © 123RF.com

GROW YOUR FAITH

Devotions to help you grow your faith in the midst of the turmoil brought on by Alzheimer's disease.

Monday: Stand Firm in Faith

Be on your guard; stand firm in the faith; be men of courage; be strong. Do everything in love. 1 Corinthians 16:13–14

Most of my life has been pretty easy compared to my father's life. He lived on a tenant farm during the lean time right after the Great Depression. Life was tough but he was raised by two God-fearing parents who went to church every Sunday and had a strong and courageous faith. His parents worked hard and raised nine children on a small dairy farm. Being a farmer in those days was difficult because modern farm machinery was still in its infancy. Most work was accomplished with a set of mules and a one bottom plow or cultivator. It took great faith to work a field and plant it in the spring not knowing what the weather would be like during the summer.

My dad told me about the bad years they had when the harvest was slim. They barely made enough to cover their planting expenses and pay the farm mortgage. Nonetheless, they were grateful because God had blessed them enough to break even. My grandparents stood firm, trusted God, and started each new crop year with the hope of a bountiful harvest.

I suppose that is how I approach my Alzheimer's situation. I stand firm knowing God will help me through the difficult years ahead as I hope for a cure. I'm so hopeful I agreed to be part of an Alzheimer's clinical trial. It may not help me but it may plant seeds that grow into a revolutionary cure for this dreadful disease. Like my grandfather, I'm hopeful for a bountiful harvest. I stand firm in my faith that He will work this situation to the good because I love Him and I'm called according to His purpose. How about you?

Prayer: Heavenly Father, help us to stand firm in the midst of this storm and grant us courage for the road ahead. Amen

Tuesday: Unwavering Faith

Without weakening in his faith, he faced the fact that his body was as good as dead – since he was about a hundred years old – and that Sarah's womb was also dead. Yet he did not waver through unbelief regarding the promise of God, but was strengthened in his faith and gave glory to God. Romans 4:19–20

Today's Scripture is a particularly promising passage from Paul's letter to the church in Rome. I like it because of Paul's description of Abraham's strong faith in the face of physical realities. "Without weakening in his faith" and "he did not waver through unbelief" stand as vivid examples of faith in the midst of uncertainty about a promised future. Abraham's faith in God was credited to him as righteousness.

Faith is often challenged by the difficult situations we face. If we hold firm, our faith will be strengthened. With each new challenge our faith muscles are stretched in preparation for the one great challenge marking our lives. Who we are in Christ is not necessarily defined by the blessings that fall our way but by the trials we faithfully endure.

Alzheimer's is such a trial that must be endured faithfully. There are good days when I know God has blessed me with clear thinking and a sense of normalcy. But the not so good days test my faith. Then I must hold firmly to His promises: He will never forsake me and all things work to the good for those who love the Lord. It is perseverance in the difficult days that make the good days such a blessing. It is also a glorious reminder God is still in complete control and He loves me. Alzheimer's can't take my faith from me. How are your faith muscles today? Stretch them by trusting God!

Prayer: Father of Abraham, grant us a strong, unwavering faith in the midst of turmoil and strife. Amen

Wednesday: Faith Worthy of the Gospel

Whatever happens, conduct yourselves in a manner worthy of the gospel of Christ. Then, whether I come and see you or only hear about you in my absence, I will know that you stand firm in one spirit, contending as one man for the faith of the gospel without being frightened in any way by those who oppose you.
Philippians 1:27–28

My favorite book of the New Testament is Paul's letter to the Philippians. My fondness stems from the uplifting tone of his letter and Paul's expression of love and admiration for the Philippians. This passage reminds me to conduct myself in a manner worthy of the gospel of Christ no matter what is happening in my life. Paul places a tough directive on our hearts as he writes to his beloved church.

After my diagnosis of early-onset Alzheimer's, I had some tough decisions to make regarding my finances, possessions, career, and life. Most decisions were pretty easy to make and I did them readily. But the one difficult decision dealt with my faith. How would I react given this new development in my life? Would I turn away from God and blame Him? Would I draw closer to Him knowing His perfect plan was intact? I struggled with these questions for only a short time because if I had to have Alzheimer's, I wanted God with me all the way!

God gave me 55 fantastic years of healthy living. How could I complain about 5-10 years of declining health? Besides, I knew by my faith and His word, He was not finished with me yet. He still had more work for me to do. Maybe the disease just allowed me to trust in Him more so I could conduct myself worthy of the gospel of Christ. Whatever the reason, I stand firm in my faith; nothing will disrupt my relationship with Christ. Not even Alzheimer's! How about you?

Prayer: Gentle Christ, help us to stand firm in our faith. Amen

Thursday: Faith Develops Perseverance

Consider it pure joy, my brothers, whenever you face trials of many kinds, because you know the testing of your faith develops perseverance. James 1:2–3

I was a helicopter pilot in the United States Marine Corps over 35 years ago and can still remember the rigors of flight training. One memorable event was the Dilbert Dunker, a makeshift cockpit on rails designed to crash into a pool of water. The flight student is strapped into the cockpit and released down the rail into water where it turns upside down. The trainee must release his harness, push out of the cockpit, and swim to the surface using only one breathe of air. It is a pretty scary exercise but is fairly simple to execute if one remains calm. The intent of the exercise is to teach trainees to react calmly under stress and gain confidence in their ability to exit the cockpit after a crash water landing. This is one of the many tests a flight student undergoes before climbing into an actual aircraft. These training events determine the perseverance of the trainee for future flight operations.

The same can be said about our Christian faith. According to James, we must face many types of trials testing our faith and building perseverance in our Christian walk. These trials develop a more resilient faith enabling us to endure anything happening in our lives. It may seem silly but I look at Alzheimer's as just another trial I'll endure to reinforce my firm faith in Christ. It may not be the trial I would have chosen on my own but we seldom get the chance to choose the trials we undergo! Throughout my Christian walk, He has been preparing me for this particular trial. Like the rigors of flight training, I've been prepared. Christ is with me all the way! Are you prepared? If not, He'll get you ready.

Prayer: Lord Jesus, thank You for Your preparation up to this point. Help me endure this trial in a manner worthy of Your calling. Amen

Friday: Stand in Faith or Not at All

If you do not stand firm in your faith, you will not stand at all.
Isaiah 7:9

I love to watch the *Dirty Harry* movies where Clint Eastwood stars as Detective Harry Callahan. I love these movies because I always know where Detective Callahan stands when it comes to law enforcement and the apprehension of known criminals. He doesn't play favorites, politics, or games. He always stands on the side of justice. If you stand on the other side, well, you're just likely to make his day. To Harry, it seems pretty clear what is right and wrong.

The book of Isaiah is pretty clear cut as well. You definitely know where Isaiah stands regarding his relationship with God and how the children of Israel are to turn from their sinful ways. Isaiah doesn't sugarcoat his prophetic message. He stands firm on the holiness and absolute authority of God. He reminds the rulers if they don't stand firm in faith, then they will not stand at all. There are no stipulations or conditions allowing them to sin or slide on their faith. They either stand firm upholding God's covenant or they don't.

It really isn't much different today. We either stand firm in our faith relying on God's strength for whatever comes our way or we don't. I don't know about you, but I stand firm in my faith knowing God is in complete control no matter what the circumstances.

Having Alzheimer's doesn't change my faith in God one bit. It simply reinforces my complete reliance on His perfect power to sustain me. I choose to stand firm in my faith so Alzheimer's can just make my day! How about you?

Prayer: Heavenly Father, may our faith and reliance on You sustain us in the days ahead as we choose to stand firm. Amen

Saturday: Hold Firmly to Faith

Therefore, since we have a great high priest who has gone through the heavens, Jesus the Son of God, let us hold firmly to the faith we profess. Hebrews 4:14

My son, Ben, bought a 300 magnum rifle years ago to hunt coyotes and deer. After buying the rifle, a friend commented I'd better hold firmly to the stock since a 300 magnum kicks quite a bit. I thanked him for his advice but soon forgot it. The next weekend Ben and I were zeroing in the scope for deer season. We set up a target and loaded the rifle. I got in the prone position, aimed, and gently squeezed the trigger. The round went off and the rifle kicked sharply causing the scope to ram into my head just above the eyebrow. You see, I forgot to hold firmly to the stock. Not only did I get a nice scar but my pride was wounded in front of my eldest son. But it was an invaluable lesson for him on how hard a 300 magnum kicks!

Holding on firmly is good advice especially when it comes to our faith. Perhaps that is what the writer of Hebrews was trying to get across to the Jewish converts who were being tempted to convert back to Judaism. He was reminding them to hold firmly to the faith established by the great high priest Jesus Christ, the Son of God.

I can still remember the first few weeks after being diagnosed with Early-onset Alzheimer's. I'd go to bed at night holding the Bible and hoping my faith was still intact. Holding firmly to the Bible gave me comfort because I had done this before when faced with situations completely out of my control. Holding firmly to the faith you profess is prudent advice no matter what the situation. So, what are you holding on to?

Prayer: Lord, help us to hold firmly to the faith we profess in spite of anything Satan throws our way. Amen

Sunday: Be Still to Affirm Your Faith

Be still, and know that I am God; I will be exalted among the nations, I will be exalted in the earth. The Lord Almighty is with us; the God of Jacob is our fortress. Psalms 46:10–11

It is time to set aside our busy schedules and focus on being still before the Lord. This time of stillness and reverence builds our faith by allowing the Holy Spirit to refresh our souls. It is a precious time that gently reminds us of how holy our God is and how much He truly loves each of us. It is an opportunity to quietly reflect on who we are in Christ and reaffirm the faith we so gladly profess.

For me, being outside during the quiet of the morning provides a beautiful reminder of the continual presence of the Lord as I see His fingerprints all around me. In the calmness of the early hours I reflect on His grace and how wonderful it is to be a child of God. I often forget how truly blessed I am and this early morning time gently reminds me of God's grace.

On this day I eagerly await the time when I can fellowship with other Christians and worship God in a congregational setting. There is something special about gathering together on Sunday mornings to praise God with other Christians. It seems so simple yet there is nothing that fills my heart with such joy. My faith is strengthened as I look at my brothers and sisters in Christ. I know each one has something going on in their lives but they are able to put it aside and come together to worship God. It is such an encouragement and I pray I will be able to continue worshipping for a long time.

Alzheimer's may cause me to forget things but when I walk into our church I feel whole again. My spirit is renewed and I can endure another week no matter what changes may occur in my life! Be still today and affirm your faith as well.

Prayer: Lord and Savior, refresh our spirits and our faith. Amen

Dean Fikar © 123RF.com

A COOPERATIVE SPIRIT

Devotions to help you develop a willing and cooperative spirit
when Alzheimer's disease hits home.

Monday: A Willing Mind

And you, my son Solomon, acknowledge the God of your father, and serve him with wholehearted devotion and with a willing mind, for the Lord searches every heart and understands every motive behind the thoughts. If you seek him, he will be found by you; but if you forsake him, he will reject you forever. 1 Chronicles 28:9

Have you ever worked with someone who had great ability but their heart wasn't in the job? In most cases, I'd rather the person just leave. In fact, the job generally went much smoother and faster without them. It's sad when a person has been given so much ability but has such a poor attitude. Perhaps that is what King David was relaying to Solomon about his relationship with God as he passed on the throne to his son.

King David was a man after God's own heart so he knew how important a man's heart was to the Lord. Serving God with wholehearted devotion and a willing mind was an absolute necessity in order to rule with wisdom and goodness. David's advice holds true today. God wants us to serve Him with this same zeal and spirit.

So how does this impact us as we deal with Alzheimer's? It simply means we must continue to serve the Lord. We don't blame God for what has happened. We graciously ask Him to use us as He chooses.

Our relationship with God should be strengthened as we draw closer to Him because of our illness. He still remains Lord of our lives and nothing changes that fact. Continue to seek Him and He will be found because His love for us endures forever. Having Alzheimer's disease doesn't change that one bit!

Prayer: Father, may we serve You with all our hearts, all our minds, all our strength, and all our spirit because You are our God. Amen

Tuesday: Eager Willingness

Now finish the work, so that your eager willingness to do it may be matched by your completion of it, according to your means.
2 Corinthians 8:11

Alzheimer's has a funny way of changing the way you tackle tasks. I generally start out pretty gung-ho as I begin a simple project. However, my mind doesn't always follow the same path as my spirit. To compensate, I break a project down into little steps which I write down. It is sort of a mini-checklist for me to follow as I get involved in the task at hand. As I finish each step, I check it off. This assures me of completing all the critical steps. Plus it allows me to walk away, or wander off as I sometimes do, then jump right back into it. I didn't used to have to do this but things have changed since my diagnosis!

This isn't precisely what Paul was preaching to his flock at Corinth but it is close. Paul wanted the believers in Corinth to continue in their giving with eagerness as they had done the previous year. Paul understood their desires and good intentions started out strong but had a tendency to wane as time passed. He wanted to make sure the Corinthians would stay focused and continue their generosity. It is not likely they suffered from Alzheimer's but they had other issues which distracted them. Paul's letter provided them encouragement to continue on with their previous work.

Like the Corinthians, we need encouragement as well. My loving wife often provides me prompts when I become distracted. I thank God for her help and for giving me a willing spirit that takes prompting so well. Take Paul's advice and develop some eager willingness in your life today.

Prayer: Lord, thank You for sending people our way who provide encouragement so we might complete what we have started. Amen

Paul M. Hornback

Wednesday: There Is Willingness

For if the willingness is there, the gift is acceptable according to what one has, not according to what he does not have.
2 Corinthians 8:12

In Paul's letter to the Corinthians, he pens a profound passage beginning with the words "...if the willingness is there." The words surprised me because I have always focused on the part that says, "...the gift being acceptable according to what one has, not according to what he does not have." I imagine this is a common problem with others who rush over the first part of the verse. The first part of the passage is the heart of the matter. Our *willingness* to give is critical if our gift is to be acceptable. A humble willingness, a right spirit, and a genuine desire to give results in a pleasing offering to the Lord.

After struggling with early-onset Alzheimer's for quite a while, I finally had no choice but to retire earlier than I wanted. After retiring, our income changed dramatically. We struggled with what we could afford to give to the Lord through our local church. Our willingness to give was still strong but our resources had diminished. This passage provided comfort because I knew I had a willing spirit and a genuine desire to continue giving but my offering would be less. It helped me understand my gift would still be acceptable in the eyes of the Lord because of my heartfelt desire to continue giving.

Alzheimer's has a way of changing your financial situation but it should not change your heartfelt desire to give to the Lord's work. You still belong to Christ and He loves you dearly. Don't let Alzheimer's change your heart or stifle your spirit!

Prayer: Lord Jesus, continue to move in our lives in such a manner as to nurture our willing spirits so we may be of service to You and our gifts will be acceptable in Your eyes. Amen

Thursday: A Weak Body with a Willing Spirit

Watch and pray so that you will not fall into temptation. The spirit is willing, but the body is weak. Matthew 26:41

Have you ever felt like the disciples at Gethsemane: Tired, exhausted, and completely run down with no energy left to stay awake, let alone pray? I've been there numerous times in my life. In today's passage, Jesus tells his disciples to watch and pray so they don't fall prey to temptation.

Didn't Jesus know they would fall asleep when He left them? Yes, Jesus knew exactly what would happen because the disciples were relying on their own strength. They could not comprehend the magnitude of what Jesus was about to face. Perhaps Jesus wanted them to remember these specific words which He spoke to them so they could write about it later.

It is a brutal reminder of how important a willing spirit is to the Lord. Jesus fully understands our bodies are frail and weak but if our spirits are strong, we won't fall spiritually asleep. Alzheimer's is just another indication of how weak our bodies are today. We must rely on God's strength to continue the path He has prepared for us.

In today's passage, the disciples were trying to do everything in their own strength. They had not yet received the power of the Holy Spirit in their lives. But the Holy Spirit is the key to maintaining a willing spirit in the midst of a weak body. So even though Alzheimer's has a grip on my weak body, God holds my spirit tightly and it is stronger than it has ever been! Don't let Alzheimer's dampen your spirit or willingness to serve God. He is in complete control and His strength is more than sufficient for the task at hand.

Prayer: Father God, help us maintain a strong and willing spirit even though our bodies are frail and weak. Amen

Friday: Willing to Share

Command them to do good, to be rich in good deeds, and to be generous and willing to share. 1 Timothy 6:18

I love the encouraging words of Paul as he writes to his beloved friend Timothy in today's passage. When Paul left on his fourth missionary journey, he instructed Timothy, his son in the faith, to care for the church at Ephesus. This passage penned by Paul was aimed at rich folks in the Ephesus church. Timothy was to command them not to put faith in their wealth but to do good deeds, be generous, and be willing to share the blessings God had bestowed upon them. By doing these things, the rich would be able to "take hold of the life that is truly life."

These words of wisdom hold true for us today since in the eyes of most of the world's population, we are rich beyond all measures. Of course, the key once again is to have a willing spirit. Our willingness to share our money, possessions, and faith define who we are in Christ. It enables us to grab hold of a life that is truly a life worthy of the gospel.

Our willingness to follow Christ's commands shouldn't be impacted by our circumstances. The underlying issue is whether or not we are willing to do as Christ commands. I don't know about you but I want to be a man after God's own heart. I deeply desire to have a willing spirit the Lord can use no matter the circumstances. Alzheimer's may limit certain things we are able to accomplish but it doesn't eliminate everything we are capable of doing. Being willing to share in whatever manner we are able will help we will have a life embraced by Christ. That is what I truly desire!

Prayer: Lord Jesus, foster within us a willingness to share all You have given us so we might live a life worthy of Your calling. Amen

Saturday: Because You Are Willing

Be shepherds of God's flock that is under your care, serving as overseers – not because you must, but because you are willing, as God wants you to be; not greedy for money, but eager to serve; not lording it over those entrusted to you, but being examples to the flock. 1 Peter 5:2–3

As I write these words the last of the 33 Chilean miners who were trapped underground for 69 days have been safely rescued. The last man out was the shift foreman who oversaw the miners while trapped 2000 feet below the surface of the earth. He rationed food and water for 17 days until a small hole was drilled to their location and initial contact made. While heroic efforts occurred above the surface, similar efforts were conducted below. The trapped miners encouraged one another, discussed their fears, and maintained a hopeful attitude. This hopeful and encouraging spirit was initiated by the caring foreman whose leadership helped the men endure the horrid conditions while trapped below ground.

Perhaps Peter had something similar in mind when he penned today's passage providing instructions for the church elders. They were to be overseers because they were willing and eager to serve in a humble manner. We are all elders in one way or another since we are charged with exemplifying Christ in our lives.

Having Alzheimer's doesn't change who we are in Christ nor does it change the fact we are to be willing servants. Certainly things become more difficult but by maintaining a willing spirit we assist our caregivers and set a humble example for those we love. Just like the Chilean miners who were trapped below the surface, we are trapped in our collapsing minds. But don't lose hope for God is still at work to free our spirit from a weak body!

Prayer: Heavenly Father, we are trapped in a collapsing mind and we desperately need Your help to maintain a willing spirit. Amen

Sunday: Be Still to Strengthen Your Will

Be still, and know that I am God; I will be exalted among the nations, I will be exalted in the earth. The Lord Almighty is with us; the God of Jacob is our fortress. Psalms 46: 10–11

A willing spirit and a humble heart are all I need to be still before the Lord. A willing spirit helps me set aside this time as a priority in my schedule. A humble heart allows God to have my full attention as I approach Him without a hidden agenda. Being still before the Lord refreshes my spirit and anchors my willingness to serve Him in whatever capacity He directs.

This time of stillness is absolutely necessary for a real relationship with the Lord. It is during these quiet moments my "true north" is reaffirmed. Perhaps that is why Sunday was created to be a day of rest so our spirits would be refreshed through worship, prayer, and stillness. God's plan was for us to set aside one day a week so we would rest and truly focus on Him. The only way to truly know God in a personal way is to be still before Him.

These times of being still before the Lord have become even more precious since I was diagnosed with early-onset Alzheimer's disease. I desperately need the time to allow the Holy Spirit to speak to me, remind me how much God loves me, and strengthen my spirit. Without these quiet moments, the future fears of this disease steal my trust and peace in the Him. Please take time today to sit beside the still waters, lie in green pastures, and be still before the Lord. God will renew your spirit if you are willing to be still. His grace, love and mercy will certainly surround you. Then you will know He is your God!

Prayer: Father, help us find time in our busy lives to be still. Refresh our souls, renew our spirits, and remind us of our salvation. Reset our true north so we might humbly serve You more. Amen

Foottoo © 123RF.com

GODLY WISDOM

Devotions to help you seek God's wisdom for critical decisions when Alzheimer's disease strikes.

Paul M. Hornback

Monday: Fear of the Lord Is the Beginning of Wisdom

The fear of the Lord is the beginning of wisdom; all who follow his precepts have good understanding. To him belongs eternal praise. Psalm 111:10

Any study of wisdom should start with today's Scripture from Psalms. The Psalmist asserts "the fear of the Lord" is the beginning of wisdom. The use of the word *fear* has a different connotation than that of being terrified of something. I look at "fear of the Lord" like I do fear of my earthly father. I was fearful I would disappoint him with my decisions in life; I would not live up to the moral standards by which he lived his life; I would not grow to be the honorable and generous man he was; and I would not honor his legacy of learning. He was a remarkable man and I wanted to walk in his footsteps.

Perhaps this is what the Psalmist had in mind when he wrote today's Scripture. The beginning of wisdom rests at the feet of our heavenly Father. If we follow His precepts we will have good understanding.

Because of Alzheimer's, my decision-making abilities have been impacted. It is difficult for me to make a big decision. Then I struggle with whether or not each decision is a wise one. Thankfully, all I need do is read my Bible and talk with my heavenly Father when I lack wisdom. He guides me and brings godly people into my life to help. Thus, listening to the wise counsel of others, praying about it, and seeking His guidance are the steps to ensure my decisions are wise. Alzheimer's may change our decision-making ability but it doesn't change our heavenly Father's ability at all!

Prayer: Heavenly Father, grant us wisdom and understanding for all our decisions, big and small. We trust You alone. Amen

Tuesday: The Lord Gives Wisdom

For the Lord gives wisdom, and from his mouth come knowledge and understanding. Proverbs 2:6

Solomon was the wisest man to ever walk the face of the earth. He asked for only one monumental thing from the Lord. Solomon asked for wisdom sufficient to lead God's people properly. It stands to reason God gave him wisdom far beyond what anyone has yet to attain.

Much of the Book of Proverbs is attributed to Solomon and wisdom is a major theme throughout the text. Today's passage reminds us the Lord gives wisdom. From His mouth come knowledge and understanding. I could certainly use all the wisdom, knowledge and understanding God will dish out!

Since being diagnosed with early-onset Alzheimer's, I have found my storehouse of wisdom is lacking in many areas. As a result, I must rely on prayer, the Scriptures, meditation, and wise Christian counsel to fill my wisdom voids. Prior to my illness, I prided myself on my acute analytical and decision-making abilities. Since Alzheimer's has a foothold in my brain, both of these attributes have been seriously affected. Thankfully, I am not ashamed to ask for help in making major decisions now. I simply pray and ask God for wisdom and assistance in knowing the right path to take.

Today's passage from Proverbs provides the foundation for facing a lack of wisdom, knowledge, or understanding in anything. Seek the Lord's advice. Set aside selfish pride and simply ask for help. God has yet to turn anyone away empty-handed. Solomon asked and God replied. So can you!

Prayer: Heavenly Father, You are the alpha and omega in all things including wisdom. Give us wisdom to meet today's needs. Amen

Wednesday: Godly Instruction

Listen to my instruction and be wise; do not ignore it. Blessed is the man who listens to me, watching daily at my doors, waiting at my doorway. For whoever finds me finds life and receives favor from the Lord. Proverbs 9:33–35

Have you ever wished you had Solomon as a personal advisor when a major decision loomed? Wouldn't it be great to have someone wise to help you make the right choice? Well, why settle for the apprentice when you can have the Master?

Today's passage reminds us to listen wisely to the Lord's instruction. But how do we listen so as to not miss anything the Lord sends our way? Proverbs instructs us to watch and wait. This means we need to pray daily and during our prayers, wait for His response. This seems pretty simple doesn't it?

Why then is it so hard to pray and wait for God's response? Perhaps because we want things in our time, we want it now, and we want it easily! God doesn't necessarily work according to our schedule but He certainly provides the instruction and guidance we need. He may respond through Scripture, a trusted friend, an event, or a change in our hearts. God works in mysterious ways but He always provides what we need if we simply call on Him. The key is searching for His wisdom and waiting for His instruction before making a decision.

Alzheimer's can certainly be a scary situation but you can trust the Lord to help you navigate the treacherous waters ahead. Seek His wonderful wisdom and comforting counsel and you will find favor with the Lord. Remember, having Alzheimer's won't change God's promises one bit!

Prayer: Precious Lord, provide us godly instruction as we seek Your counsel in our daily lives. We wait patiently at Your doorstep. Amen

Thursday: Wisdom in Taking Advice

Pride only breeds quarrels, but wisdom is found in those who take advice. Proverbs 13:10

My father was a very wise man. He had both street smarts and book learning. The street smarts came from living during extremely difficult times. He never went to college or formally finish high school. The book learning came from his never ending thirst for reading and his continual education during a 22 year career in the Army. I can remember seeing him with a book in his hands almost every night.

When I was a teenager, my dad and I would talk for hours about politics, the Vietnam War, famous people, history, religion, and life in general. Because he was knowledgeable about so many things, I sought his counsel when I had to make difficult decisions impacting my future. Unfortunately, I did not always take his advice because of my petty pride. Pride had a way of coming between us as I grew older. In almost every case, his advice was spot on. If I had heeded it, I would have avoided much sorrow and heartache in my life.

Today's passage reinforces what I learned the hard way. Wisdom is found in those who take advice! Of course, it is vitally important to take God's advice. The Scriptures are pretty clear on that point! Proverbs cautions us about listening to wicked and foolish people which can get us into trouble. Therefore, it is important to seek out wise Christian counsel when faced with major decisions. This can be your spouse, a trusted friend, a pastor, or a lawyer. Heed their advice but pray about it as well. God will affirm the advice if it aligns with His will and plan for your life.

Prayer: Father God, help us to take advice from godly people You send our way to counsel us on decisions we need to make. Amen

Friday: Get Wisdom

Get wisdom, get understanding; do not forget my words or swerve from them. Do not forsake wisdom, and she will protect you; love her, and she will watch over you. Wisdom is supreme; therefore get wisdom. Though it cost all you have, get understanding.
Proverbs 4:5–7

I am amazed at the contestants on *Jeopardy* and how they are able to rapidly recall stored knowledge across a host of differing categories. I definitely do not possess the knowledge of most of these contestants. However, knowledge alone does not equal understanding or wisdom.

Today's passage from Proverbs reminds us to get wisdom and understanding even if it costs all we have in life. Wow, that is a pretty bold statement isn't it? For all practical purposes wisdom is supreme. Proverbs advises us to get wisdom because it will protect and watch over us. This is sound advice especially in light of all the scam artists who prey upon older people with diminished mental capacities or dementia.

Having wisdom (or at least access to someone with wisdom) certainly protects you from the snares of evil individuals. Perhaps this is in part what today's passage implies. Seeking wisdom, both from the Scriptures and from a trusted Christian friend or family member, will keep you from evil. Alzheimer's certainly impacts our ability to win at *Jeopardy* but it doesn't mean we have to lose at life! God has ways to offset the debilitating effects of Alzheimer's disease. We need to seek Him, get wisdom and understanding, and trust in Him. His word is true and He's faithful no matter what befalls us!

Prayer: Gracious Father, You alone are our rock and fortress. We depend on You for wisdom in whatever manner You choose to give it. Remind us to seek You first and our path will be made straight. Amen

Saturday: Wisdom for Perseverance

If any of you lacks wisdom, he should ask God, who gives generously to all without finding fault, and it will be given to him.
James 1:5

I love the book of James so much that in all of the Sunday school classes my wife and I have taught or been associated, we have studied the book of James at least once. James offers a straight forward (often times 'in your face') look at how we should live Christian lives. That is why I love James so much.

Today's Scripture bluntly states if you lack wisdom all you need do is ask God and it will be given to you. Pretty straight forward isn't it? This passage follows right on the heels of James saying we should consider it "pure joy" whenever we face trials of many kinds. Wisdom enables us to persevere through whatever trial or circumstance we may encounter.

Wisdom is definitely the mark of maturity for persevering through situations that may not be to our liking. Alzheimer's is certainly a trial requiring wisdom, perseverance, and faith to endure. All of these are readily available if we humbly ask God to provide them according to His glorious grace and goodness. In fact, that is the focal point of today's passage.

If we lack wisdom, we need to ask God and it will be given to us. James does not beat around the bush when it comes to trials, tests, faith, perseverance, and wisdom. They are all linked to how we are to live our lives as Christians. Godly wisdom allows us to faithfully persevere through the many trials and tests we encounter in life. You see, God hasn't changed and his promises still hold true. Alzheimer's is just another trial in life He most certainly will help you through!

Prayer: Father, give us wisdom and strength for this trial. Amen

Sunday: Wisdom from Stillness

Be still, and know that I am God; I will be exalted among the nations, I will be exalted in the earth. The Lord Almighty is with us; the God of Jacob is our fortress. Psalms 46:10–11

What a wonderful week it has been as we focused our thoughts on words of wisdom from our heavenly Father. Now it is time to be still before Him and exalt Him above all the earth. When it comes to wisdom, He is the alpha and omega, the perfector of knowledge, the generous giver of understanding, and the ultimate source of sound instruction. He is worthy of our praise because He is the one true God.

If you lack wisdom in any area of your life, if you have big decisions to make, or if you are uncertain about what lies ahead, ask for God's wisdom and discernment. Be still before Him and quietly allow His wisdom to speak to you in whatever manner He chooses to impart His precious pearls. Being still before God pushes out the worries of a troubled life, the deceitfulness of worldly wealth, and the desire to have other things. If we can just be still and focus on Him alone, our lives will be filled with the joy of His holy presence. Our hearts will rejoice and our spirits will be renewed as the Holy Spirit moves quietly in the stillness to calm our souls while bringing perfect peace to our lives.

He eagerly waits for you to run to His open arms. He wants you to share everything a precious child would share with his loving father. Don't delay spending time with Him today. Be still and seek His presence. You won't be disappointed!

Prayer: heavenly Father, help us to be still before You today and exalt Your holy name. Comfort us, fill us with Your presence, and grant us wisdom for the days ahead. We desperately need Your insight to make major decisions so we humbly ask for Your guidance. Thank You for Your grace and mercy in our lives. Amen

Tina Wiley © 123RF.com

ACCEPT HELP

Devotions to help you accept help from others which will improve your daily life with Alzheimer's disease.

Monday: Two Are Better Than One

Two are better than one, because they have a good return for their work. If one falls down, his friend can help him up. But pity the man who falls and has no one to help him up! Ecclesiastes 4:9–10

I love the outdoors and hiking in rugged terrain. I suppose it is the adventure and challenge of doing something new and difficult enticing me to answer nature's call. Recently, my two sons and I went with some close Christian friends to hike in Tennessee in an area with lots of rocks, waterfalls, and stream beds. Since my diagnosis of Alzheimer's, I had not been hiking in very difficult terrain because my sense of balance has been impacted.

The trip was an absolute joy and the scenery was breathtaking. The terrain was pretty rugged and at times I had to rely on the help of one of my sons to climb up rock ledges, hop from one boulder to another, and cross wet stream beds. At first I thought I'd be embarrassed and have my pride hurt because I needed help. However, I soon realized in order for me to enjoy this spectacular outing it was an absolute necessity to have help. I actually enjoyed having my boys walking beside me and offering their hands in particularly difficult areas.

Today's Scripture indicates it is better to have two so if one falls, the other can help him up. How very true this is when hiking but more importantly, in everyday life. Alzheimer's can impact our abilities in different areas so it is essential to accept assistance. Set aside foolish pride, embrace the help of others, and thank God for helpful friends. Alzheimer's does change us but we still have lots of life left to live!

Prayer: Thank You Father for the help You send our way. Amen

Tuesday: Unexpected Help

When Apollos wanted to go to Achaia, the brothers encouraged him and wrote to the disciples there to welcome him. On arriving, he was a great help to those who by grace had believed. Acts 18:27

God often provides help in ways we may not expect. Today's passage describes such an event occurring in the early church. Apollos was in Ephesus speaking boldly about the Lord Jesus. When he wanted to go to Achaia, the brothers in Ephesus wrote the brothers in Achaia and greased the skids so to speak. Apollos was welcomed in Achaia where he was a great help to the believers. While in Achaia, he vigorously refuted the Jews in public debate using Scripture to prove Jesus was the Christ.

Apollos was an unexpected help in the Roman province of Achaia but what might have happened if they had not accepted his help? Would the early church have suffered a major setback? Thankfully we don't have to wonder about it because Apollos was accepted wholeheartedly by the brothers in Achaia.

Like the early church, those of us afflicted with Alzheimer's disease are in a battle. This battle cannot be won alone and will definitely require the assistance of others. But we have a choice to make. We can graciously accept the help of others or we can attempt to go it alone. Today's passage from Acts provides assurance we should welcome the help of others. As for me, I decided early on to set aside foolish pride and accept the help of loved ones and good Christian friends whenever it is offered. I certainly don't want to be a burden on anyone but I also know I cannot survive this battle alone. So accept help from others and your future will be filled with God's grace!

Prayer: Lord Jesus, thank You for the unexpected help of good friends at just the right time to meet our individual needs. Amen

Wednesday: Help for the Journey

I plan to do so when I go to Spain. I hope to visit you while passing through and to have you assist me on my journey there, after I have enjoyed your company for a while. Romans 15:24

Paul was quite the traveler and accomplished many missionary journeys to help establish the early church. However, Paul did not accomplish his travels without the help of others. Today's passage presents Paul's plans to pass through Rome on his way to Spain and his request for assistance from the church in Rome. Without the help of his Christian brothers and sisters, Paul would have been less effective in spreading the gospel throughout the lands bordering the Mediterranean Sea. We also know Paul had a thorn in the flesh that caused him great anguish. As such, Paul received help in many different ways as he spread the gospel.

The other day, my wife and I drove to a seminar at which she was presenting. I drove most of the way but I did need her help navigating and making decisions at crucial points. You see, Alzheimer's has impacted my decision-making ability. As a result, I am not afraid to ask for and accept help in areas where my abilities are degraded. Like Paul, I realize in order for me to be successful, I need the assistance of others. I rejoice in the fact I am still able to drive and I mostly welcome my wife's assistance. I fully understand at some point I will no longer be able to drive. In fact, I have difficulty driving at night so I no longer attempt night driving in unfamiliar places. Alzheimer's may be my "thorn in the flesh" but with the help of others I will continue forward!

Prayer: Lord Jesus, thank You for the example of Paul and how he requested and readily accepted the help of others. Help us to be more like Paul as we need help from time to time. Amen

Thursday: Help from a Faithful Brother

With the help of Silas, whom I regard as a faithful brother, I have written to you briefly, encouraging you and testifying that this is the true grace of God. Stand fast in it. 1 Peter 5:12

The Scriptures are full of references where God's chosen people relied on the help of others to continue God's work on earth, complete a specific task assigned by God, and to spread the gospel. Today's passage is the final greeting in First Peter where he acknowledges Silas' help in the writing of his letter. Silas may have been a scribe who helped record Peter's thoughts as well as the bearer of the letter to its destination. It is a perfect example of one brother helping another in an area where one was lacking.

Alzheimer's disease impacts individuals in different ways. An early diagnosis can help identify the affected areas so adjustments can be made to help compensate for declining abilities. The key is to maintain a willing spirit and graciously accept assistance from others. In the case of Peter, his letters may not have been written or delivered without the help of Silas. Peter was able to put aside foolish pride and humble himself knowing he could not do all God required on his own.

When Alzheimer's strikes you cannot do all life requires on your own. Therefore it is perfectly acceptable to seek help from others. You certainly want to be as independent as possible but in areas where the disease has degraded your abilities, you shouldn't be afraid to ask for assistance. Peter asked for help. Why shouldn't you do the same?

Prayer: Heavenly Father, help us to know our limitations and to humbly ask for help where and when we need it. Amen

Friday: An Ever-Present Help

God is our refuge and strength, an ever-present help in trouble.
Psalm 46:1

I can always find hope and encouragement during difficult times by reading the Psalms. No matter how hopeless the situation may seem from my earthly understanding, God always provides hope through His word. You see, if God has helped in the past and He is the same yesterday, today, and tomorrow, then I can expect His help in my situation.

After being diagnosed with early-onset Alzheimer's disease, I struggled with the fears everyone faces. What would happen at work, how would I deal with my finances, what would I do with my property, and how would I plan for my future? These concerns weighed heavily on my heart. I prayed to God for His help and wisdom to address these issues and He responded in glorious ways. I applied for disability retirement and it was approved in record time (the work issue was resolved). I went to a trusted Christian lawyer and he helped my wife and I decide what to do with our home, our legal matters, and certain parts of our finances (the finances were under control). Out of the blue, an auctioneer approached me about handling some of our property (the property issue was settled).

We all need help in situations that seem hopeless. Our first step has to be to go to God in prayer. We must lay out all our concerns and ask for His help. He is our strength and He will guide us. For me personally, it was getting past the whole pride issue because I have always been able to manage things on my own. Now I've learned God's wisdom is a far better than mine because He has my best interests at heart. He is my rock, my fortress, and my hope! Is He the same for you?

Prayer: Father, thank You for Your help in all matters. Amen

Saturday: A Wife of Noble Character

A wife of noble character who can find? She is worth far more than rubies. Her husband has full confidence in her and lacks nothing of value. She brings him good, not harm, all the days of her life. Proverbs 31:10–12

The book of Proverbs is filled with wisdom and sound advice for living one's life. But the closing epilogue personifies the wife of noble character for which every man searches. Today's Scripture describes the blessed state of the husband of such a noble woman. She brings him only good in his life and does nothing to harm him. Her husband places his confidence in her and as a result he lacks nothing.

I have been blessed with such a noble wife and she is worth far more than anything money could buy. I trust her with all I have accumulated in life. After being diagnosed with early-onset Alzheimer's disease, our lawyer suggested we place all of the property we planned on keeping in my wife's name. This way if anything happened to me my wife would already have the property in her name so it would be legally hers. This was a significant step easily done because I have a noble wife. We also took care of other matters our lawyer suggested so my wife would have full authority over all our affairs. Again, this was done because I know she would "watch over the affairs of our household" in a wise and prudent manner.

I believe God allowed me to meet a noble woman 38 years ago. He gave me the wisdom to marry her. God must have known all along what was going to happen in my life and how important it was I marry a Proverbs woman. She helps me every day and I am a blessed man because of her!

Prayer: Heavenly Father, thank You for sending us noble people to help us in our times of need. Amen

Sunday: Reflection in Stillness

Be still, and know that I am God; I will be exalted among the nations, I will be exalted in the earth. The Lord Almighty is with us; the God of Jacob is our fortress. Psalms 46:10–11

This week we have focused on welcoming the help of others to improve our daily lives. Now it is time to be still before the Lord and thank Him for the help He graciously sends our way. It is important to take time each week and reflect on the ways God has touched your life through the kindness of others. As you remember these special acts of kindness and helpfulness, make sure you thank your heavenly Father for sending His faithful servants along your path. We often take for granted the generous gifts our gracious Father delivers to us daily. By simply being still before Him, He gently reminds us of all He has done and continues to do for each of us.

It is ironic how much I took for granted during the years before Alzheimer's began to impact my life. I never really required anyone's assistance. I could easily handle everything on my own so I usually refused the help of others. When someone did graciously lend a hand, it didn't seem like a big deal so I took it for granted. That has all changed. Now I truly appreciate assistance in areas I am no longer able to manage on my own. Each week I am both amazed and humbled by the goodness and grace of God. In spite of all that has happened to me, He still finds ways to bless me through the help of others. He is truly my rock and fortress and I will exalt Him above all things. Take time today to be still before the Lord, praise His holy name, and strengthen your relationship with Him.

Prayer: Lord God, You are the one true God who always looks upon us with compassion. Thank You for Your everlasting love, grace, and mercy in our lives. You are our rock and fortress. Amen

George Robertson © 123RF.com

FRIENDSHIPS

Devotions to help you nurture friendships that make a difference for your daily battles with Alzheimer's disease.

Monday: A Friend Closer than a Brother

A man of many companions may come to ruin, but there is a friend who sticks closer than a brother. Proverbs 18:24

Proverbs is filled with amazing insights when it comes to living out our daily lives. Today's passage reminds us to choose our companions carefully; otherwise they will ruin our lives. This is sound advice and it aligns closely with what my parents said concerning my teenage friendships.

Friends can be a blessing or burden depending on their character and relationship with Christ. A friend with a deeply rooted relationship in Christ will be a friend who sticks closer than a brother. This type of friend will exhibit love, joy, peace, patience, kindness, goodness, faithfulness, gentleness, and self-control. Now isn't that the kind of friend you would love to have in your life? This kind of friend will never harm you in any way. They always have your best interests at heart and never act from selfish motives.

Good Christian friends are important when Alzheimer's strikes. As our reasoning skills become impaired, we can be conned due to our disability. Often, an individual of "many companions" can be duped into handing his life savings over to an unscrupulous individual. Having a trusted Christian friend provides someone from whom we can seek sound advice. Nurturing these friendships is a priority because they are priceless. If you don't have friends like these, then get connected with a good Christian church and develop godly friendships. People with Alzheimer's are easy prey for con artists but godly friends won't let this happen to you!

Father God, thank You for friendships deeply rooted in Christ. Help us to nurture these trusted relationships. Amen

Tuesday: Do Not Forsake a Friend

Do not forsake your friend and the friend of your father, and do not go to your brother's house when disaster strikes you – better a neighbor nearby than a brother far away.
Proverbs 27:10

Proverbs provides precious pearls of wisdom for fostering friendships that will endure the test of time. Today's passage from Proverbs cautions us not to fail a friend in his time of need. Then when disaster strikes your household, you can rely on your trusted friend. This especially holds true for those of us dealing with Alzheimer's disease. Maintaining strong friendships is not only good for our emotional health but also provides the venue for social interactions. This is important so you exercise your brain through interesting conversation, playing games (like cards, board games, charades, etc.), and performing simple tasks together (like cooking, raking leaves, gardening, or reading).

Friendships formed in a Christian environment are more likely to survive difficult circumstances because of the caring nature of these friendships. Friends who are our brothers and sisters in Christ are willing to:

- Remind us of important appointments
- Drive us to the grocery or doctor's office
- Call us daily to ensure everything is all right
- Let us into our houses when we've locked ourselves out

because we trusted them with our spare key.

Like today's Scripture indicates, a true friend doesn't deny his friend in times of need. Don't be afraid to rely on your friends for help when you are struggling. They truly want to help but probably aren't exactly sure what to do. God helped foster these beautiful friendships so use them when you need help!

Prayer: Father, thank You for strong Christian friendships. Amen

Wednesday: Wounds from a Friend

Wounds from a friend are better than many kisses from an enemy. Proverbs 27:6

Ouch! Today's Scripture really hurts when you read it, doesn't it? Come on, why in the world would I prefer wounds from a friend rather than multiple kisses from an enemy? I'd much rather have my friend say lots of nice things about me even if they are simply platitudes, right? Wrong! It would be far more favorable to have a good friend tell me something I've been doing wrong especially if it can harm me or someone else.

Let's take an example that will eventually impact most everyone diagnosed with Alzheimer's disease. That's right, the coveted skill giving us independence, the ability to drive. This can be a real issue for people in the early stages of Alzheimer's disease. We want to maintain our independence but there will come a point when we will not be able to drive safely. In most cases, Alzheimer's patients don't recognize how poorly they may be driving so it takes the insights of caring family members or friends to address the issue.

I'd much rather have a friend tell me it is time to hand over my car keys because it takes the burden off my family. Plus, a friend would have no hidden agenda and would likely have my best interest at heart. So, wounds from a friend definitely applies in this situation. It is important to prepare yourself for this event and to remember today's passage from Proverbs so you don't hold it against your devoted friend. Friendships are precious. Having a friend who is willing to lay their friendship on the line to protect us is purely priceless!

Prayer: Lord Jesus, help us to be grateful for friends who are willing to risk their friendship to insure our safety. Help us to not hold their truthfulness against them when they talk boldly with us. Amen

Thursday: A Friend Loves at All Times

A friend loves at all times, and a brother is born for adversity.
Proverbs 17:17

Proverbs has a very succinct way of boiling a relationship down to a single statement. In the case of today's passage the single statement is, "a friend loves at all times." What a powerful proposition this statement is with regard to true friendship. It brings to mind the relationship David had with Jonathan, Saul's son. Jonathan became one in spirit with David and he loved him as himself (1 Samuel 18:1). He held this friendship in high regard even though his Father, King Saul, wanted David destroyed because of his arrogant jealously toward David. David and Jonathan remained friends throughout the tumultuous time of Saul and until Jonathan's death at the hands of the Philistines.

I like to think King David instructed Solomon on how precious and priceless a true friend is using the friendship he kindled with Jonathan as the ultimate example. Perhaps that is why Solomon penned the verses in Proverbs articulating the value and characteristics of a "true" friend. True friendships, like that of Jonathan and David, are hard to come by because they are nurtured through good and bad times. If you have such a friendship, then you are truly a blessed individual because your friend loves you in spite of all circumstances.

Even though early-onset Alzheimer's strikes in mid-life, a true friend will weather the storm and stand by you through thick and thin! Treasure this remarkable friendship. Thank God He has blessed you with such a wonderful relationship.

Prayer: Heavenly Father, we don't always understand why things happen in our lives but thank You for sending true friends our way so we can weather the storm together. Amen

119

Friday: Covering Offenses Saves Friendships

He who covers over an offense promotes love, but whoever repeats the matter separates close friends. Proverbs 17:9

Proverbs provides divine wisdom that pierces the heart of earthly learning. Earthly wisdom says we should tell the world whenever we have been offended or hurt. Just look at all the reality and talk shows filling our daily television schedule. Apparently, it is pretty easy to get caught up in gossip and drawn into putting down someone who has hurt you. But this is earthly wisdom not divine wisdom. Divine wisdom reminds us if we "cover over" an offense, we promote love and save friendships.

Friends are not perfect and they will commit offenses or speak harsh words about us. As Christians, we need to overlook these misjudgments and simply let them slide. This is especially important as people learn about your illness. They may not fully understand the disease or have any concept of how it impacts an individual's life. People may say, "You act pretty normal and your memory seems fine to me." They might even comment to someone, "He doesn't look or act like my grandfather who had Alzheimer's so he's just faking it."

Words like these cut us to the core! But remember, people can't possibly comprehend what is going on in your life because all they understand is the latter stages of Alzheimer's disease. You have to learn to "cover over" these offenses with love and understanding. If you fail to take the advice of today's passage and lash out in anger, you will negatively impact your friendship and your Christian witness.

Prayer: Lord Jesus, help us to cover over any offenses or harsh words spoken against us so we might be worthy of the gospel. Amen

Saturday: God's Friend

And the scripture was fulfilled that says, "Abraham believed God, and it was credited to him as righteousness," and he was called God's friend. James 2:23

Have you ever wondered what it means to be called a friend of God? Is it possible to be a friend to the creator of the universe? Today's Scripture reminds us it is absolutely possible to be God's friend because Abraham provided the perfect example of what it takes to befriend God. Abraham simply believed God in spite of all that was going on around him and as a result he was God's friend. Well then, how important is it to be considered God's friend? Astronomically important! I can't imagine having a better friend than God because He:

- Loves you unconditionally
- Is with you always
- Has your best interests at heart
- Believes in you.

Wow, that is my kind of friend! Consider this situation. Suppose you lock your wife and dog in the trunk of your car for a day. You come back and open the trunk. Who's going to be happy to see you, jump in your arms, and cover you with kisses? It won't be your wife! Your dog will wag his tail and not hold anything against you. Now I'm not comparing God to a dog but His love for us is unconditional. We don't lock God in the trunk per se but we do tend to lock Him out of our lives. However, He always rejoices when we return to Him.

He is a true friend and longs to have a closer relationship with you. Believe in God and even Alzheimer's can't come between you and Him! That is my kind of friend.

Prayer: Loving Father, thank You for being our eternal friend. Your perfect friendship and love are all we need. Amen

Sunday: Stillness Strengthens Friendship

Be still, and know that I am God; I will be exalted among the nations, I will be exalted in the earth. The Lord Almighty is with us; the God of Jacob is our fortress. Psalms 46:10–11

Have you ever spent time with a friend when all you did was sit quietly and say nothing? Perhaps it was during a difficult time like the loss of a loved one, a broken relationship, or even a serious illness. I can remember one such event in my life. After a pretty serious car wreck, while I was convalescing at home, a dear Christian brother came and sat with me. We barely said two words to each other but his presence provided me strength and fortified our friendship.

Perhaps you are going through a difficult time right now as you struggle with the effects of Alzheimer's in your life. If you are, remember your perfect friend is sitting patiently by your side. He will not leave you alone, He loves you unconditionally, and His grace is sufficient for all you are going through. Be still and know He is the one true God who never changes and understands all you are facing. He may be the only one who understands your unique situation and He will always remain your friend. Earthly friends are important but having a heavenly friend surpasses the bonds of earthly friendships. So be still before God today and share your feelings, hurts, and desires with the only one who truly knows who you are and what you are going through. You won't be disappointed!

Prayer: Heavenly Father, You are the only one who understands all the changes taking place in our lives. You understand our fears and concerns. Help us to be still before You today knowing You alone can provide the comfort and strength we desperately need to continue. Thank You for being our eternal friend and savior. Amen

Robert Crum © 123RF.com

PRAYER LIFE

Devotions to help you keep prayer as an integral part of your life as you struggle with Alzheimer's disease.

Monday: Let the Godly Pray

Therefore let everyone who is godly pray to you while you may be found; surely when the mighty waters rise, they will not reach him. Psalms 32:6

King David was a man after God's own heart because he spent time with the Lord daily. Today's passage underscores how important prayer was to David; so important he admonished the godly to pray and seek the Lord while He could still be found. Of course, God never forsakes us but our willingness to seek Him occasionally wanes.

Have you ever been through a dry period when you didn't seek the Lord on a regular basis? How did you feel? Probably like the mighty waters of dread were reaching flood stage in your life and you were drowning! I've been there and I don't want to return to those days of dread and drowning.

As you face the effects of Alzheimer's, you may feel prayer is just not worth it anymore because God has already abandoned you. Nothing could be further from the truth! He is with you and waits patiently to talk with you.

If you are a godly person, make it a habit to pray every day no matter how you feel. Put it on your daily to-do list so you don't forget. If you aren't a godly person, then perhaps now is a good time to seek the Lord and talk with Him about the rising waters of Alzheimer's disease. Trust me, you won't be disappointed. No one can comfort you like God. Without Him in my life, I'd be lost and filled with fear because of my illness. God is my friend and hiding place from Alzheimer's!

Prayer: Prince of Peace, fill us with the desire to talk with You daily and to make prayer a priority in our lives. Amen

Tuesday: Pray Three Times a Day

Now when Daniel learned that the decree had been published, he went home to his upstairs room where the windows opened toward Jerusalem. Three times a day he got down on his knees and prayed, giving thanks to his God, just as he had done before.
Daniel 6:10

Have you ever met someone truly dedicated to prayer? Daniel was certainly such a man. Daniel continued to pray faithfully even when it was unlawful to pray to anyone except the King. Why did Daniel do this? Why was it so important to him not to break his daily prayer routine? Perhaps prayer was what kept Daniel on the right course and serving God.

If you have ever sailed a boat or piloted an aircraft you understand how easy it is to be blown off course. You must constantly check your position to determine how far off course you are and then apply corrections to get back on track. Prayer serves as a status check to determine if you are on course or not. If you are off course, prayer provides the feedback to get you back on course. Pilots and sailors don't just check their course once a day as they continue to their destination. They check it numerous times and make corrections along the way.

The same was true for Daniel. He prayed three times a day to make sure he was on course with the Almighty. How about you? Have you been blown off course and need a correction? Alzheimer's disease can easily blow you off course if you don't stay connected with God. He is our true north and the only one who can plot your path, keep you on course, and guide you through the storm. Talk with Him today and get back on course. He won't leave you adrift in the Alzheimer's sea!

Prayer: Heavenly Father, You are our true north. Keep us on course so we might serve You in spite of the storm. Amen

Wednesday: Patient in Affliction, Faithful in Prayer

Never be lacking in zeal, but keep your spiritual fervor, serving the Lord. Be joyful in hope, patient in affliction, faithful in prayer. Share with God's people who are in need. Practice hospitality.
Romans 12:11–13

Have you ever had a period when you lacked the zeal to get up in the morning? It is devastating to think you have nothing to contribute. Perhaps that is why Paul reminded the Roman Christians not to lose their zeal and keep their spiritual fervor.

This hits close to home as we face the life changing impacts of Alzheimer's. We must fight the tendency to throw in the towel and stay in bed. We need to remain physically active, pursue mental activities, and continue vibrantly serving the Lord. By doing this, our zest for life will continue as we fulfill a godly purpose in our lives. Paul further instructed the Roman church to be joyful in hope, patient in affliction, and faithful in prayer.

Paul provides prudent advice for those of us dealing with Alzheimer's by insisting we be joyful in hope and patient in affliction. This may seem difficult considering all we face but Paul prepares us by reminding us to be faithful in prayer. Prayer proves to be the catalyst for joy and patience. In spite of all Alzheimer's brings into our lives, it should never push out our prayer time. Prayer keeps us centered on Christ, sets our priorities for the day, and allows us to focus on the concerns of others by interceding for them. Prayer is so powerful it makes me feel normal again and part of something so great even Alzheimer's can't touch it! That is why I get out of bed in the morning! How about you?

Prayer: Lord, restore our zeal for life by instilling a deep desire to pray and spend time with You. Amen

Thursday: Pray on All Occasions

And pray in the spirit on all occasions with all kinds of prayers and requests. With this in mind, be alert and always keep on praying for all the saints. Ephesians 6:18

Growing up as a kid in Baltimore, I loved to play baseball. The kids on my block would play all the time no matter what the season. One summer my dad signed me up for little league baseball and I was thrilled! I was a pretty decent player but I did have one handicap. During slow uneventful games, I would lose focus and my mind would wander. On one occasion, while playing third base, I lost focus and the batter hit a hot grounder right at me. The ball bounced up and hit me right on the mouth. Blood came rushing out from my lip and the game was stopped momentarily as the coaches and umpire assessed my situation. After the game was over, my dad gently reminded me to keep my head in the game and always remain alert.

Perhaps this is exactly what the Apostle Paul was trying to get across to the Ephesians. He wanted them to pray in the spirit on all occasions, be alert, and always pray for the saints. Paul was instructing them to keep their heads in the game and remain attentive by praying on all occasions.

It is ironic how Alzheimer's has impacted my ability to focus. As a result, I have a tendency to forget what I'm doing and flit from one thing to another. To prevent this during prayer, I write down my prayer concerns so I don't forget them. This was kind of annoying at first but I learned it's a small price to pay to keep my head in the game. So keep on praying in whatever manner will help you. And by all means, keep your head in the spiritual game!

Prayer: Holy Spirit, help us keep our heads in the game by praying often and gently remind us when we start to lose focus. Amen

Friday: Devote Yourself to Prayer

Devote yourselves to prayer, being watchful and thankful. And pray for us, too, that God may open a door for our message, so that we may proclaim the mystery of Christ, for which I am in chains. Pray that I may proclaim it clearly as I should. Colossians 4:2–3

Paul was a huge advocate of prayer. Many of his letters to the early church requested prayer for opening the door for the gospel message. Paul's prayer warriors were critical to the success of the early church. Paul did not care how many people attended worship or how much was collected. His focus was spreading the gospel and developing the church.

Paul's reasoning reminds me of an old farmer's adage, "Don't worry about the mule going blind; just keep loading the wagon." It simply means keep working at your task and don't worry about something which may or may not happen in the future. Paul wasn't concerned about how large the churches would grow or if they'd be there 100 years after he died. He was focused on getting the gospel out.

So how does this apply when Alzheimer's strikes your life? Don't worry about what may or may not happen. Just stay focused on what God wants you to do today. It might simply be praying for your church and pastor so the gospel will be proclaimed in a clear and devout manner. Devoting yourself to prayer may be the critical link to your church's success in its spiritual battle for unsaved souls. So keep loading the wagon and don't worry about the mule going blind!

Lord Jesus, help us to not worry about how Alzheimer's might affect us in the future but keep us focused on praying and completing the task You have assigned us. Amen

Saturday: Pray Always

Then Jesus told his disciples a parable to show them that they should always pray and not give up. Luke 18:1

Do you have days you just don't feel like praying? I think we all have days like this but today's Scripture reminds us we are to "always pray and not give up." Jesus often taught His disciples using parables so they might understand heavenly concepts using earthly situations. In today's passage, Jesus tells of the widow who constantly confronts an unrighteous judge about granting her justice against an adversary. The judge finally gives in and grants her justice.

The parable is difficult to grasp. On the surface it seems if we continually confront God on an issue we will eventually wear Him down and get action. Of course, this is not always the case. There is a much deeper lesson within this parable. If something is weighing on our hearts, God wants to hear about it no matter what. It is through our prayers we will draw closer to Him and eventually understand His guidance concerning our situation. By constantly remaining in prayer, we follow the advice of our Lord to "always pray and not give up." Prayer is the heart of the issue in today's passage.

As you face the challenges of Alzheimer's disease, it is important to remember God wants to hear about your challenges and concerns. If it is on your mind, keeps you awake at night, or hinders your daily living, then He wants to hear about your frustrations. God is caring and compassionate so you won't tire Him out no matter how much you call on him. Besides, as scary as Alzheimer's can be, it won't scare Him away!

Prayer: Precious Lord, hear our prayers and bend Your ear to our frustrations. Thank You for listening like no one on earth can. Amen

Sunday: Pray in Stillness

Be still, and know that I am God; I will be exalted among the nations, I will be exalted in the earth. The Lord Almighty is with us; the God of Jacob is our fortress. Psalms 46:10–11

Did you ever wonder why prayer is so important? Why it is mentioned so many times in the Bible? Why Jesus spent precious time in prayer with His heavenly Father? Perhaps it is because prayer provides purpose for our lives.

When we consistently spend time in prayer we position ourselves to understand God's ultimate purpose for our lives. We begin a dialogue allowing God to change our selfish desires into His perfect desire for us. God uses these special moments to refine us, refocus us, and reveal His unique plan for us. This week we focused on the following prayer principles:

- Godly people pray
- Pray often throughout the day
- Be faithful in prayer and patient in affliction
- Pray on all occasions
- Be devoted to prayer
- Pray always and do not give up.

Now it is time to be still before God and quietly pray for His direction and His perfect will in your life. He patiently waits for you to bow in His presence and pour your heart out to Him. Don't worry about what you will say or how you will say it. It doesn't matter as long as you set aside some time to be with Him. It's like the Nike running shoe commercial: Just Do It! It's the physical fitness your spiritual body desperately needs. So spend time in prayer today and draw close to Him.

Prayer: Holy Father, may our prayers draw us closer to Your perfect purpose for our lives so we might please only You. Amen

Francis De Casa Gonzalez © 123RF.com

CHRISTIAN COMMUNITY

Devotions to help you maintain a community of Christian brothers and sisters to support you in your faithful fight against Alzheimer's disease.

Paul M. Hornback

Monday: One Day in Your Courts

Better is one day in your courts than a thousand elsewhere; I would rather be a doorkeeper in the house of my God than dwell in the tents of the wicked. Psalm 84:10

There is something special about God's house. It always brightens my spirit no matter what else is happening. I know there must be biblical principles and psychological doctrine explaining this phenomenon. However, I understand it as simply feeling the Lord's love and presence which permeates His house. The minute I walk through the doors of our little Methodist church, I can feel His spirit moving as He welcomes me home. It is somewhat like returning from a deployment (if you served in the military) or coming home after a long vacation or extended business trip. You walk through the door of your house or apartment and the euphoria of being home just overwhelms you. It is a warm, wonderful feeling and I never grow weary of being in God's house.

In today's passage, the Psalmist asserts better is one day in His house than a thousand days somewhere else. This is especially true after my diagnosis of early-onset Alzheimer's disease. The church has become a safe sanctuary for me. It is a holy place I can go and not worry about the changes occurring in my life. I know God's house will be filled with caring people who love and understand what I am going through.

I pray you have a church that provides you safe haven. God's house is there just for you. It is a place where Alzheimer's can't break the bond between you and Christ!

Prayer: Lord Jesus, thank You for allowing us the privilege to be in Your courts and to find a safe sanctuary from the devastating impacts of Alzheimer's. We are truly grateful for this special place. Amen

Tuesday: Dwell in the House of the Lord

One thing I ask of the Lord, this is what I seek: that I may dwell in the house of the Lord all the days of my life, to gaze upon the beauty of the Lord. For in the day of trouble he will keep me safe in his dwelling; he will hide me in the shelter of his tabernacle and set me high upon a rock. Psalm 27:4–5

There is something special about being in the God's house. It never ceases to amaze me how awesome it is to be in His house. In fact, when I'm going through a difficult time I often think about my church. It reminds me of something my father once told me about a very tough time he had during World War II. Surprisingly it wasn't during a skirmish with the Germans; instead it occurred one cold night while on sentry. During his watch he grew afraid and began to think of his church back home. He remembered how wonderful it was to be surrounded by people who genuinely loved him and he felt safe. It's funny how often we think about the safety and love of God's house when in danger or difficult situations.

Perhaps that is what King David was thinking when he wrote today's passage. Maybe you are going through a difficult period right now as you read this devotion. Alzheimer's has a way of making our lives more difficult and frightfully uncertain. I find comfort in going to the "house of the Lord" even in my mind. I kneel at the oak altar and ask God to hide me from the disease while keeping me safe.

Take a moment today and spend some time at His altar. Ask for His help as you face the difficult challenges of your disease. Dwell in His house today and forever!

Prayer: Heavenly Father, help us remember the days in Your tabernacle so we might gain strength for the days ahead. Amen

Wednesday: Continue Meeting Together

Let us not give up meeting together as some are in the habit of doing, and let us encourage one another all the more as we see the day approaching. Hebrews 10:25

How important to spiritual well-being is meeting together on a regular basis? The writer of Hebrews thought it was absolutely essential. There are two important reasons for this: fellowship and encouragement. Fellowship provides caring Christian company to foster spiritual growth and hold us accountable to live godly lives. Furthermore, from this close Christian community we receive encouragement for enduring difficult days plus we are given an opportunity to encourage others during their days of struggle.

This is especially true for those of us suffering from Alzheimer's disease. A key recommendation for Alzheimer's patients is to continue participating in social activities and enjoying the company of close friends. There are no closer friends than your brothers and sisters in Christ. As a Christian, I belong to three small groups that lovingly support my spiritual wellbeing. More importantly, these groups allow me an opportunity to encourage and pray for others. I have found the more time I spend encouraging and praying for others, the less time I spend dwelling on my current situation.

This is exactly what the writer of Hebrews was saying in today's passage. As long as we continue to meet together and make a conscious effort to encourage one another in Christ, our spirits will not be broken. Alzheimer's disease can be a spirit breaking event but not if you have a close Christian community to meet with regularly. So, go to a meeting!

Prayer: Lord of All Creation, create in us a steadfast spirit that encourages and prays for those we meet in need. Amen

Thursday: Dwell in His House Today

Surely goodness and love will follow me all the days of my life, and I will dwell in the house of the Lord forever. Psalm 23:6

I absolutely love the 23rd Psalm since it was one of the first passages I learned as a young boy. Perhaps it is one of your favorite Psalms as well. Today's passage has special significance since I now struggle with early-onset Alzheimer's disease. Each time I read it, I find comfort knowing I can dwell in the house of the Lord forever. This not only means after I die but right now!

It is simply amazing God allows each of us to dwell in His house in the present sense. By dwelling in his house, we have the opportunity for "goodness and love" to follow us all the days of our lives. Dwelling in the house of the Lord is the only place to be. He provides comfort when life is less than ideal, consideration when others can't possibly understand how the disease is affecting us, and compassion because we are hurting inside. Since the Holy Spirit lives within every Christian, we are dwelling in His house today and are thereby granted the comforts bestowed upon a member of His royal family now.

Alzheimer's has a way of stealing peace but only if we forget who we are in Christ and in whose house we reside! In God's house, He is in charge; He is the master of the house and nothing comes into His house to wreak havoc on members of His family. I belong to Him, I reside in His house, and He has promised me abundant life. All I need do is trust in Him. Alzheimer's can dull my senses but it can't steal the comfort of dwelling in His royal house! I encourage you to take up residence in His house today. You won't be turned away.

Prayer: Prince of Peace, we dwell in Your house forever and are truly grateful. Amen

Friday: Entering His Gates

Enter his gates with thanksgiving and his courts with praise; give thanks to him and praise his name. For the Lord is good and his love endures forever; his faithfulness continues through all generations. Psalm 100:4–5

Do you think God cares how we enter His house? What is important is that we show up, right? Today's Scripture suggests we should enter His courts with thanksgiving and praise. We do this because the Lord is good and His faithfulness spans all generations!

As I read today's passage, I immediately thought of Carlene Hughes who attended our church for decades. He always greeted me with a huge smile, hug, and word of encouragement. As he grew older and age took a toll on his health, he never let his spirit wane. Even when he could barely move using a walker, his face would brighten when he got out of the car and entered the church. He stands as a vivid reminder of how God wants us to worship in His courts. On days when I don't feel like going to church, the image of Carlene moving slowly in his walker with a glorious grin on his face inspires me to go. This is especially true given the reality of Alzheimer's disease which often causes me to forget people's names and sometimes not know exactly what to say. Nonetheless, I enter God's house with a smile on my face and a song in my heart!

Listen my dear friends, we never know who may be watching and later in their life be encouraged because we joyfully endure difficulty. I want to be remembered as a man with a thankful heart, a praiseful spirit, and an enduring love for the Lord who entered His courts with a smile. That is much better than just someone who had Alzheimer's disease!

Prayer: Lord, may we always enter Your courts with praise. Amen

Saturday: Rejoice in His House

I rejoiced with those who said to me, "Let us go to the house of the Lord." Psalm 122:1

Today's Scripture is actually part of a "song of ascents" ascribed to King David. I would expect nothing less than rejoicing when David speaks of going to the house of the Lord. I can visualize the young David singing and even dancing with joy as he worships his God.

Is this the way you behave on your way to church on Sunday morning? Do you sing a hymn of praise or a contemporary Christian song as you drive to worship? Do you arrive at church already having worshiped in song along the way? God deeply desires we arrive at His house in a joyous state of mind fully prepared to worship and praise Him. It's funny we have Christian CD's to play in our stereos but we are generally too rushed on Sunday morning to sing along and prepare our hearts for worship. Music is a vital part of any Sunday morning worship experience. It places our hearts and minds in a praiseful state as we lift our voices to God.

Since I have been struggling with Alzheimer's disease, one of my great joys is to sing familiar hymns and contemporary songs of worship. The words flow through my spirit and even if I'm a little off key it really doesn't matter because I sing these words to my Lord in praise. Music really helps those of us suffering from Alzheimer's so listen to Christian music often. Then, when you worship, sing out in a joyful manner as you praise God. He is listening and He truly loves a joyful singer!

Prayer: Heavenly Father, we deeply desire to arrive at Your house ready to worship but so many times we allow other things to steal our joy. Help us to get ready for worship so we might praise You. Amen

Sunday: Pray in Stillness

Be still, and know that I am God; I will be exalted among the nations, I will be exalted in the earth. The Lord Almighty is with us; the God of Jacob is our fortress. Psalms 46:10–11

This week we have explored how wonderful it is to dwell in the house of the Lord and the spirit in which God wants us to worship Him. Today is the day most Christians go to church for worship and it has been a vital part of my life for over 30 years. Whenever I miss a Sunday service, my week seems empty and meaningless. Perhaps this is because my spirit had not been refreshed through worship with other believers.

There is nothing magical about worship attendance. However, there is something biblical about resting and worshipping on the Sabbath. From a biblical standpoint, dwelling in the house of the Lord is exactly where we need to be at least one day a week. It is the perfect place to revive our spirits and refresh our souls. In His house, we worship the One whose blessings and grace engulf us every day of our lives.

Now that I struggle with Alzheimer's, His house has more significance. In His house I gain strength and support for serving Him. In the stillness of our corporate prayer time, I feel His spirit moving among the members of our congregation as He comforts and strengthens those who need His caring touch. I pray you are part of a congregation that prays so you feel His presence during worship. If you are, be grateful for dwelling in His house of prayer. If you aren't, find a church where prayer is paramount. Then worship the Lord and be refreshed in His house!

Prayer: Almighty Lord, thank You for Your universal church giving us a place to worship You and feel Your presence. Amen

Wasin Pummarin © 123RF.com

GRACE ABOUNDS

Devotions to help you discover how God's grace surrounds your life as you live with Alzheimer's disease.

Monday: The Grace of God

*For I am the least of the apostles and do not even deserve to be
called an apostle, because I persecuted the church. But by the grace
of God I am what I am, and his grace to me was not without effect.
No, I worked harder than all of them – yet not I, but the grace of
God that was with me. 1 Corinthians 15:9–10*

Paul has a perfect way of expressing how glorious the grace of
God is in life. Saul, before his conversion and name change,
persecuted the early church with a vigor that surpassed all of the
Pharisees. He was a "dirty dog" to the early Christians but because
of the grace of God his life was changed. God used Paul's zeal to
further His kingdom. God's grace can channel a person's gifts, once
used for evil, to spread God's goodness.

Grace is a wonderful gift none of us earn but all are allowed to
receive. It does not matter whether you are sick or healthy, rich or
poor, naïve or street smart, or a hard worker or a bum. Grace comes
upon you no matter what circumstance you are facing. Grace is
God's glorious gift.

As I struggle with Alzheimer's disease, I more fully understand
how truly wonderful His gift of grace is in my life. There was a time
when I felt I had to earn grace by serving God in extraordinary ways.
I worked on Emmaus Walks, spoke in churches, chaired committees,
and filled in for our pastor all in an effort to gain grace! Now that my
abilities are diminishing, I have come to understand God's grace
isn't going to diminish accordingly. By the grace of God I am what I
am and His grace continues in me. God's grace is something
Alzheimer's can't change. Accept His grace today!

*Prayer: God of Grace, thank You for Your loving grace that is
not earned but flows freely to all of us. Amen*

Tuesday: Grace Abounds To You

And God is able to make all grace abound to you, so that in all things at all times, having all that you need, you will abound in every good work. 2 Corinthians 9:8

Have you ever wondered where grace is in your life? I have to admit I've wondered about God's grace given my struggles with Alzheimer's. But today's Scripture reminds us God's grace abounds in all things at all times. God's grace never goes away even when we face life changing situations.

You may not feel like grace is abounding in your life but God pours His grace upon you nonetheless. That is what Paul wanted the Corinthians to understand. Grace isn't just at work when we are healthy, wealthy, and wise. It continues even if we are sick, poor, or not playing with a full deck!

Paul does add an important caveat to God's abounding grace. Grace is given so you will abound in every good work. God's grace is poured out so we might serve Him and continue His work here on earth. It's funny how often we miss God's grace until we start serving Him. When we develop a servant's heart, we are no longer self-centered human beings who try to manipulate God to get all the things we want. Instead, we are focused on serving Him in whatever manner He deems acceptable. Then the scales fall from our eyes and we see God's grace all around us.

I can testify to this for as long as I'm serving Him, I don't focus on how Alzheimer's is impacting me. It doesn't matter if I'm sick because God's grace abounds. Then I'm able to abound in every good work! How about you? Can you see God's grace? If not, just open your eyes because it's there!

Prayer: Father of Grace, help us to see Your grace at work in our lives so we might continue Your work here on earth. Amen

Wednesday: Grace Is Given

But to each one of us grace has been given as Christ apportioned it. Ephesians 4:7

In Paul's letter to the Ephesians, the word grace appears twelve times. Perhaps the Apostle Paul wanted the Ephesians to fully appreciate God's eternal purpose and glorious grace in their lives. God's grace doesn't just enter your life by itself. Riding on grace's coattail is God's ultimate purpose for your life. Grace is a great gift from God because it's free, pure, and life changing. The trick is you have to accept it; you have to be willing to make the decision to choose grace.

Once you accept grace then you begin to make godly choices like walking in the spirit, reading God's word daily, saying no to temptations, talking with God, serving God, and living in a manner worthy of the gospel. Grace is just the start of a life spent in communion with Christ. So what has that got to do with your struggles with Alzheimer's? First, grace has still been apportioned to you just like the Ephesians. Second, grace is still working in your life even though you may not necessarily feel it doing anything.

I can say this because I see God's grace working all around me. It is working in the Sunday school class my wife and I lead. I see it in the faces of the young adults as they begin to trust God more in their daily lives. This in turn helps me see God's purpose in my life. I realize His grace is sufficient to enable me to teach and relate to these young adults even when I'm struggling with the impacts of Alzheimer's. What is God doing in your life today? He still has a plan for you and Alzheimer's doesn't change that at all!

Prayer: Lord, may Your grace be apportioned to each of us today so we might continue to fulfill Your purpose in our lives. Amen

Thursday: Seek the Treasure

See to it that no one misses the grace of God and that no bitter root grows up to cause trouble and defile many. Hebrews 12:15

I'm a movie fanatic. One of my favorites is *Oh Brother Where Art Thou.* In this movie three convicts escape from a chain gang and go in search of a treasure supposedly hidden by one of them. The three men develop a bond through misadventures they share while on the run. One of the convicts is captured but is reunited with the other two in a theater where his new chain gang has been allowed to view a moving picture. He whispers a warning to his colleagues saying, "Do not seek the treasure." Apparently he has revealed the secret location of the hidden treasure and the long arm of the law will be waiting for them should they seek the treasure's location.

Sometimes grace can be just like the hidden treasure the convicts were seeking. In today's Scripture, the writer of Hebrews cautions the Jewish converts to "see to it" no one misses the grace of God. That is why I seek out some remnant of God's grace in my life every day. It really doesn't take much effort to discover the footprints of grace in your life. For example, I had an appointment with my psychologist today and it is snowing pretty heavily so I worried about getting there. Out of the blue his secretary called to assure me it was okay to miss the appointment due to the weather. You see, Alzheimer's has made it extremely difficult for me to make even simple decisions. However, God knows how difficult this is so in His grace He took care of it. Now this may not seem like a big deal to you but for me it was pretty substantial. Plus it gave me peace and time to write today's devotional. His grace is all around us so by all means "do seek the treasure!"

Prayer: Prince of Peace, please help us to seek out the footprints of Your grace surrounding us every day. Amen

Friday: Grace Strengthens the Spiritual Heart

Do not be carried away by all kinds of strange teachings. It is good for our hearts to be strengthened by grace, not ceremonial foods, which are of no value to those who eat them. Hebrews 13:9

There is much emphasis today on maintaining a healthy heart. Doctors tell us to maintain a low cholesterol level, watch our blood pressure, and take a low dose aspirin every day. We are to eat a diet low in fat, high in fiber, and low in cholesterol. Furthermore, we should exercise five days a week insuring we reach our target heart rate to strengthen the heart muscles.

These are certainly excellent recommendations for a physical heart but what about a spiritual heart? The writer of Hebrews had a few healthy words of advice concerning the spiritual heart. First, he cautioned them not to be carried away by all kinds of strange teachings. The Christian faith was simple and wasn't tied to legalistic conditions. Second, he warned their spiritual hearts were strengthened by grace not by ceremonial foods which have no "spiritual" value when eaten.

These wonderful words still hold true today. When we partake of God's grace our spiritual hearts become much stronger. But there are conditions when it comes to God's grace. You have to recognize, receive, and remember it. Recognizing grace is pretty simple because God showers us with His grace every day. Receiving grace is simply accepting God's gift in the manner in which it has been provided to you. Remembering how God's grace impacted your life is the final step and one we must never forget. By doing all three your spiritual heart will be strengthened. What are you waiting for? His grace abounds for you. Therefore recognize, receive, and remember!

Prayer: Father, help us recognize, receive, and remember the wonderful acts of grace You provide for us every day. Amen

Saturday: More Grace for the Humble

But he gives us more grace. That is why Scripture says: "God opposes the proud but gives grace to the humble." James 4:6

James, the brother of Jesus, is a meat and potatoes kind of guy. He is very direct when it comes to living according to Jesus' teachings. I would have loved to have heard James speak and teach as he was one of the pillars of the early church. Of course, now we have his book which was written to instruct and encourage members of the Jerusalem church.

Today's Scripture states God gives us more grace to deal with everything the world throws at us. I don't know about you, but I like the idea of "more" of the good stuff. I'd like more cream and sugar with my coffee, more ice cream with my blackberry cobbler, and more gravy with my biscuits. But most of all, I want more grace to help me deal with all the challenges of Alzheimer's disease. You know what I'm talking about: help to make decisions, to clear the fog on bad days, to remember what I was going to do, to write out the bills, or to balance the checkbook. Well, God does just that! He gives us more grace but it seems to flow more freely to those who are humble.

So, where to do you fall on the humble spectrum? Are you leaning toward the proud side by being too high and mighty to ask for help? Or are you leaning toward the humble side and realizing you could use some help with daily activities? I want to have my needle pegged on the humble side so God's grace will flow freely in my life. Do you want more grace or more pride? The choice is yours but you'd better grab all the grace you can because living with Alzheimer's takes more grace than anyone can imagine!

Prayer: Holy Lord, help us to choose humility over pride every day so Your grace may flow freely in our lives. Amen

Sunday: Grace in Stillness

Be still, and know that I am God; I will be exalted among the nations, I will be exalted in the earth. The Lord Almighty is with us; the God of Jacob is our fortress. Psalms 46:10–11

This week has been filled with Scriptures relating to God's glorious grace in our lives. His grace is all around us every day. All we need do is recognize it, receive it, and remember it so our spiritual hearts will be strengthened.

Now it is time to be still and reflect on the glorious wonders of His wonderful grace. But do you have trouble finding the time and willpower to be still long enough to feel His presence? Perhaps you are afraid of being still before the Lord so you stay busy until you fall exhausted into bed. Either way, finding time to be still before God can be an act of grace all by itself! There isn't anything to be afraid of and it really doesn't take much time. Ten or fifteen minutes can be more than enough to disconnect from the worries of this world and reconnect with your heavenly Father.

Since my diagnosis of Alzheimer's, I treasure these periods of stillness because I don't have to talk much. All I need do is utter His name and grace seems to take care of the rest of our conversation. In these quiet times, I know He is God because He doesn't require stunning speech or perfect prose. All he requires is my undivided attention. His grace pierces through the heart of Alzheimer's disease. In the stillness I realize He is the Lord Almighty. He is in complete control of all things! So Alzheimer's, where is your sting and where is your victory? I've got grace! How about you?

Prayer: Blessed Redeemer, calm our spirits and help us be still before You today so we can truly exalt You above all other things in our lives and on this earth. Amen

Photographieundmehr © 123RF.com

CONTINUE TO SERVE

Devotions to help you find new ways to serve God in spite of living with Alzheimer's disease.

Monday: Serve the Lord

*Now fear the Lord and serve him with all faithfulness. Throw
away the gods your forefathers worshipped beyond the River and in
Egypt, and serve the Lord. But if serving the Lord seems undesirable
to you, then choose for yourselves this day whom you will serve...But
as for me and my household, we will serve the Lord.*
Joshua 24:14–15

Joshua was a strong man of courage and character, the type of
individual we call a "man's man." Joshua and Caleb were the only
two who believed with the Lord's help, Moses and the Israelites
could possess the land flowing with milk and honey. You have to
admire Joshua, not just because of his courage and character, but
because of his unfaltering faith.

In today's passage, Joshua has to remind the Israelites to fear
the Lord and serve Him with all their faithfulness. He lays down a
gauntlet to them saying, "Choose for yourselves this day whom you
will serve." It sounds like something John Wayne would have said to
his men just before heading into a fierce fight. Perhaps John
Wayne's screen characters were cut from the same mold as Joshua.
You always knew where John Wayne stood on an issue. The same
was true for Joshua; he made it clear he and his household would
serve the Lord!

So Pilgrim, where do you stand? Has Alzheimer's crept in and
stolen your faithfulness? Are you wavering on "whom you will serve
today?" Will you serve the disease of Alzheimer's by giving up,
losing hope, and doing nothing? Or will you continue to serve your
Lord in faithfulness knowing He is in complete control of
everything? As for me and my household, we will serve the Lord
just like Joshua did!

*Prayer: Lord, strengthen our faith so we and our households
will serve only You. Amen*

Tuesday: Servant of All

Sitting down, Jesus called the Twelve and said, "If anyone wants to be the first, he must be the very last, and the servant of all."
Mark 9:35

It is funny how Jesus knew exactly what the disciples were talking about even when He wasn't within earshot of their conversation. This is precisely what happened on the road to Capernaum as the disciples argued about who among them was the greatest. It's pretty typical of a group of men to try and determine the pecking order after they have been together for a short period of time. Perhaps you've been in a similar situation at work, a social group, or even church.

Some people just have to be first. However, Jesus had a slightly different approach. He taught the Twelve to be first, you must be last and a servant to all. Wow, that is a pretty revolutionary concept! But what has that got to do with Alzheimer's disease? It simply means for as long as we are able, we should continue to humbly be of service to our families, friends, and faith. Just because we are sick doesn't mean we should play first fiddle and be pampered. Instead, we are to be last and a servant to all.

Now here's the tough part. I've told my oldest son when I can no longer function reasonably then it is okay to place me in a long term care facility of my family's choosing. In this way, I will certainly be last and not a burden to my family. Besides, I probably won't know the difference. I know that is a pretty tough pill to swallow for some folks who struggle with this disease. But it's precisely what I conclude from Jesus' words in today's passage. So don't be afraid to be last!

Lord Jesus, help us to truly understand what it means to be first by being last and serving others in spite of our disease. Amen

Wednesday: Serve in Love

You, my brothers, were called to be free. But do not use your freedom to indulge the sinful nature; rather, serve one another in love. Galatians 5:13

In high school, I played on the tennis team and was pretty good within our region. The key to being good at tennis is to have a fast and accurate serve. If your serve gets in the box with speed and spin then it's considered a deadly serve. To develop a great serve one must practice, practice, practice. Practice makes it easier to serve well with accuracy and speed.

The same is true for Christianity. To be a great Christian, one must be good at serving. To be good at serving, one must love, love, love. The more you love, the easier it is to serve. Perhaps that is what the Apostle Paul was trying to tell the Christians in Galatia. By not having to be slaves to the law and therefore being free, they should not indulge in sinful acts. Instead, with love in their hearts, they should serve their fellow man. So it is with those of us afflicted with Alzheimer's disease. As long as we have love in our hearts, then we can serve and bless our fellow man. The key to serving is love. The key to love is Christ. Alzheimer's really doesn't have a say in the matter.

How is your serve? Is it off a bit since your diagnosis of Alzheimer's? Have you been reluctant to serve because you are embarrassed or you are mad at God? Do not become a slave to Alzheimer's. You belong to Christ and He is your master. He still loves you despite the disease. So get out there and serve. You will find favor in His heavenly eyes.

Prayer: Precious Jesus, help us to find new and exciting ways to serve You in spite of our ailments. You alone hold the key to shape our serving into to something beautiful and loving. Amen

Thursday: Serve Wholeheartedly

Serve wholeheartedly, as if you were serving the Lord, not men, because you know the Lord will reward everyone for whatever good he does, whether he is slave or free. Ephesians 6:7–8

Do you have days when you just seem to go through the motions from sunrise to sunset? Your heart just isn't in tune with whatever happens to be on your schedule for the day. Perhaps it is work, school, or even married life. You get up in the morning and just muddle through the tasks of the day.

The Apostle Paul probably saw much of this type of living during his lifetime which may have spurred him to pen today's passage. Paul wanted to ensure the Christians in Ephesus understood, whether slave or free, how important it was in the eyes of their Lord to serve wholeheartedly. He wanted these new Christians to be shining stars in all aspects of their lives. If they did this, they would stand out against the darkness of society. Paul wanted them live the practical daily life of a believer so they could continue to work out the purposes of God while here on earth. Paul does not offer any qualifiers to his statement on "serving wholeheartedly" other than slave or free. He did not imply only the healthy, rich, or employed were to serve. Absolutely not! We are all wholeheartedly to serve no matter what our condition or health.

Even with Alzheimer's I have found ways to serve with my whole heart. Granted, there are many tasks I can no longer accomplish but there are still ways I can serve. How about you? Are you serving God wholeheartedly or just going through the motions? Remember, God has something special in store for those who serve Him wholeheartedly!

Prayer: Lord, give us a servant's heart so we might serve You wholeheartedly in whatever manner You deem worthy. Amen

Friday: Serve Him Only

Jesus said to him, "Away from me, Satan! For it is written: 'Worship the Lord your God, and serve him only.'" Matthew 4:10

Today's Scripture from Matthew comes at the end of Satan's temptation of Jesus. Jesus was led by the Spirit into the desert and after fasting for forty days and nights, he was tempted by Satan in three ways. Satan's last temptation was to tell Jesus He could have all the kingdoms of the world if He would worship and serve only him. Jesus rebuked Satan by quoting Scripture and reaffirming He would only serve His Father.

Isn't it funny how often we are tempted and even diabolically deceived into serving other things in our lives? You might wonder what kinds of things pull us away from serving the Lord. The list is long and lascivious and includes careers, food, houses, cars, hobbies, gambling, drinking, shopping, material possessions, physical fitness, dieting, poor health, sexual pleasure, greed, and other seemingly simple pleasures. Anything controlling your mind, schedule, and pocketbook to such an extent you cannot live without it becomes your master and you serve it.

What is the poison in your life which robs you of time with the Lord? If you can't find time for prayer, Scripture, and service then something else is ruling your life! After being diagnosed with Alzheimer's I realized how much "things" were choking my spiritual airway. My property, cars, career, and healthy body had all demanded too much of my time. Their firm grip on my spirit now has been severed. I worship and serve them no more! How about you?

Prayer: Heavenly Father, You are the only one we should worship. Help break the strongholds on our lives stealing away our precious time from serving, worshipping, and learning about You. Amen

Saturday: Serve a Living God

How much more, then, will the blood of Christ, who through the eternal Spirit offered himself unblemished to God, cleanse our consciences from acts that lead to death, so that we may serve the living God! Hebrew 9:14

Isn't it wonderful Christ offered himself up for us sinners so we might be saved from death because of the atrocious acts of disobedience we commit? I wonder if this statement sounds a bit too harsh to you. The writer of Hebrews didn't! He assured us the unblemished blood of Christ would cleanse our consciences from acts leading to death. However, he added a crucial caveat, "So that we might serve the *living* God!"

It's important to remember He's a *living* God and not some stone faced statue or papier-mâché deity. Serving a *living* God makes a world of difference. So, how can you serve a living God now that you are struggling with Alzheimer's? What kinds of things can you possibly do? Well here's a short list:

- Pray for your family, friends, and fellow Christians daily
- Write letters or cards to lonely shut-ins
- Call folks who are going through a difficult time and offer encouragement
- Volunteer to be a church greeter on Sunday morning
- Help fold Sunday bulletins for your church
- Ride along with the minister when he makes home visits
- Help serve communion at your church.

These are but a few ways you can serve which require a limited amount of time, effort, and mental ability. Even though your abilities may be diminishing, you can still serve in some way. Our living Lord looks longingly for your service to Him. So get up and serve the Living Lord!

Prayer: Living Lord, help us find new ways to serve You that are truly worthy of the special sacrifice You made for each of us. Amen

Paul M. Hornback

Sunday: From Stillness to Service

Be still, and know that I am God; I will be exalted among the nations, I will be exalted in the earth. The Lord Almighty is with us; the God of Jacob is our fortress. Psalms 46:10–11

It is Sunday and time to take a few special moments to be still before the Lord and know He is God. I don't know about you, but Sundays seem to be the busiest day of the week for me. I have to find time to review the Sunday school class material which I teach, get breakfast ready for the family, help get lunch going so it's ready when we get back from church, fix a small breakfast snack for our young adult Sunday school class, and get myself ready for church. Therefore, on Sunday mornings I get up at the regular time instead of sleeping in so I can have some precious quiet time with the Lord.

There's something special about the stillness on Sunday mornings that seems to quiet the soul and empower the spirit. It is during these wonderful quiet moments on Sunday I am tenderly renewed through prayer so I might continue to serve in a joyful manner. I pour out my heartfelt concerns about the disease I'm facing and ask for strength for the days ahead. During these moments, I also receive inspiration about new ways to serve my Lord as well as things to write about.

How about you? Do you spend time on Sunday mornings being still before the Lord? Is this where you find your inspiration for serving? If not, I pray you will spend some quiet time before the Lord today. Ask Him in what ways you can serve. He is waiting patiently for you to come and simply be still before Him. You won't be disappointed!

Prayer: Sovereign Lord, these quiet moments are so precious to the life of our spirits. Help us to be still before You and to refresh our souls so we might serve You more willingly and joyfully. Amen

Colin Young © 123RF.com

WAIT UPON THE LORD

Devotions to help you realize patience is a precious virtue in your fight against Alzheimer's disease.

Paul M. Hornback

Monday: The Watchman Waits

I wait for the Lord, my soul waits, and in his word I put my hope. My soul waits for the Lord more than watchmen wait for the morning, more than watchmen wait for the morning. Psalm 130:5

As a young first lieutenant in the United States Marine Corps, while our squadron was deployed in the North Atlantic in the winter aboard a Helicopter Landing Ship, I was often assigned flight deck duty after flight operations had been secured for the day. The Flight Deck Watch Officer had to conduct hourly rounds to ensure helicopters were securely chained to the deck with blades tied down. Since the deck was generally icy and the skies dark because of wintery overcast conditions, the trip around the deck was extremely dangerous due to the rough seas. I still remember how great it was to see morning break because the daylight lit the deck making the aircraft check much easier and safer. This helped me understand and appreciate today's passage regarding the watchmen eagerly waiting for morning.

So what are you eagerly waiting for in your life? Are you waiting for a cure for Alzheimer's, a miracle drug to soften the symptoms, or perhaps a doctor who will give you a different diagnosis? I know this type of waiting is tempting because I ventured into that cavern on occasion. However, I didn't linger very long. Instead I decided to wait upon the Lord and put my faith, hope, and trust in Him alone. Do I want a cure, a new drug, or even a miracle healing? Absolutely! I'm just not going to wait around idly and let life pass me by. That's why I choose to wait on the Lord, plus do my part by taking my medication, participating in a clinical trial, remaining healthy, and staying active. I firmly believe God has a plan and I want to be an active participant. So, what are you waiting for?

Prayer: Precious Savior, let us patiently wait for You. Amen

Tuesday: Blessed Are Those Who Wait

Yet the Lord longs to be gracious to you: he rises to show you compassion. For the Lord is a God of justice. Blessed are all who wait for him! Isaiah 30:18

In today's society, waiting can sometimes be considered a four letter word. We stand impatiently in front of the microwave waiting for our lunch to cook and wonder why it is taking so long. I can remember my mom cooking the noon meal and spending over an hour getting it ready! Boy would she have loved to have had a microwave oven back in the 1960s! But I must admit her lunches tasted much better and were probably more nutritious than what I cook in the microwave.

It's ironic how impatient we have become. Technology has made our lives so much easier yet we aren't satisfied. In today's passage, Isaiah reminds Israel the Lord is gracious and compassionate while blessing those who wait for Him. Perhaps Israel was impatient and wanted things much sooner than God's perfect plan allowed. So they became rebellious in the sight of the Lord and judgment loomed in their future.

So how does today's passage help us who are suffering from Alzheimer's? First, the Lord is still a God of grace and compassion. I see evidence of these qualities every day, don't you? Second, God continues to bless those who wait for Him. What does it mean to wait for God when you're afflicted with Alzheimer's? It means to go on living while praising Him during the dementia storm. He is fully aware of your condition and has put things in motion for your good. All you need do is trust in Him and wait patiently for His perfect outcome. So wait for Him, accept His grace, and be blessed today.

Prayer: Gracious Lord, help us to wait for You. But as we wait may we praise You all along the way for You are gracious and compassionate. Amen

Wednesday: Wait for the Gift

On one occasion, while he was eating with them, he gave them this command: "Do not leave Jerusalem, but wait for the gift my Father promised, which you have heard me speak about." Acts 1:4

One of the strange effects of Alzheimer's in many people is the inability to come up with the right words during conversation. It can creep up unexpectedly and when it hits, it seems like the break in conversation last for minutes. My wife has assured me the duration of my pauses has been a few seconds at most. It's funny how often we perceive a period of waiting as being astronomical long but to others this same period is dramatically diminished in duration.

This same concept applies to waiting for God to move in situations where we have asked for His help or guidance. We perceive the wait as being extremely long while God sees it as only a blink of an eye. This must have been true for the disciples as they waited in Jerusalem for the gift Jesus spoke about in today's Scripture. It must have seemed like an eternity as they worried about what might happen next. The gift of the Holy Spirit finally came and empowered them for the rest of their lives. You see, God isn't necessarily worried how long we have to wait because He knows waiting builds perseverance, patience, and persistence into our character.

God is much more concerned about your character than your changing circumstances. Conversely, when you are waiting, you are more concerned with your immediate circumstance than with your character. So how is your character doing as you wait for God to respond to something you've asked for? Continue to wait patiently and don't give up for He is faithful. Besides, your character depends on your patience!

Prayer: Father, help us wait patiently for the wonderful gift we need to help us in our hour of need. Amen

Thursday: Take Heart and Wait

I am still confident of this: I will see the goodness of the Lord in the land of the living; be strong and take heart and wait for the Lord.
Psalm 27:13–14

I love the Psalms because of the positive and powerful promises the passages contain. Today's passage certainly brings out the positive position of the Psalmist who confidently takes heart and waits for the Lord. One of the strange characteristics of Alzheimer's disease is you will experience some "not-so-good" days when it is overwhelming. These "not-so-good" days can take a toll on your emotional health.

I suppose your attitude regarding the disease impacts how you face your "not-so-good" days. Do you waste away the good days worrying how the "not-so-good" days will impact you? Or do you live life to the fullest with a strong heart on the good days knowing with confidence God's strength will carry you through the "not-so-good" days? I choose the latter and opt to live the good days with all the gusto I can muster knowing His goodness prevails especially in the "not-so-good" days.

During the "not-so-good" days, I wait confidently on the Lord knowing His goodness still surrounds me even though the fogginess prevails. On these days I try to read encouraging Scripture from the Psalms. I also get outdoors where the beauty of God's creation reminds me He is still in complete control. Thus I am reassured the "not-so-good" days will pass and the good days will return. So take heart today and wait upon the Lord. His goodness fills the land and fills our hearts as well!

Prayer: Merciful Lord, help us enjoy the good days with gusto and trust in Your strength during the "not-so-good" days. Amen

Friday: Wait Patiently

I waited patiently for the Lord; he turned to me and heard my cry. He lifted me out of the slimy pit, out of the mud and mire; and gave me a firm place to stand. Psalm 40:1–2

As a teenager growing up on my dad's cattle farm, one of my chores was to feed hay to the cattle each day during the winter. Since the ground would get extremely muddy, my father didn't want me driving the tractor in the fields or barn lot for fear of creating muddy ruts. Because of his concerns, I had to carry bales of hay to the field by hand. The problem with this was my gum boots would often get stuck in the mud. When this happened I had to set the bales down and pull my boots out of the mud and try again. I can remember how impatient I was for spring to finally arrive and dry out the barn lot so I could feed hay easier and use the tractor once the ground was firm.

Today's passage reminded me of my days on the farm and how easy it was to get stuck in the mud of the barn yard. Sometimes our lives can easily become mired in the muddy pit called Alzheimer's disease. We become impatient with God and upset with our dwindling capabilities. We wonder why we can't function like we did before our illness. But, just like my experiences in the mud of the barnyard, we can learn coping strategies enabling us to get on with life. The key is to patiently try different methods of sidestepping our inabilities.

There are strategies you can use to offset the limitations of Alzheimer's. I rely on checklists to keep me on track during the day. It is a coping strategy that has helped me maintain some independence. Patience is the key and my checklists are a firm reminder God can help me if I will let Him.

Prayer: Lord of Compassion, help us out of the muck and mire of confusion and uncertainty that can overwhelm us at times. Amen

Saturday: Wait for Salvation

I wait for your salvation, O Lord, and I follow your commands. I obey your statutes, for I love them greatly. I obey your precepts and your statutes, for all my ways are known to you. Psalm 119:166–168

Being an avid gardener, I can't wait for spring to arrive so I can play in the gardens surrounding my home. Long before I begin planting new seedlings and bulbs, I have to prepare the gardens for new plants. Mulching, weeding, soil preparation, and composting must be done to start the planting process. All this happens in the early springtime.

Today's passage from the Psalms implies the Psalmist has to wait for the Lord's salvation but he doesn't just sit by idly. In fact, he follows the Lord's commands, loves His statutes, and obeys His precepts. Just like the gardener who prepares his ground for the long awaited spring, the Psalmist prepares his heart and mind for his long awaited salvation. Like a gardener and the Psalmist, those of us with Alzheimer's disease wait for a miraculous salvation but we must also prepare the ground as well. So, how do we do this? Here are just a few ways I prepare ground so to speak:

- Take my medicine and vitamins every day
- Participate in a clinical trial to help find a cure
- Eat healthy foods and exercise daily
- Try new coping strategies for memory loss
- Write, read, and work mentally challenging puzzles
- Keep my doctor and therapist appointments.

Remember you can't sit idly by and expect the disease to go away. Like the Psalmist, you must prepare your heart and mind. Then wait for the Lord to bring your salvation!

Prayer: Lord, help us prepare the ground for Your salvation. Amen

Paul M. Hornback

Sunday: Wait and Be Still

Be still, and know that I am God; I will be exalted among the nations, I will be exalted in the earth. The Lord Almighty is with us; the God of Jacob is our fortress. Psalms 46:10–11

I walked outside this morning and wandered through the gardens here at the Hornback Homestead. In the stillness of the morning, I noticed the first few stalks of green stems breaking through the cold winter ground proving spring is just around the corner. Tulips, daffodils, white bells, and crocuses have waited all winter for just the right time to start their slow steady climb from deep beneath the frigid garden soil.

Springtime is a special time for me because it slowly sets the stage for an incredible transformation that occurs annually in my gardens. I have waited patiently all winter for the first signs of spring to emerge. The wait is over and once again I am reassured God is in complete control of all things.

This week we have examined Scriptures related to waiting on the Lord. It is now time to be still before Him and wait for His reassurance He is in complete control of our lives. Like the flowers waiting for spring, we also wait on the Lord knowing He is God, He is among us, and He is to be exalted above all things. Alzheimer's can be a fierce foe but it trembles before the Lord Almighty who is our fortress in times of trouble. He alone controls our lives and we wait patiently in His comforting arms. Be still and know He is God alone!

Prayer: Lord Almighty, You are exalted above all nations and all things on this earth. You are our only fortress, salvation, and comforter. May we be still before You today knowing You alone are God and are worthy of all our praise! Amen

Markus Gann © 123RF.com

A SLOWER PACE

Devotions to help you learn to slow your pace down as you live with Alzheimer's disease.

Monday: Quiet Waters

The Lord is my shepherd, I shall not be in want. He makes me lie down in green pastures, he leads me beside quiet waters, he restores my soul. Psalm 23:1–3

I have been an avid hiker my entire life. Being outdoors and walking through forests, hills, mountains, and wilderness terrain brings me joy and peace. Nothing is more thrilling than hiking in rough terrain and discovering a stream in the wilderness. In my youth, I would hike as quickly as possible so I could cover more ground in a day. I would simply pass by a stream and not give it a second thought. As I've grown older and more mature, I've learned to hike at a slower pace and enjoy the scenery. Now when I come upon a stream in the wilderness, I stop to enjoy the beauty and serenity of its calming waters. Perhaps that is what the Psalmist had in mind as he wrote the words, "He leads me beside quiet waters."

God often brings quiet waters into our lives so we can be refreshed, restored, and revitalized for the path ahead. Dealing with Alzheimer's is much like an arduous hike in the wilderness. The key to survival is taking it slowly and enjoying the journey as much as possible. There will be rough terrain but there will most certainly be gentle bubbling brooks of beauty along the way. These waters may take the form of a beautiful sunrise, a quiet walk in the garden, an especially touching prayer time, or a surprise visit from an old friend. Take time to allow God to lead you to your quiet waters and pause to have your soul restored.

Prayer: Wonderful Father, thank You for Your eternal guidance leading us beside still waters where our souls are gently refreshed. Help us pause and enjoy the calming beauty of Your gifts. Amen

Tuesday: Safe Pasture

Trust in the Lord and do good; dwell in the land and enjoy safe pasture. Psalm 37:4

While working as an engineer for the Department of the Army, I prided myself on being able to manage multiple projects, assist other engineers, and still meet my deadlines. This was truly multitasking and I loved it! I was dwelling in the work environment, trusting God to empower me, doing good deeds, and enjoying safe pasture. I understood exactly what the Psalmist was writing about in today's Scripture.

Prior to my diagnosis, I started having trouble multitasking, I began making mistakes, I had difficulty focusing, and I was missing deadlines. It was a relief when I got my diagnosis because I finally understood what was happening to me. Perhaps something similar led to your diagnosis as well.

It is strange how Alzheimer's disease takes away our ability to multitask. Of course, this isn't all bad. Now, I enjoy focusing on one task at a time like making dinner, writing a devotion, making a home repair, or working in the garden. I have found I can still dwell in the land, do good deeds, and enjoy safe pasture but at a much slower pace. I am much happier now as I go through my daily routine. Life is much simpler and saner. I wonder how I ever survived in the hustle and bustle of a fast-paced government engineering office.

How about you? Are you slowing down and not trying to do as much as you used to do? I pray you are because that's what God wants. Do this and He will keep you in safe pasture.

Prayer: Good Shepherd, help us dwell trustingly in the land of Alzheimer's while allowing us to do good deeds and enjoy Your safe pasture. Slow our pace down so we can focus on You. Amen

Paul M. Hornback

Wednesday: My Soul Pants for God

*As the deer pants for streams of water, so my soul pants for you,
O God. My soul thirsts for God, for the living God. Where can I go
and meet with God? Psalm 42:1*

When my son Ben was young, we would often go hiking in
search of waterfalls along the Skyline Drive and the Blue Ridge
Parkway. This is a beautiful area with some very rough terrain. I
remember one 12 mile hike during which we saw three waterfalls. It
was an incredible day that started out cool but reached 98 degrees in
the afternoon. I did not pack enough water and by 11:00 we were
completely out. By 2:00 we were panting for water and our pace had
diminished dramatically. We finally can upon a clear pool of water
at the base of the first waterfall and jumped in to cool our bodies.
We drank the refreshing clear water and were revitalized for the hike
ahead.

I have never forgotten how thirsty we were on that hike. It
helped me understand how deeply the deer pants for water in today's
passage. The Psalmist compares the deer's panting for water to our
soul's panting for God. After being diagnosed with Alzheimer's, I
fully understood how much my soul panted for God. I needed Him
more than water, more than life itself. I felt I was trying to race away
from the disease but couldn't. I was tired, thirsty and searching for
answers. God reminded me He was right alongside me. Like the
clear pool of water that refreshed my son and me, all I had to do was
slow down, dive into His word, and be refreshed.

Is your soul panting for God? Are you searching for answers?
Slow down and let Him refresh you today. Open His word and seek
His presence. You will pant no more!

*Prayer: Savior, refresh our panting souls and quench our thirst
for You, the one and only living God. Amen*

Thursday: Morning Satisfaction

Satisfy us in the morning with your unfailing love that we may sing for joy and be glad all our days. Make us glad for as many days as you have afflicted us, for as many years as we have seen trouble.
Psalm 90:14–15

Mornings are an especially wonderful time here at the Hornback Homestead as I usually rise early for prayer and Bible reading. It wasn't always this way as I'd often stay up late and sleep until the last possible moment. I'd shave, eat breakfast, say a quick prayer, and have my first cup of coffee on the 45 minute drive to work. I remember how frazzled and frenzied the days were back then.

Today's Scripture reminds us to take time in the morning so we might be satisfied with His unfailing love. If we do this we will find joy and be glad all our days. In order to be satisfied in the morning we must slow our lives down and connect with the Lord before we start our daily routine. This has been especially beneficial for me since I now suffer from Alzheimer's. I generally wake up early, start the coffee, read from my study Bible, spend time in prayer, and then walk outside and enjoy the majesty of His amazing creation. This puts things into perspective and helps me start my day right.

Slowing down, spending time with the Lord, and enjoying His splendor has made living with Alzheimer's so much easier. As the Psalmist said, it make us glad for as many days as we are afflicted, for as many years as we have trouble. Isn't this what you really want? To be glad and joyful in spite of what has happened in your life. So, get up and be satisfied in the morning. His unfailing love awaits you!

Prayer: Lord of Heaven and Earth, satisfy us in the morning as we spend time with You. Bring joy and gladness into our lives with Your unfailing love. Amen

Friday: Choose What's Better

"Martha, Martha," the Lord answered, "You are worried and upset about many things, but only one thing is needed. Mary has chosen what is better, and it will not be taken away from her."
Luke 10:41–42

Remember the episode with Mary, Martha, and Jesus when He came to visit them? Martha was busy making preparations and Mary was sitting at Jesus' feet listening to what He had to say. Martha comes to Jesus and asks, "Lord don't you care my sister has left me to do the work by myself? Tell her to help me!" How many of you identify with Martha in this passage?

I was most certainly a Martha most of my life. I was busy doing something which absolutely had to be done. There was little time to be still and spend time with the Lord. I was "worried and upset about many things" and honestly believed if I worked hard enough and long enough it would solve all my problems. All I needed was a little help from the Lord to keep everyone else focused and working hard like me! I can even remember praying for the Lord to light a fire under some folks so we could get a project finished on time.

How about you? Are you worried, frustrated, and upset about things out of your control? Has Alzheimer's robbed you of your peace of mind and joy for life? Then take the advice of our Lord and choose what is better. Slow down a bit, sit at His feet, and spend some time listening to Him. Read His word, pour out your heart to Him in prayer, and listen silently for His reply. Make this a habit you practice every day. Do this and you will choose just like Mary did. Besides, life will be better and it won't be taken away from you!

Prayer: Lord, may we always sit at Your feet and listen intently for Your words of encouragement so joy will fill our hearts. Amen

Saturday: Do Not Be Burdened

It is for freedom that Christ has set us free. Stand firm, then, and do not let yourselves be burdened again by a yoke of slavery.
Galatians 5:1

Jewish Christians in Galatia were attempting to persuade the Gentile converts to follow the Old Testament practice of circumcision in order to confirm salvation. The Apostle Paul was adamant the gospel of Christ was based solely on grace through faith in Jesus Christ. The bondage of legalism taught by certain Jewish Christians tended to pervert the gospel of grace that gave new life and freedom to all believers. Paul penned today's passage in his letter to the Galatians so all Christians would understand the freedom found in Christ.

What does today's passage dealing with the "yoke of slavery" have to do with living under the auspices of Alzheimer's? Simply put, we are no longer burdened by what we "used to be able to accomplish" because things aren't the same anymore. Like the new covenant Christ established so we could be saved from the legalism of Judaism, we are now freed from the burden of doing all the complicated things we used to do. Multitasking is out so just accept it. The pace of living is much slower now so simply accept it. The ability to comprehend multiple conversations is out so learn to accept it. We are no longer bound to the things we used to be able to do so free yourself from the burden of trying to accomplish those things.

It is okay not to be like you were before. It is important to accept this new condition and change your life accordingly. Don't beat yourself up because you can't do what you once did. Christ gives you the freedom to be who you are now!

Prayer: Lord, help us accept who we are now and live in the freedom You have given us. Amen

Sunday: Slow Down and Be Still

Be still, and know that I am God; I will be exalted among the nations, I will be exalted in the earth. The Lord Almighty is with us; the God of Jacob is our fortress. Psalms 46:10–11

This week has been a tough week of coming to grips with all that is going on in our lives. Although we are still the same people we were before we were diagnosed with Alzheimer's, we definitely have new limitations. It is extremely important we learn to slow down, reduce stress, and concentrate on one thing at a time. This may be a challenge because you are so used to multitasking, going at breakneck speeds, and living independently.

Be assured you can change because I certainly did. Slow your pace down and enjoy the freedom of no longer being yoked to our cultural rat race. Find time to be still so you can:

- Walk beside the quiet waters
- Dwell in safe pasture
- Pant for God like the deer pants for water
- Find satisfaction in every new morning
- Choose what is better by spending time at His feet
- Not be burdened by your old ways.

The Lord is waiting patiently for you to slow down, sit a spell at His feet, and allow Him to lead you gently beside His quiet waters. Can't you just hear the babbling brook as He beckons you to stop and place your feet in the cool clear water? Take time today to be still before the Lord and worship His majesty. He is waiting to welcome you into His presence.

Prayer: Lord of All, let us be still before You today so we might pause to enjoy Your quiet waters and dwell in Your safe pastures. Our souls pant for You and nothing else can quench the longing in our hearts. Fill our spirits with Your presence. Amen

Bennymarty © 123RF.com

A DAILY ROUTINE

Devotions to help you develop a daily routine to bring order to the foggy days of Alzheimer's disease.

Paul M. Hornback

Monday: A Wife of Noble Character

She gets up while it is still dark; she provides food for her family and portions for her servant girls. She considers a field and buys it; out of her earnings she plants a vineyard. She sets about her work vigorously; her arms are strong for her tasks. Proverbs 31:15–17

I love today's passage from Proverbs because it epitomizes a wife of noble character. It describes a woman filled with wisdom, integrity, honor, righteousness, and dignity who is worth more than rubies to her husband. She rises early in the morning to start her daily routine and sets about her work vigorously. Perhaps this is in part why she is worth so very much in the eyes of her husband and children.

There are positive benefits to maintaining a consistent daily routine. This is particularly true when you struggle with Alzheimer's. A consistent daily routine keeps me on track especially on days when I flitter about aimlessly. To avoid this, I have developed a daily schedule I follow pretty consistently. This schedule has specific things I do in the morning (shave, take medication, fix breakfast, read Bible, pray, check email, work on devotional, visit Mom, feed dogs, walk, and do dishes). In the evening I also have a list of things I do as well (fix supper, feed dogs, clean up dishes, read, lay out clothes, take shower, lock up the house, and pray). These routines are the same for each day of the week.

Now this may seem somewhat silly but it helps me maintain a familiar daily structure while keeping me focused on what's important. Proverbs is filled with good advice like keeping a daily routine just like the "Wife of Noble Character." It works for me so it may work for you as well!

Prayer: Lord, gives us each a daily routine we can easily follow to bring order to our lives. Amen

Tuesday: Job's Regular Custom

When a period of feasting had run its course, Job would make arrangements for them to be purified. Early in the morning he would sacrifice a burnt offering for each of them, thinking, "Perhaps my children have sinned and cursed God in their hearts." This was Job's regular custom. Job 1:5

Job was a godly man and there was no man like him on earth. He was blameless and upright, shunned evil, and feared God. Job not only kept himself righteous before God but he also acted for the righteousness of his family as evidenced in today's passage. Two vital concepts stand out in this Scripture. First, Job did his duty early in the morning which implies he got up early as a normal part of his routine. Second, his sacrificial duty was a regular custom and it defined who he was in the Lord. Perhaps this is why the Lord held Job in such high regard.

I find comfort in having a special time for God in my daily routine. In fact, I have it itemized on my morning and evening schedule for each day of the week. I don't want Alzheimer's to creep in and steal these precious periods from my life. Perhaps this may seem a little precocious but it helps me maintain focus on what's important. Like Job, I want this time early in the morning and late in the evening to be part of my regular custom.

How about you? Do you have a daily routine that includes time with the Lord? Perhaps you read Scripture from the Bible, follow a daily devotional like the Upper Room, or just spend quiet time in prayer. Whatever your special time alone with God entails, make it your regular custom just like Job.

Prayer: Precious Father, thank You for the special time we spend with You every day. May it define who we are in You. Amen

Wednesday: Jesus' Custom

Jesus then left that place and went into the region of Judea and across the Jordan. Again crowds of people came to him, and as was his custom, he taught them. Mark 10:1

Jesus was a marvelous teacher in all aspects. He had a way of mesmerizing a crowd by the comforting words He spoke and the parables He used to superimpose godly wisdom upon earthly understanding. No wonder people flocked to hear Him speak. The interesting thing about the Lord was He taught the crowds "as was his custom." So if the Lord did it back then when He walked this earth, then He is still doing it today. Now He teaches through His word with the help of the Holy Spirit. The key is to be in His presence. Today we do this by reading and studying the Holy Bible.

After being diagnosed with Alzheimer's disease, the Bible took on new meaning in my life. It became my way of focusing on something bigger than my disease. I'm still learning new things and I know my brain is benefitting from this process. I encourage you to read your Bible daily, ask the Holy Spirit to help your learn new insights, and to pray about what you've read.

Alzheimer's works on our brains in negative ways but the word of God works on our brains in positive ways. It's funny how I can read a book or a magazine and have trouble following what I've read. However, when I read the Bible I have no trouble following or understanding the passages. Perhaps it's because it is the living word of God and Alzheimer's can't break down what has been divinely created. So read it, learn from it, and let it saturate your mind!

Prayer: Holy Spirit, come live in our hearts and minds so we might read and continually learn from the Holy Scriptures. Amen

Thursday: This Has Been My Practice

In the night I remember your name, O Lord, and I will keep your
law. This has been my practice: I obey your precepts.
Psalm 119:55–56

The 119th Chapter of Psalms was probably written by an
Israelite of exemplary piety who constructed the Psalter as a massive
alphabetic acrostic. Today's passage comes from the section entitled
Zayin. It describes God's word as being a constant comfort and
gentle guide for whatever circumstances befall life. The Psalmist
reminds us to keep God's law and obey His precepts so it will be
"our practice."

Perhaps you wonder how to do what the Psalmist prescribes. All
you do is practice, practice, practice! As a Marine second lieutenant
going through Navy flight school, I was required to learn emergency
procedures for each training aircraft. The only way to learn these
procedures was to memorize the steps and practice them over and
over. So it is with our ability to keep God's law and obey His
precepts. We must first learn His words and then practice following
them until they become burned into our brains. By reading His word,
meditating on His word, and spending time with Him daily, we
begin a process that puts us on a path toward righteousness.

Just like memorizing and practicing emergency procedures, you
can learn and practice His perfect precepts. By doing this you will
have constant comfort and a gentle guide in whatever circumstances
befall your life including Alzheimer's disease. There is no better
guide or more perfect companion through the uncertain maze of
Alzheimer's than our Lord Jesus Christ. So pick up the Bible and
practice, practice, practice!

Prayer: Gentle Guide Jesus, help us abide in Your presence,
read Your word, and practice Your precepts every day. Amen

Friday: As Was His Custom

As his custom was, Paul went into the synagogue, and on three Sabbath days he reasoned with them from the Scriptures, explaining that Christ had to suffer and rise from the dead. "This Jesus I am proclaiming to you is the Christ," he said. Acts 17:2

Do you ever wonder what folks will write or say about you after you leave this earth? Perhaps you don't want to think about the words people will use to describe your actions once you die. In today's passage the Apostle Luke describes Paul as one who reasoned with the Jewish people that "this Jesus" was the Christ using the Scriptures. Interestingly, Luke adds the caveat "as his custom was" inferring Paul routinely went to the synagogues to reason and proclaim Christ.

Perhaps we should examine the actions we routinely conduct and determine if they are worthy of the gospel. I'm sure this is an exercise many folks would rather excuse themselves from conducting. As Christians, it is vital we step outside ourselves and examine who we are in the eyes of others. Would people see you as simply a sports enthusiast, golf pro, couch potato, yard and garden ape, save the whale warrior, or political activist? Now don't get me wrong, there is nothing wrong with any of these activities but is this how you want to be remembered?

Alzheimer's has been a rude awakening for me because I know I have a limited amount of time remaining. Therefore, I want to draw closer to the Lord, share His story more, and be a man after God's own heart. So, "as was his custom," do what is worthy of the gospel and create a destiny of divinity in your life!

Prayer: Precious Lord, help us routinely proclaim the gospel and humbly serve You so we are people after Your own heart. Amen

Saturday: Avoid a Habit of Idleness

Besides, they get into the habit of being idle and going about from house to house. And not only do they become idlers, but also gossips and busybodies, saying things they ought not to.
1 Timothy 5:13

In Paul's first pastoral letter to Timothy, he cautions him about young widows who can easily get into the habit of being idle. According to Paul, idleness leads to all types of mischief and ungodly activity. Perhaps Paul should not have limited his idle caution to only young widows. As the old saying goes, "idle hands are the devil's workshop."

Having a daily routine filled with beneficial activities is essential to your wellbeing and positive attitude. This is especially true when Alzheimer's strikes. Idleness allows your mind to wander off into a frenzied state of worry about the disease. Following a routine schedule fills your day with meaningful activity and keeps idleness at bay.

My daily routine has specific time for prayer, Bible reading, meditation, and quiet walks where I connect with God's wonderful creation. My weekly schedule is highlighted with time for worship, Sunday school, small group fellowship, and corporate prayer meetings. By interweaving opportunities for fellowship during the week, I maintain a social connection with good Christian friends which boosts my spirit and allows me to stay socially active. Alzheimer's disease can impact the brain in ways that cause an individual to want to stay at home. Remaining active socially, mentally, and physically does much for the emotional well-being of Alzheimer's patients. So avoid the tendency toward idleness because Paul's instruction to Timothy is still sound advice for us today!

Prayer: Lord of Heaven and Earth, it is our humble prayer to live lives filled with righteousness so we might be better servants. Amen

Paul M. Hornback

Sunday: Scheduling Stillness

Be still, and know that I am God; I will be exalted among the nations, I will be exalted in the earth. The Lord Almighty is with us; the God of Jacob is our fortress. Psalms 46:10–11

This week we have explored how important it is to maintain a daily routine filled with interesting activities, quiet time for prayer, physical exercise, mentally stimulating activities, social interactions, Bible reading, and meditation. These daily routines provide a familiar format that flows easily within our day to day living. Maintaining an established weekly schedule is also important as it can remind us of opportunities for fellowship, worship, corporate prayer, and social connection. It is also essential to schedule opportunities to be still before the Lord.

Scheduling times of stillness is absolutely vital to maintain our healthy relationship with our Lord. He eagerly waits for these precious moments so He can have our full attention. It is during these quiet moments He softly speaks to our souls and refreshes our weary spirits. It is then we can pour out our heart, and present our requests to Him; He will listen like no one else has ever listened. He alone provides the comfort and compassion we so earnestly desire. He understands all we are going through and how Alzheimer's is impacting our lives.

So make sure you schedule in time every day to be still before the Lord. You won't be disappointed because I know you'll find a caring, compassionate, and understanding Savior who loves you dearly. And that's something Alzheimer's can't steal from your life!

Prayer: Lord of Life, help us remember to always spend time with You alone every day. Bless these times of stillness and draw us closer to You, listen to our prayers, and comfort us. Amen

Timothy Mainiero © 123RF.com

A GENTLE SPIRIT

Devotions to help you battle the frustration brought on by
Alzheimer's disease by fostering a gentle spirit.

Paul M. Hornback

Monday: Be Completely Humble and Gentle

As a prisoner for the Lord, then, I urge you to live a life worthy of the calling you have received. Be completely humble and gentle; be patient, bearing with one another in love. Ephesians 4:1–2

The Apostle Paul has a way of grabbing your attention and bringing you down off your high horse. Today's passage does all that in just two short sentences. Paul reminds the Ephesians he is a prisoner for the Lord. I'm not sure if you have ever been incarcerated, visited an inmate in prison, or been part of a prison ministry. Although I've never been incarcerated, I have done some prison visitation and I've been part of a ministry team that went into a state prison. It is a humbling and heart wrenching experience to go behind bars and talk with prison inmates who have turned their lives over to Christ. These men now minister to other inmates and spread the gospel of Christ inside the prison walls.

It takes a very special individual to do this type of ministry, someone with a gentle and humble heart. But honestly, isn't that the type of heart all Christians are to have once we come to Christ? The fruit of the spirit includes gentleness, love, and patience. Christ paid a high price so we would no longer be slaves to sin and so the Holy Spirit could reside within each of us. Once the Holy Spirit takes up residence in our hearts, then the fruit of the spirit can begin to flow in our lives. It has been my humble prayer even though I am a prisoner of Alzheimer's, God, through the Holy Spirit, would keep my heart humble and gentle. This way I might be patient, bearing all things in love. That is my earnest prayer for you as well.

Prayer: Holy Spirit, keep our hearts humble and gentle so we might be patient, bearing one another in love as our Lord requests. Amen

Tuesday: Clothe Yourselves with Gentleness

Therefore, as God's chosen people, holy and dearly loved, clothe yourselves with compassion, kindness, humility, gentleness, and patience. Colossians 3:12

I have loved jogging ever since I left the Marine Corps over 30 years ago. As a civilian engineer working for the U.S. Army, running three or four miles every day at noon gave me an opportunity to break away from the hectic pace of work, enjoy the beauty of nature, and converse with God. I cherished those runs since they helped me maintain my sanity in the fast-paced environment in which I worked.

Whenever I changed into my running clothes, everyone knew to leave me alone because I was about to leave for a short run. I am not a marathoner but when I put on those running clothes I certainly felt like one. The clothes helped me get my mind around the personal race I was about to run. Paul's letter to the Colossians reminds them to clothe themselves properly because they were God's chosen people. Since they were holy and dearly loved people of God, they should be wearing compassion, kindness, humility, gentleness, and patience. It is amazing how Paul used this analogy of clothing to remind us to "put on" these spiritual articles of clothing daily.

If I can put on gentleness, then the other attributes will flow naturally from my gentle spirit. After being diagnosed with Alzheimer's, I worried about developing an uncooperative spirit as the disease progressed. As I prayed about this God kept reminding me of today's passage. Now I try to clothe myself spiritually with gentleness so it will always be a part of who I am in Christ. It is a simple reminder God is in control of who I am and Alzheimer's must bow to what God wants in me!

Prayer: Lord, clothe us every day with holy gentleness. Amen

Paul M. Hornback

Wednesday: A Gentle and Quiet Spirit

Instead, it should be that of your inner self, the unfading beauty of a gentle and quiet spirit, which is of great worth in God's sight.
1 Peter 3:4

The other day my wife bought me six young chicks. I placed the chicks in the basement in a large plastic tub with plenty of chick starter and water. I also put a white heat lamp over the tub to keep the chicks warm. After a few days I noticed the chicks were always on edge and agitated anytime I came near them. I decided to try a red heat lamp so the light would not be as bright on them all the time. After a few hours I went down to the basement and to my surprise the chicks had calmed down, were resting contently, and were not agitated at my presence. The red light made all the difference.

If we want to develop gentle and quiet spirits we must be under the right type of light, the light of Christ. There we can mature into gentle, humble, patient, kind, and quiet servants. This is exactly what the Apostle Peter was talking about in today's passage. The unfading beauty of a gentle and quiet spirit is pleasing and of great worth to God. A Christian with a gentle spirit is easily molded by God. This type of individual is not agitated by people who wrong them, unpleasant situations, or difficulties that crop up in life.

Staying in the light of Christ makes dealing with Alzheimer's so much easier. I don't have to lash out or be upset because I feel like life has thrown me a curve. All I need do is bask in the "Light of our Lord" and take pleasure in His presence. He will continue to fill all my needs just like I did for the chicks under the red light!

Prayer: Lord of Light, keep our spirits gentle and quiet so we might also be of great worth to You. Amen

Thursday: A Gentle and Humble Hearted Master

*Take my yoke upon you and learn from me, for I am gentle and
humble in heart, and you will find rest for your souls.
Matthew 11:29–30*

My father was a career Army man so we moved constantly as he
was transferred from one duty station to another. When my dad
finally retired, we moved to a small farm in Kentucky. I started high
school and began to adjust to farm life which was quite different
from life near Army posts. There was plenty of hard manual labor
but we did have a small John Deere tractor we used to plow fields,
plant tobacco, harvest hay, and do general farm tasks. However,
some of our neighbor farmers still used mules to do much of their
crop work. One old farmer, Mr. Wells, always rode his mule to and
from the tobacco patches he cultivated. One hot summer day, I
watched Mr. Wells use his mule to cultivate a tobacco patch while I
was hoeing. He was very gentle with the mule and he stopped at the
end of each row to give his mule a rest.

As I read today's Scripture this image filled my mind because,
like Mr. Wells, Christ is a kind and gentle master. As we take
Christ's yoke upon us we work for a master who is gentle and
humble in heart. This remains true even though we are experiencing
the challenges of living with Alzheimer's disease. Christ understands
all we are going through and he adjusts our yoke accordingly. You
see, even thought our work may be different than it was before the
disease struck, we still have work to do for His kingdom. Mr. Wells'
mule was old and he no longer plowed, pulled a wagon, or helped
harvested crops but he was still able to cultivate tobacco. Mr. Wells
knew his mule's limitations just as Christ knows ours. Remember,
He is a gentle master and He loves you dearly!

*Prayer: Gentle Master, adjust our yokes so that we might serve
You in some wonderful way. Keep us gentle and humble in heart.
Amen*

Paul M. Hornback

Friday: Pursue Gentleness

But you, man of God, flee from all this, and pursue
righteousness, godliness, faith, love, endurance, and gentleness.
1 Timothy 6:11

Paul's first letter to Timothy contained instructions for leading the church at Ephesus but it also contains sound advice for living the Christian life. Today's Scripture reminds us to flee from ungodly ways of living and to pursue godly attributes. As I read the passage, I recalled a time after I left the Marine Corps when I made the conscious decision to stop cursing. In the Marines, it was a habitual way of communicating and emphasizing certain instructions that was more acceptable in the eyes of most Marines.

I struggled with breaking this habit for about a year but finally began to make headway. The secret was not only to avoid using the words but to replace the habit with something else. At the same time I began to read the books on positive thinking written by Norman Vincent Peale. The combination of pursuing positive thinking and the conscious act of fleeing from the use of curse words seemed to do the trick. Eventually I overcame the urge to curse.

As Paul so aptly put it, not only do you have to flee from ungodly activity but you must pursue godly activity to replace it. As I struggle with many of the impacts of Alzheimer's disease, I find the same is true. If I desire to avoid aggressiveness, controversy, and quarreling in my daily life, then I have to pursue gentleness, kindness, and peacefulness each day. In order to accomplish this, I must spend time with the Lord in prayer and reading His word. Only then will His gentle spirit and humble heart guide my daily actions.

Prayer: Gentle Savior, help us flee from all ungodly ways of living so we might pursue Your gentle spirit and draw closer to You. Amen

Saturday: Gentleness Evident to All

Let your gentleness be evident to all. The Lord is near.
Philippians 4:5

Alfred Hitchcock was a master of mystery when it came to directing films with a sense of the macabre entwined. For nearly fifty years he was the dean of movie directing and no one had his knack for suspense. To keep audiences intrigued he often made cameo appearances in his films. For example, in *The Birds* he's found walking past the pet shop with two white terriers; in *North By Northwest* he's spotted missing a bus during the opening credits; and in *Shadow of a Doubt* he's playing cards on the train. Alfred Hitchcock was truly an innovative film maker who knew how to engage the audience.

In today's passage from Paul's letter to the Philippians, Paul says our gentleness should be evident because the Lord is near. Is your gentleness evident to all? When I ask this I don't just mean to your family or your close friends. How about the people you encounter in the doctor's office, while waiting in a long line at the supermarket, or even while you are stuck in traffic? Will your gentleness be evident to all these people as well? Hopefully gentleness will flow from deep within you no matter where you are or what you are doing. That way if the Lord made a cameo appearance in your life today, He would not be disappointed in your actions.

Alzheimer's can weigh heavily on my spirit if I allow it to have a foothold in my thoughts. I have to remind myself daily who I am in Christ so my gentle nature will overpower the negative impacts of the disease. I do this not just because Christ might be waiting in the shadows to make an appearance but because that's what Christ expects of me. How about you?

Prayer: Lord, help us be gentle servants in all we do. Amen

Paul M. Hornback

Sunday: Gentleness in Stillness

Be still, and know that I am God; I will be exalted among the nations, I will be exalted in the earth. The Lord Almighty is with us; the God of Jacob is our fortress. Psalms 46:10–11

This week our area was hit by severe thunderstorms with high winds, torrential rains, tornadoes, hail, and massive flooding. This was a record breaking month for thunderstorms and tornadoes across much of the United States. This morning, the storms have quieted down and there is a gentle rain falling. It is quite a contrast from the previous day's aggressive weather.

I sat on the front porch drinking coffee and was amazed at the gentleness of the rain and the stillness of the morning. I took time to be still before the Lord. I thanked Him for who He is, for safety throughout the week of horrific weather, and for His many blessings in my life. I also thought about how wonderful gentle rains are in comparison to aggressive thunderstorms. It helped me understand why God simply adores a gentle spirit while He abhors an aggressive and quarrelsome spirit.

This week we have focused on pursuing a gentle spirit that both delights God and is pleasing to our loved ones. Now it is time to be still before the Lord and allow the Holy Spirit to gently rule our hearts. As we all know, the Holy Spirit enables the fruit of the spirit to flow in our lives and gentleness is a fruit of the Holy Spirit. I pray you will take time every day to be still before the Lord to thank Him for His love, grace, and mercy; to seek out His will for your life; to ask for His help in living with Alzheimer's; and to pursue gentleness from the Holy Spirit. God will be pleased if you do this daily!

Prayer: Lord of Grace, may Your Holy Spirit reign in our hearts and keep us gentle in all the things we do and say so we might be pleasing in Your sight and a blessing to our families. Amen

Dimaberkut © 123RF.com

COMING TO GRIPS

Devotions to help you learn to accept a diagnosis of Alzheimer's disease and the changes it brings.

Paul M. Hornback

Monday: Set of the Sail

Direct me in the path of your commands, for there I find delight.
Psalms 119:35

There is an old sailor's adage that says, "Tis the set of the sail and not the gale that determines the way you go." If you have been sailing you understand how important the set of the sail is with respect to the direction your boat will travel. Perhaps the Psalmist understood this premise because he wrote in today's passage to find delight you must direct yourself along the path of God's commands.

There is truth in the old adage and the Psalmist's words when applied to life after a diagnosis of Alzheimer's. First, you must acknowledge the fact you have the disease. There's no use denying it because Alzheimer's is not going away just because you choose not to accept it. In fact, you will probably do yourself more harm by ignoring the diagnosis. You see, the gale is most certainly Alzheimer's disease and the sail is your attitude. Once you've acknowledged the boat you are in, then you can set your sail in the right direction. You can begin to make plans for the future, treasure the days ahead, let go of the superfluous things, and research your options.

After my diagnosis I read extensively on Alzheimer's, touched base with the Alzheimer's Association, and picked the brain of every doctor I could. As a result, I'm staying on a perfectly set course because the "set of my sail" is moving me in the right direction. The gale may be Alzheimer's disease but the sea I am on belongs to God! He alone can direct me to the only safe harbor in the storm. Trust Him and set your sail!

Prayer: Heavenly Father, You alone know our future and You alone can move our boat to still waters. Help us through this storm. Amen

Tuesday: Advice and Instruction

Listen to advice and accept instruction, and in the end you will be wise. Proverbs 19:20

My wife and I have a fairy tale marriage. She believes I'm a prince and I believe she's a princess! Honestly, we have a wonderful marriage and we've only had a few arguments I can remember over the past 38 years. The last argument we had occurred four years ago. It centered on my desire to help a young parolee who had a history of drug abuse, stealing, and lying because I was convinced he had changed. My wife knew the young man and his wife as she'd dealt with the family and many like them in her position as the county school system's Family Services Director. She tried to explain to me I was wrong about the young man and he was back to using drugs. I failed to heed her advice and even verbally lashed out at her. As usual, I was wrong and the young man took me for a couple of thousand dollars because I wasn't willing to listen to her sound advice or accept her wise instruction. In the end, I wasn't wise at all but just a thoughtless fool.

This particular lesson taught me much about listening to advice and accepting instruction when it came to dealing with my diagnosis of early-onset Alzheimer's disease. This time I was going to be wise and not repeat my previous mistakes. Although there is no cure for Alzheimer's disease, there are things you can do to make your life easier, to plan for the future, and to stay healthy but first you have to acknowledge the diagnosis. Then listen to your doctor's sound advice and wise instructions like today's passage from Proverbs indicates. Just because you have Alzheimer's doesn't mean you can't be wise if you are willing to listen to the sound advice of others.

Prayer: Wise Father, help us listen to those who You have brought into our lives to provide us sound advice and instruction. Amen

Paul M. Hornback

Wednesday: A Straight Course

Folly delights a man who lacks judgment, but a man of understanding keeps a straight course. Proverbs 15:21

After completing Officer Candidate School in 1977, I was commissioned a second lieutenant in the United States Marine Corps. Next, I attended The Basic School where all new Marine officers learn the fundamentals of leadership. One of the programs included land navigation and orienteering. During this course, young officers learned how to navigate over unfamiliar terrain. The key to land navigation is to understand how to read a map and compass to follow a course to a predetermined destination. Some of my fellow Marine officers were former Boy Scouts which made land navigation pretty easy for them. However, many were not and the navigation course was pretty difficult. These young officers just didn't trust the map and compass and blindly headed off in the wrong direction. These officers lacked good judgment, were unable to keep a straight course, and got lost because they were foolish!

Perhaps that is what today's passage from Proverb's infers. If you understand your circumstance then you can keep a straight course through it. The same is true for navigating Alzheimer's disease. Understanding the disease and how it impacts your life is fundamental to being able to set a straight course through the disease. Knowledge will be your key to charting a course that not only helps you but helps prepare your family for what lies ahead. Remember, God is on your side! He alone can help you prepare yourself mentally and spiritually for the road ahead. So don't let folly cloud your judgment. Learn all you can and move forward in the right direction. With God's help you will keep a straight course!

Prayer: Lord of Understanding, help us maintain the straight course You have prepared for our journey with Alzheimer's disease. Amen

Thursday: Pay Attention and Gain Understanding

Listen, my sons, to a father's instruction; pay attention and gain understanding. I give you sound learning, so do not forsake my teaching. Proverbs 4:1–2

As a young boy growing up in Baltimore, I could not get enough of my dad's wisdom. I would listen to every word he said as he talked about work, Army life, and family. I especially loved to hear his opinions about current events and politics which I absorbed like a sponge. Then the teenage years came and his wisdom seemed trivial. About the time I got my first car, we stopped having long conversations and talked only about chores or during counseling sessions when I had disobeyed him. Unfortunately, the time I needed him most I pushed him away. Obviously, I did not heed the advice of today's passage from Proverbs. I failed to pay attention and gain understanding from someone with real life experience.

Perhaps this lesson applies to you as you deal with a diagnosis of Alzheimer's disease. First comes acceptance, then comes instruction, and finally you gain understanding for the road ahead. I can't emphasize enough how important it is to learn everything you can about the disease and how others have learned to cope. There is much good advice available to those who are willing to reach out for help.

Proverbs teaches wisdom and understanding which will add years to your life. With Alzheimer's, every year is a blessing and you need to capitalize on the "good years" that occur during the early stages of the disease. God provides wisdom if you will only pay attention. Seek His wisdom and the wisdom of those he puts in your path. If you don't, it will be foolish!

Prayer: Father, give us wisdom and understanding to help us deal with this disease as we acknowledge what is happening to us. Amen

Friday: Start Rebuilding

Come let us rebuild the wall of Jerusalem, and we will no longer be in disgrace. I also told them about the gracious hand of my God upon me and what the king had said to me. They replied, "Let us start rebuilding." So they began this good work. Nehemiah 3:17–18

The wall surrounding the city of Jerusalem and the city itself were in ruins. Nehemiah got word about the state of the city and he wept. He mourned, fasted, and prayed to his heavenly Father to grant him favor before the king so he might return to Jerusalem and rebuild the wall. King Artaxerxes granted his request and Nehemiah returned. He inspected the wall and saw firsthand all the damage. Then he had to get the people to recognize and acknowledge the state of the city. Once they understood, they could rebuild the wall under his leadership.

The same is true regarding Alzheimer's disease. Once we acknowledge our state and accept our diagnosis, we can move forward to rebuild our lives. You see, the people of Jerusalem weren't just rebuilding the wall for themselves; they were rebuilding it for future generations. So it is for us as we prepare for our future and the future of our families.

After I came to grips with my diagnosis, I saw an attorney to get my affairs in order, transferred property to my wife, found a clinical trial, and started this series of devotions for Alzheimer's patients. Like Nehemiah, I was more concerned for those who would live on after me. So examine the walls of your life, take stock of your situation, and begin to make plans for the future. But don't forget to ask God for His guidance and His favor just like Nehemiah did in today's passage!

Prayer: Father, help us rebuild our lives after our diagnosis so that we might be better servants for You and for our families. Amen

Saturday: Hold on to His Hand

For I am the Lord your God, who takes hold of your right hand and says to you, do not fear; I will help you. Isaiah 41:13

The words from Isaiah have always been an encouragement to me. Today's passage reminds us to call upon the Lord who is always beside us holding firmly to our right hand. The day I finally received my diagnosis of early-onset Alzheimer's, I was relieved God was by my side. It came after a year of tests, doctor visits, and trips to out-of-state clinics.

Accepting the diagnosis was by no means an easy thing to do. It required me to admit my mind was no longer as healthy and functional as it once was. I also had to acknowledge I had a disease with no known cure. However, it didn't mean my life was over or I had to walk this road alone. Like Isaiah said, God would take hold of my right hand and I'd have nothing to fear for He was going to help me. And God did exactly that!

Accepting the diagnosis simply reminded me how much I needed God's help to live my life. And let me set one thing straight, there is still lots of living left after a diagnosis of Alzheimer's. Will it be different? Yes. Will there be changes? Yes. Will God be there to help you with the transformation? Absolutely! God will not leave your side so you need not fear the future. God is in complete control and He alone can help you through the challenging times ahead. After I accepted my diagnosis and acknowledged the state I was in, I simply began to rely on God more fully. So, fear not, hold on to His hand, and continue to walk with Him. He won't let you down!

Prayer: Hallowed Father, we need You now more than ever. Hold our hands tightly and guide us through the days ahead. Amen

Paul M. Hornback

Sunday: Stillness Provides Acceptance

Be still, and know that I am God; I will be exalted among the nations, I will be exalted in the earth. The Lord Almighty is with us; the God of Jacob is our fortress. Psalms 46:10–11

This morning was a picture perfect morning. I walked outside and the birds were singing, the mist was beginning to lift from our pond, and the air was fresh. I stood in the yard gazing at the majestic scenery laid out before my eyes, sipped my hot cup of morning coffee, and thanked God for another breathtaking morning. Other than the birds singing, the morning was quiet. Nothing shattered the silence and majesty of the new day.

Standing outside surrounded by the beauty of God's creation made it especially easy to be still before the Lord and know He is God. In the stillness of the morning, I could feel His presence and I was reminded He alone is my fortress. This week we focused on the importance of accepting a diagnosis of Alzheimer's disease. Now it is time to be still before the Lord, exalt Him above all things on this earth, and surrender our condition over to Him. He is truly our fortress.

Somehow the quiet of this glorious spring morning reminds me each new day is a beautiful blessing from God. Although I may face daily challenges from the effects of Alzheimer's on my brain, God will help me find ways to cope so He will be glorified through my condition. Remember, accepting the diagnosis and acknowledging you need God's help to continue living your life opens the door for God to respond in powerful ways. He stands by your side ready and waiting for you to take hold of His hand so He might help you!

Prayer: Holy Father, You alone are our helper as we struggle with the challenges Alzheimer's brings to our lives. Help us to focus on You as You move powerfully in our lives. Amen

Krzysztof Wiktor © 123RF.com

MAINTAIN BALANCE

Devotions to help you maintain balance in the confusing world
of living with Alzheimer's disease.

Monday: Listening Versus Preparations

She had a sister called Mary, who sat at the Lord's feet listening to what he said. But Martha was distracted by all the preparations that had to be made. She came to him and asked, "Lord, don't you care that my sister has left me to do the work by myself? Tell her to help me!" Luke 10:39–40

We all remember Luke's recounting of what happened when Jesus came to Mary and Martha's home. Today's passage reminds us how Mary sat at the feet of Jesus listening to His teachings while Martha was distracted with the preparations required for entertaining guests. We've all been in the same boat as Martha; distracted from what is important because we were too focused on the needs of the moment. We lacked the ability to balance what "needs to be done" with what is truly important. Was Jesus saying to Martha preparations and work did not need to be done? Absolutely not! Instead, Jesus was reminding Martha that sitting at His feet and listening was far more important at this particular moment.

The same is true when Alzheimer's strikes your life. There are lots of preparations that need to be done but they must be balanced with moments of stillness and joy. Maintaining balance is absolutely essential because you don't want to become "worried and upset about many things" and forget to continue loving your family, spending time with the Lord, and enjoying the good days. If you grasp anything from today's passage let it be this one thought: The Lord knows exactly what our priorities should be and He will certainly set us straight if we will only ask Him!

Prayer: Lord, remind us each day to live our lives with balance so we don't get tied up in the preparations of life rather than the living of a God-centered life. Amen

Tuesday: Balance Brings Success

Plans fail for lack of counsel, but with many advisers they succeed. Proverbs 15:22

My wife and I enjoy walking in the evening at a park near our home. One day we encountered a lady with a large dog whose husband was having car trouble. We cut short our two mile walk and went to see if we could help. After saying hello, we discussed his problem which entailed the shift mechanism's inability to move from Park into Drive. He had already contacted a tow truck using OnStar but he had no way to get himself, his wife, and their dog back home. I offered to get my van and drive them all back home which he readily accepted.

On the way home I kept trying to figure out what was wrong with his car because I had a similar problem in one of my past vehicles. Unfortunately, I just couldn't remember since my mind was all jumbled up on that particular day. Upon arriving at home, I "Googled" the car problem and found a quick fix that would at least get his car moving. I drove to his location and sure enough it worked. Besides doing a good deed, I discovered how truly important balance is as we approach challenges from living with Alzheimer's disease.

Since I couldn't rely on memory alone, I used the internet to search for a potential solution. As you deal with the limitations Alzheimer's brings to the table, finding a balance between relying on your own abilities and accepting help from other sources leads to success in day to day living. Perhaps this is what Solomon was trying to say in today's passage. No one can expect to have all the answers, remember everything, and rely on no one. We all need balance which includes accepting help from others from time to time. Perhaps that is why Solomon was so wise!

Prayer: Lord, help us bring balance to our lives in all things. Amen

Wednesday: Seek Balance in Your Life

Yet a time is coming and has now come when the true worshipers will worship the Father in spirit and truth, for they are the kind of worshipers the Father seeks. God is spirit, and his worshipers must worship in spirit and in truth. John 4:23–24

Max Lucado weaves a wonderful tale about learning to dance by only reading a book on dancing. He surmises we can learn the fundamentals of dance by simply following the instructions in a book but it will be purely mechanical until you add music to the newly learned dance steps. There is definitely a balance between knowing the sequence of dance steps and moving rhythmically with the music. If you've watched "Dancing with the Stars" you know exactly what I'm talking about!

Today's passage reminds us God also requires balance in our worship. John says the balance is between the truth of the Scriptures and the presence of the Holy Spirit. The Father seeks those who worship both in truth and in spirit and this balance is pleasing to Him. When it comes to dealing with Alzheimer's disease, we must also seek balance in order to please those who love and care for us. Alzheimer's requires us to balance the pace at which we live our lives given the physical and mental limitations the disease brings.

The initial impacts of Alzheimer's may not be the same for everyone but they probably include loss in the areas of mental focus, concentration, short term memory, reasoning, and decision making. Learning to constructively balance your remaining abilities with the limitations brought on by the disease makes the Alzheimer's dance all the more challenging. So get out there and dance but don't forget to pace yourself!

Prayer: Father, help us find the right balance in our lives. Amen

Thursday: Balance Between Ask, Seek, and Knock

Ask and it will be given to you; seek and you will find; knock and the door will be opened to you. For everyone who asks receives; he who seeks finds, and to him who knocks, the door will be opened.
Matthew 7:7–8

Today's passage is part of Jesus' Sermon on the Mount. This particular passage reminds us to ask, seek, and knock as we live our Christian lives humbly serving Christ. It's interesting how these three words form the acronym "ASK" (Ask, Seek, Knock). This simple acronym is gentle reminder of the balance we need to live in a Godly manner.

- Ask implies continual communication with Christ through focused prayer and daily conversations
- Seek requires reading and studying His holy word to gain Godly wisdom, discernment, and encouragement
- Knock acknowledges our human effort in serving and taking action once we've talked it over with God and understand His guidance from Scripture.

The balance between these three thoughts from the Sermon on the Mount paints a beautiful picture of living a Christ centered life especially for those struggling with Alzheimer's disease.

- Ask Christ for help as you struggle with the disease
- Seek wisdom from His word as your memory and decision-making ability wane
- Knock on the doors of your caregiver and loved ones as you require assistance in conducting your personal affairs and daily tasks.

You see, Christ knows all you are going through and all you need do is ASK and he'll be there to help and comfort you!

Prayer: Gentle Savior, help us to ask, seek, and knock as we live our lives focused on humbly serving You. Amen

Friday: A Balanced Ministry

The blind receive sight, the lame walk, those who have leprosy are cured, the deaf hear, the dead are raised, and the good news is preached to the poor. Blessed is the man who does not fall away on account of me. Matthew 11:5–6

Today's passage from Matthew recounts Jesus' response to John the Baptist's disciples who asked Jesus if He was the one who was to come or should they expect someone else. Jesus' response reminds us He balanced His ministry on earth with healing the sick and preaching the good news. The healing part of His ministry reinforced the good news for which the world desperately hungered. The good news of God's love and grace made possible the healing miracles performed by Christ.

Balance was important to Christ's ministry on earth and it is also important when facing Alzheimer's. Because the disease generally strikes during the mid-life years (50 – 60 years of age), those diagnosed with Alzheimer's are faced with a difficult future. Balance is required to continue serving the Lord while maintaining mental and physical health.

To continue serving I exercise daily, eat a Mediterranean diet, take all my medications, read my Bible, pray for healing, and participate in a clinical trial. I balance my healthy living with continued service by teaching Sunday school, attending worship, helping at our church's food pantry, ministering to young adults, and participating in other outreach ministries. Alzheimer's may have a foothold in my brain but the Lord has a stronghold on my spirit. The same can be true for you!

Prayer: Lord, give us balance in our lives like You had balance in Your ministry while You walked this earth. Help us stay mentally and physically healthy so we might continue to serve You. Amen

Saturday: God Made One as Well as the Other

When times are good, be happy; but when times are bad, consider: God has made the one as well as the other. Therefore, a man cannot discover anything about his future. Ecclesiastes 7:14

I just returned from a wonderful but exhausting hiking trip to the mountains in western North Carolina with friends from my church. Our first route was probably the most strenuous as it was a five mile hike up and down mountains. It was hot and I had not fully recovered from the recent drug infusion from my Alzheimer's clinical trial. Needless to say, I was always last on the trail forcing my friends to slow their pace down. The scenery was beautiful making it a good day but my body was exhausted which made it sort of a not-so-good day. As I hiked, the book of Ecclesiastes kept coming to mind.

Today's Scripture infers there will be good and bad days. If you are struggling with Alzheimer's you fully understand the truth of these words. Since God has made one as well as the other, we have to learn to balance the good with the bad. I could have whined and complained because I was not yet strong enough to hike at a normal pace but then I might have overlooked the spectacular beauty of the mountains. I could have stayed home and simply told my friends I was not well enough to hike the strenuous trails but then I would miss out on the spectacular scenery and friendly fellowship of this trip. Instead, I chose to take a chance and balance my limited strength with my desire to enjoy God's glorious creation. Like Ecclesiastes says, none of us can discover what the future holds but we can enjoy the present as we learn to balance the good times with the bad times. So be happy knowing God is in complete control and go take a hike!

Prayer: Lord of all Creation, helps us balance our lives in such a manner we can handle the good with the bad. Amen

Sunday: Stillness to Bring Balance

Be still, and know that I am God; I will be exalted among the nations, I will be exalted in the earth. The Lord Almighty is with us; the God of Jacob is our fortress. Psalms 46:10–11

This week we have focused on the concept of balance in our lives as we learn to deal with the impact of Alzheimer's. Maintaining balance is absolutely essential if we are to adapt to the challenges the disease brings. Balance provides a sense of stability as we learn to accommodate:

- Our remaining abilities and the limitations of the disease
- Independent living while accepting assistance from others
- Serving the Lord by maintaining a healthy lifestyle
- Good times and bad times that co-exist in our lives.

Now it is time to be still before the Lord and know He is the God of all things. Take some time to acknowledge who He is and thank Him for His everlasting presence in your life. He alone can help you deal with the many challenges you are experiencing because of Alzheimer's. He alone understands the impact these challenges have on you personally. Our Lord is a personal God. He knows full well the pain, heartaches, and struggles the disease brings into your life and the lives of those closest to you.

Open up to Him, pour your heart out to Him, and He will comfort you like no one else. I know this is true because I have poured out all my frustrations, anxieties, and fears before Him. He assures me He is in complete control and all I need do is trust in Him. He is my rock and my fortress and I will have peace. How about you? Spend some time with Him today and be peacefully balanced in your life!

Prayer: God of Jacob, come be our fortress and bring us balance in our lives so we might adjust to living with Alzheimer's. Amen

Jon Bilous © 123RF.com

MEDITATE ON HIS WORD

Devotions to help you discover new ways to read and meditate on God's word when Alzheimer's disease strikes.

Monday: Meditate on the Word of God

Do not let this Book of the Law depart from your mouth;
meditate on it day and night, so that you may be careful to do
everything written in it. Joshua 1:8

I love to watch old movies. I have watched many movies twenty
or thirty times. At one time in my life, I could even quote large
portions of the dialogue from some of my favorite movies like *Top
Gun, You've Got Mail, A Few Good Men,* and *As Good As It Gets.*
One day God laid on my heart the desire to spend more time reading
and memorizing Scripture and less time watching movies. This
occurred a few years before some difficult times struck my family
and long before I had Alzheimer's disease. The Scriptures I
memorized help me through difficult times far more than the petty
movie lines.

On nights I don't sleep very well, I try to meditate on some of
the passages I learned years ago. These Scriptures bring me comfort
because they assure me God is in complete control, His word is still
true, and He cares deeply about me. Although I remember some
famous lines from the movies I've watched, I know from experience
they provide little in terms of encouragement, strength, and comfort
when facing the trials of life.

It is uncanny how powerful the word of God can be in your life
if you will read it, meditate on it, and remember it. By doing so, you
can more easily endure Alzheimer's disease. But remember,
Alzheimer's does not describe who you are in Christ. Only God's
word describes who you are in Christ. It is the only thing worth
memorizing and meditating on!

Prayer: Lord Jesus, help us to read, understand, memorize, and
meditate on Your holy word so we might draw closer to You and
gain strength for the rocky road ahead. Amen

Tuesday: Let the Word Dwell in You Richly

Let the word of Christ dwell in you richly as you teach and admonish one another with all wisdom, and as you sing psalms, hymns and spiritual songs with gratitude in your hearts to God.
Colossians 3:16

The Apostle Paul penned these words to the Colossians to remind them followers of Christ adhered to certain rules for holy living. These rules come from the word which must first dwell in you richly if you are to teach and admonish one another with holy wisdom. Not only was this sound advice for the Colossians but it is also practical advice for Christians today; especially for those dealing with Alzheimer's disease.

Over the past few days I noticed I had become critical and argumentative with my wife and son. Perhaps this was because I had missed my morning devotional time. In fact, it had been a few days since I had spent time reading and praying. Fortunately, I did not allow this phenomenon to rule my life. Instead, I began reading the Bible more regularly so God's word would dwell in me richly and help counter the impacts of my disease.

As I struggle with the day-to-day impacts of living with Alzheimer's, I have come to realize how important it is to dip my cup in the well of the word every day. By doing this, my mind is filled with thoughts of God which in turn fills my heart with gratitude. As a result, it is hard to be critical and argumentative when I am overflowing with gratitude for God's grace in my life. So let the word of Christ dwell in you richly so your heart may be filled with gratitude!

Prayer: Precious Lord, richly fill our hearts with Your word as we read the Bible so we might overflow with gratitude. Amen

Paul M. Hornback

Wednesday: Know the Scriptures

Jesus replied, "You are in error because you do not know the Scriptures and you do not know the power of God." Matthew 22:29

My father was a voracious reader. As a young boy in Baltimore, I remember my parents buying our first set of encyclopedias when I entered junior high. When the volumes came, my dad decided to read the entire set. I don't know if he read each volume cover to cover but he had a different book by his bed every week until he had gone through all the volumes. At the dinner table each night we'd talk about what he'd read and if I questioned anything, he'd make me look it up in the encyclopedia. My dad had a thirst for knowledge.

As I entered my teenage years, we moved to a farm in Kentucky where my family attended South Fork Baptist Church. There, my dad developed a thirst for the word and began reading the Bible daily. He studied the Scriptures, devoured Sunday school books, and read Bible commentaries. We'd talk about what he read and sometimes we would get in heated discussions about religion. As I entered my rebellious years, my father spent more time in the Bible and started teaching my teenage Sunday school class. He was a great teacher and I think it helped our relationship as I saw him relate to other teenagers going through difficult situations.

I am convinced knowing Scripture and understanding the power of God can help in every situation. Now that I struggle with Alzheimer's disease, I am assured reading the Scriptures helps me cope with the challenges I face each day. There is power and hope in the word of God. All you need do is pick up the Bible and read it. So read the Bible today and find help!

Prayer: Lord, encourage us to read and know the Scriptures so we might be better equipped to fight. Amen

Thursday: Delight in the Law of the Lord

Blessed is the man who does not walk in the counsel of the wicked or stand in the way of sinners or sit in the seat of mockers. But his delight is in the law of the Lord, and on his law he meditates day and night. Psalm 1:1–2

A group of adults at our church meet once a month to dine together and write cards to folks going through difficult situations. The meal is always wonderful because we meet at the home of Susan Phelps who is an amazing and gifted cook. While eating dinner a longtime friend of mine, Jim Murray, asked about the fresh asparagus which according to my wife was absolutely fabulous. You see, neither Jim nor I are very fond of asparagus. During the conversation about the attributes and health benefits of this strange vegetable, Jim commented it wasn't likely going to be one of the foods we'd take and cook on our annual canoe trip. In his opinion, it just wasn't on par with steak and potatoes, Oreo cookies, marshmallows, and homemade wine.

As we joked about cooking asparagus over an open fire while eating Oreos, it got me thinking about God's word and how often I pack the Bible when I go on a trip. Isn't it one of the things I deeply love? Shouldn't it be carried everywhere I go? If I delight in the law of the Lord, why isn't it in my backpack or luggage? The simple truth is I've become complacent and just don't take the Bible with me when I travel. Sure I can recite plenty of Scripture but it just is not the same as reading the word and delighting in this special time with the Lord. Now that I struggle with Alzheimer's, the time I spend reading His word is even more precious and absolutely critical to my healthy state of mind.

Prayer: Gracious Savior, empower us to take Your word everywhere we go so we might delight in it day and night. Amen

Paul M. Hornback

Friday: Your Law Is within My Heart

Then I said, "Here I am, I have come – it is written about me in the scroll. I desire to do your will, O my God; your law is within my heart." Psalm 40:7–8

King David is extremely expressive as he reveals his thoughts and feelings in this Psalm. Today's passage implores us to read the word and place it within our hearts so we might truly want to do God's will. King David was very specific about how the word was to dwell in our lives. He could have said, "Your law is within my mind" rather than "within my heart." You see, the word has to move from our mind to deep within our hearts. Once the word is in our hearts it begins to change who we are in Christ. King David understood simply knowing the word of God, quoting the law, and studying the Scriptures wasn't enough. The law has to take up residence in our heart so we will delight in the Lord and desire to do His will.

As I struggle with the daily challenges of Alzheimer's disease, I find comfort in reading the Bible and allowing the words to move from the foggy corners of my mind to the warm chambers of my heart. As many of you who struggle with Alzheimer's know, the words of Scripture don't often stay in your mind. I personally have trouble remembering what I've read so I have to reread it several times. My prayer is God will allow His holy word to fill my heart and change my selfish nature. As my self-centeredness is transformed, I am more likely to conform to the image of Christ and do the will of His Father. Although Alzheimer's may impede my brain and reasoning ability, it can never change my heart where the word of God lives and thrives. So read your Bible today and ask God to etch the words on your heart.

Prayer: Father, may Your word reside deep in our hearts. Amen

Saturday: Light for My Path

Your word is a lamp to my feet and a light for my path. I have taken an oath and confirmed it, that I will follow your righteous laws. Psalm 119:105–106

I remember flying a Marine helicopter at night in the North Atlantic and landing on the deck of Navy amphibious ships. Daytime landings can be difficult when the sea is rough but nighttime landings are especially treacherous. The dark nights make the ship difficult to see. However, the landing deck has small lights providing enough illumination to guide the pilot safely on a path to avoid the obstacles, antennas, or wires that populate a naval ship. Without the deck lights, it would be almost impossible to land on the deck at night in bad weather.

The word of God is a lot like those deck lights. It provides sufficient light to navigate our way so we stay on the path God has marked out for us. Without God's word we would be lost, especially during the storms of life that inevitably come our way. One such storm is Alzheimer's and without the comforting assurance of God's word I would be lost in a sea of confusion and disbelief. His word provides daily guidance, assurance He is in complete control of my life, compassionate comfort, and hope for a useful future.

I still remember how scared I was when making my first helicopter nighttime landing in rough seas but how wonderful it felt as I turned onto the final approach to the helipad and saw the comforting glow of the deck lights. So it is with the word. It lights my path and guides me daily through the treacherous seas of Alzheimer's disease. If you need some holy light, reach for God's word and you will land safely.

Prayer: Lord, light our paths and provide us guidance as we struggle with the impacts of Alzheimer's in our lives. Amen

Sunday: Stillness through Scripture

Be still, and know that I am God; I will be exalted among the nations, I will be exalted in the earth. The Lord Almighty is with us; the God of Jacob is our fortress. Psalms 46:10–11

This week we have focused on the importance of God's holy word in our daily lives. It is now time to be still and remember He is the Lord Almighty! As you are still before the Lord today, think of your favorite Scripture from this week and simply:

- Meditate on the Scripture
- Let the words dwell richly in you
- Recite it until you know the words are part of you
- Delight in what the passage is saying to you
- Allow the words to fill the chambers of your heart
- Use the words to light your path forever.

My favorite Scripture from this week was Psalm 119:105; *"Your word is a lamp to my feet and a light for my path."* I can hear the words as if God is reminding me to trust in Him and read His word daily so my path might be fully illuminated. As I struggle with the effects of Alzheimer's disease, I am comforted by God's holy word which reminds me every day I need not fear for He is in complete control.

It is so easy to become fearful when facing the uncertainty of a future with Alzheimer's. The only way to squelch this fear is to read His word, trust His word, and allow His word to dwell richly within your heart. So spend time today being still before the Lord as you meditate on a special Scripture God has placed on your heart. Allow Him to speak to you, comfort you, and remove your fears as you exalt His holy name.

Prayer: Lord of Heaven and Earth, speak to us today through Your holy word so we might experience Your comforting presence. Amen

Alexey Stiop © 123RF.com

GOD'S BLESSINGS

Devotions to help you anticipate God's glorious blessings in your life as you deal with Alzheimer's disease.

Monday: Richly Blessed

As the Scripture says, "Anyone who trusts in him will never be put to shame." For there is no difference between Jew and Gentile – the same Lord is Lord of all, and richly blesses all who call on him. Romans 10:11–12

There is a wonderful old hymn entitled *Count Your Blessings* written by Edwin Othello Excell in the late 1890s. The closing words of the first verse say, *Count your many blessings, name them one by one, and it will surprise you what the Lord hath done.* The words of this familiar hymn ring in my head for days after singing it in worship. The words are a vivid reminder of what the Apostle Paul wrote to the church in Rome as evidenced in today's passage. "The same Lord is Lord of all, and richly blesses all who call on him" is as true today as it was when Paul wrote these words to the Romans.

We often forget how blessed we are especially during difficult times. Alzheimer's can be an extraordinarily difficult and distressing situation clouding one's life. It can be devastating but it doesn't mean God's rich blessings no longer flow in your life. The closing words of this famous hymn remind me I'm not alone in my battle with Alzheimer's disease:

So, amid the conflict whether great or small,
Do not be disheartened, God is over all;
Count your many blessings, angels will attend,
Help and comfort give you to your journey's end.

I find comfort in the simple truth God is Lord over all things. I am grateful His angels attend to me daily. I know I will have help, comfort, and rich blessings all the days of my life!

Prayer: Lord of All, thank You for Your rich blessings surrounding us every day bringing comfort and help during life's conflicts. Amen

Tuesday: Blessings for the Righteous

Blessings crown the head of the righteous, but violence overwhelms the mouth of the wicked. The memory of the righteous will be a blessing, but the name of the wicked will rot.
Proverbs 10:6–7

Blessings are often referred to as God's gift to the righteous. In fact, Proverbs tells us God's blessings crown the head of the righteous. In other words, the blessings are an outward symbol of God's favor in the life of a righteous person. In today's Scripture, King Solomon asserts the mere memory of a righteous person will be a blessing. Wow, not only are we blessed during our earthly life but even after our death the misty memory of our mortal lives will be a blessing to others!

After being diagnosed with early-onset Alzheimer's, I struggled with how God's blessings were being manifested in my life. Perhaps you are feeling exactly the same way. After my initial pity party, I came to realize how truly blessed I was because my family surrounded me with overwhelming love and support. They helped me make the necessary decisions about retirement, finances, and property; they encouraged me to write this devotional; they put their lives on hold to help me get a grip on my diagnosis; and they altered their future plans to be more available for me. God's blessings crown my head in more ways than I can possibly put down on paper. His blessings abundantly flow all around me. All I need do is stop, be still, and listen as He gently reminds me of all He has done.

Just because you have Alzheimer's doesn't mean God's blessings cease to exist. He will continue to shower you with His blessing as you continue to trust in Him. I'm blessed and I pray my mere memory will be a blessing to others.

Prayer: Father, thank You for Your never ending blessings. Amen

Wednesday: Spiritual Blessings

Praise be to the God and Father of our Lord Jesus Christ, who has blessed us in the heavenly realms with every spiritual blessing in Christ. Ephesians 1:3

Have you ever been blessed in a way you don't understand? This concept may seem radical but many of us have been blessed in this exact manner. For instance, you may have been born into a wealthy, remarkably loving, or naturally nurturing family. If so, you had no control or choice over the chosen family. This is akin to what the Apostle Paul writes to the Church at Ephesus about. Paul opens his letter with his trademark salutations and immediately asserts our heavenly Father has blessed them with every spiritual blessing in Christ.

The same fact holds true for us today. We are born into a heavenly family that blesses us beyond our understanding and outside our earthly control. I certainly don't claim to completely comprehend the full dimension of the spiritual blessings offered to us in Christ. I simply can't wrap my feeble mind around the breadth of this concept. However, I know I'm already benefitting from His heavenly blessings. Without these blessings, I would not be able to handle the daily struggles brought on by Alzheimer's.

I am convinced God's angels and the Holy Spirit protect me from harm, guide me along safe pathways, and keep me cognizant of His love, grace, and mercy in my life. These are not possible without my Father's spiritual blessing. This is quite a concept to chew on but just like Paul's assertion to the Ephesians, it is true. So simply allow His spiritual blessings to flow gently into your life as you begin to fully trust in Christ.

Prayer: Father God, thank You for Your glorious spiritual blessings benefitting us in both the earthly and heavenly realms. Amen

Thursday: Curse into Blessing

However, the Lord your God would not listen to Balaam but turned the curse into a blessing for you, because the Lord your God loves you. Deuteronomy 23:5

I can remember making a solemn vow to read the Bible cover to cover over the course of a year. I did finally finish reading the Bible but it took a little more than a year to complete the task. I still remember reading Deuteronomy primarily because I had to struggle to finish it. Today's passage from Deuteronomy stands out like a beacon in the night shining brightly in my struggle with Alzheimer's disease. You see, the Ammonites and Moabites did not aide the Israelites when they left Egypt but instead hired Balaam to place a curse upon them. The Lord turned this potential curse into a blessing for His chosen people because He loved them.

So it is when one is cursed with Alzheimer's. God still loves you and He can turn this curse into a blessing. Since being diagnosed with Alzheimer's disease:

- My relationship with the Lord has been strengthened
- I experience less stress since I had to retire
- My desire for material possessions has waned
- I enjoy the simple pleasures of life more
- I have more time to serve the Lord.

These have all been wonderful blessings with which the Lord has showered me. What Satan intended as a curse for my life has been turned into a blessing because the Lord has ultimate control over all that happens in my life! So how about you? Are you ready to allow God to turn this Alzheimer's curse into a blessing? Just turn it over to Him and let Him bless you!

Prayer: Father of Israel, turn our Alzheimer's curse into a blessing just like You did so long ago with Balaam and the Israelites. Amen

Friday: Showers of Blessings

I will bless them and the places surrounding my hill. I will send down showers in season; there will be showers of blessings.
Ezekiel 34:26

I love growing flowers in the various gardens surrounding my home. My flower fondness stems from their beauty and how they attract butterflies, hummingbirds, and bees. I have a spectacular butterfly bush with large blue flowers right outside my kitchen window. This afternoon, while preparing vegetables for supper, a lone hummingbird blessed my view from the kitchen sink. The bird gracefully darted around the butterflies to taste the nectar of each blue blossom. One might say I have been blessed on the hill my home sits upon.

This brought to mind today's passage where God promised His people wonderful blessings under a restored relationship with Him. I am blessed with many wonderful gifts from God:

- A beautiful home surrounded by lovely gardens
- A beautiful and devoted wife who loves me dearly
- Three grown children who are the apples of my eye
- Four faithful long-haired Chihuahuas who comfort me
- A wonderful church family who prays for me
- A cadre of doctors who care for me diligently.

I feel blessed even though I deal with the daily struggles of Alzheimer's. You see, God's blessings still abound if you will look for them and thank Him for His never ending goodness. God will continue to shower you with blessings even in the midst of your struggles and difficulties. His holy word promises He will never forsake you and God will continue to bless you as long as you honor Him!

Prayer: Sovereign Lord, thank You for Your continual shower of blessings in our lives. You are an Awesome God! Amen

Saturday: Blessings beyond Comprehension

He will love you and bless you and increase your numbers. He will bless the fruit of your womb, the crops of your land – your grain, new wine and oil – the calves of your herds and the lambs of your flocks in the land that he swore to your forefathers to give you.
Deuteronomy 7:13

Today's passage from Deuteronomy reminds us of God's beautiful promise to the Israelites to bless them, their children, the work of their hands, and the land He promised their forefathers. It was a blessing beyond human comprehension because it encompassed not only earthly concerns but also spiritual realms. This was the one true God who lavished favor on His chosen people and created a nation where they would find bountiful blessings from His hand.

So how does this promise impact those of us afflicted with Alzheimer's disease? For me it is simple. As a Christian, His promise still holds true for me as I know He will bless me in ways far beyond my human comprehension. For instance, I am blessed to have been diagnosed with Alzheimer's in the United States of America where:

- Research is working toward a cure, not just a way to reduce the symptoms
- Clinical trials and new experimental drugs abound
- Social Security Disability is now more readily available to early-onset Alzheimer's patients
- Support groups and adult day care facilities are prevalent
- Medical care is second to none.

The Lord has His hand in all of these things so we might be blessed and supported in our affliction. God is wonderful and we are blessed, truly blessed in this United States of America. Thank Him this day for His bountiful blessings.

Prayer: Lord, thank You for blessings beyond comprehension. Amen

Sunday: Be Still and Remember His Blessings

Be still, and know that I am God; I will be exalted among the nations, I will be exalted in the earth. The Lord Almighty is with us; the God of Jacob is our fortress. Psalms 46:10–11

This week we have concentrated on recognizing God's never ending blessings in our lives. Now it is time to be still and exalt the Lord with an attitude of gratitude for the blessings He graciously sends our way. He deeply desires each of us to be truly thankful for all He does in our lives.

This morning I walked outside into the cool crisp air and was greeted by a beautiful morning sunrise. Now having a beautiful sunrise isn't necessarily a unique experience but having a cool crisp morning with a beautiful sunrise in the middle of the summer is quite rare in Kentucky. I was amazed at how fall-like the morning seemed and was truly grateful for the unseasonably cool temperatures. I walked to the chicken house to let the hens out; they were all huddled together in an attempt to ward off the morning chill. The walk was quite refreshing as I meandered around the gardens on my way back to the patio door. I thought how God had blessed me with such a beautiful morning.

This week I have been blessed with creative insights and words to write the week's devotions, a buyer for my 1966 Mercury Comet Cyclone, an opportunity to help a friend in financial need, morning visits with my mom, and wonderful walks in the evening with my wife. It has been a truly marvelous week even though my daily struggle with Alzheimer's persists. So how has your week unfolded? Is there any special blessing that stands out from this week? God has been graciously kind and now it is your opportunity to exalt Him in worship and praise.

Prayer: Exalted Lord, thank You for a great week filled with Your many blessings and constant reminders You care. Amen

Juan Nel © 123RF.com

NEVER GIVE UP HOPE

Devotions to help you focus on ways to maintain hope amidst the daily demands of Alzheimer's disease.

Paul M. Hornback

Monday: Reason for Hope

But in your hearts set apart Christ as Lord. Always be prepared to give an answer to everyone who asks you to give the reason for the hope that you have. But do this with gentleness and respect, keeping a clear conscience, so that those who speak maliciously against your good behavior in Christ may be ashamed of their slander. 1 Peter 3:15–16

My wife and I recently went to New Orleans for a conference. From our hotel, we walked to an open air market in the French Quarter where vendors were selling everything from handmade jewelry to potted plants. One particular vendor was selling pictures of famous New Orleans' landmarks. A unique photo caught my wife's eye and we just had to buy it. It was a photograph of an above-ground crypt with a beautiful granite angel kneeling at the tomb with its wings folded over the crypt. The angel's wings embraced the tomb as if protecting it while the angel knelt in prayer. I was reminded how God has His angels' wings folded around each of us so we are protected.

As I struggle with Alzheimer's disease, I know, just like Peter wrote in today's passage, my hope rests in Christ who sends His angels to continually watch over me. They keep me from doing something dangerous to my health and well-being and constantly remind me who I am in Christ. Alzheimer's may slowly erode away my mental faculties but it has no hope of breaking the stronghold Christ and His angels have on my spirit! So when you struggle with the daily limits brought on by Alzheimer's, remember His angels surround you with spiritual protection and comfort. God is watching out for you!

Prayer: Lord of Hope, send your angels to watch over us and keep us safe as we struggle with the daily impacts of Alzheimer's. Amen

Tuesday: Hope in God Alone

*Find rest, O my soul, in God alone; my hope comes from him.
He alone is my rock and my salvation; he is my fortress, I will not be
shaken. Psalm 62:5–6*

I just completed an eighteen month Phase III clinical trial for
Alzheimer's disease. The drug I received was administered every
two weeks intravenously. The drug worked well and appeared to
ease my symptoms and improve my memory. The team at the
University of Kentucky Sanders Brown Center on Aging were
extremely hopeful the trial might be extended and the participants be
allowed to continue on the medication. Unfortunately, that was not
the case and my infusions ended. I was disappointed because the
drug seemed so beneficial to my health.

Today's passage from Psalms reminded me my hope really isn't
in the clinical trial or its medication. My hope rests in God. He is my
rock and I will not be shaken! When I decided to participate in a
clinical trial it was not for my own personal benefit but to help later
generations in their struggles with Alzheimer's. At the time I started
the trial, I had no idea if I'd get the drug or the placebo. My motives
were pure and unselfish. Besides, I knew the trial would end and it
would be many years before the treatment might be available for the
public provided it proved beneficial. The reality is I had little hope
of getting the drug after the trial was over.

It is easy to place our hope in manmade medicines because they
are tangible. However, our hope should never rest in these earthly
elements. Our hope should only rest in the God who created us and
deeply knows our every need. Where is your hope today? Put it in
God and you won't be disappointed.

*Prayer: Everlasting God, may our hope always rest in You
alone for You are the only rock on which we need to rest! Amen*

Wednesday: Hope in a Forever Faithful Lord

Blessed is he whose help is the God of Jacob, whose hope is in the Lord his God, the Maker of heaven and earth, the sea and everything in them – the Lord, who remains faithful forever.
Psalm 146:5-6

I recently sold a 1995 Ford Ranger pickup truck to a young man who needed a vehicle get to work. He had no cash so I took a risk and allowed him to make payments for a year to pay the truck off. I really didn't need the truck since I have a newer Ford Ranger so I sold it well below book value. The old 1995 Ford Ranger had been a faithful truck and had never broken down while out on the road. I had planned on keeping it to use around the yard and farm until I could no longer drive. However, as I got to know the young man who moved to Kentucky from California, I realized all he needed was a chance to improve his life. The Ranger was not a pretty truck but it was reliable and would serve him well for at least a couple of years. The young man felt blessed to have found transportation at an extremely reasonable price.

Today's passage from the Psalms reminds us we are blessed if our help and our hope is in the Lord, the God of Jacob. Just like my young friend, we all need help and hope in our lives as we struggle with the demands of daily living. For those of us dealing with Alzheimer's disease, the demands can be challenging. But our Lord is an awesome God in whom we can place our trust since He remains faithful forever. My old Ranger was a faithful truck but it didn't hold a candle to the faithfulness of my Lord and Savior in whom my hope remains. If you are struggling today, place your hope in the Lord Almighty for He is faithful forever!

Prayer: Maker of Heaven and Earth, our help and hope remain in You alone for only You are truly faithful forever. Amen

Thursday: Hope Defeats a Downcast Spirit

Why are you downcast, O my soul? Why so disturbed within me? Put your hope in God, for I will yet praise him, my Savior and my God. Psalm 42:5

When I woke up this morning, I have to admit I was rather downcast about having early-onset Alzheimer's disease. I really didn't want to take the medications I've been taking for two years now, I didn't want to eat a healthy breakfast, and I didn't want to go visit with my mom. However, these are all part of my morning routine so I did them anyway although my enthusiasm was lacking. I suppose today's passage from the book of Psalms was written especially for folks who are feeling downcast.

After visiting my mom, I sat down at my computer to start writing. I opened my email first and read a message that singer and songwriter Glenn Campbell has Alzheimer's disease. Campbell recently made his condition public so he could continue to perform and audiences would know the truth about his medical condition. Interestingly enough, the title of the article was *"Glenn Campbell Looks Forward with Gratitude."*

It made me think about why I was in such a funk about my condition. I was having a "not-so-good day" and needed some divine inspiration. Today's passage reminded me my hope must remain in God alone and I should be praising Him with a grateful heart. By praising Him my spirits are uplifted and my enthusiasm for life returns. Are you downcast today as well? If so, stop whatever you are doing and begin to praise the Lord for who He is and all He's done in your life. Nurture a grateful heart and your hope will return once again!

Prayer: Savior and God of Hope, refresh our downcast spirits and renew our hope in You. Let us praise You for all You have done in our lives and for the awesome God You truly are. Amen

Friday: Hope in His Unfailing Love

His pleasure is not in the strength of the horse, nor his delight in the legs of a man; the Lord delights in those who fear him, who put their hope in his unfailing love. Psalm 147:10–11

I don't know about you, but I'm sure glad the Lord doesn't delight in the legs of a man since my legs are pretty scrawny! In fact, I had been called "Bird Legs" by many of my Marine buddies. There are certain good qualities about having bird legs because I can run like a scared chicken and walk as fast as strutting ostrich! This morning a dear friend saw me out walking on the trail by Creek Front Park in Hodgenville and asked if I could walk with her up the hill by the Baptist Church. Apparently my bird leg stride was what she needed to pace her walk and get her heart rate up to the desired level. However, these same bird legs of mine don't look great in a pair of shorts at the beach!

Thankfully the Lord looks at other attributes in a man rather than his legs. Today's passage from the Psalms reminds us the Lord delights in those who fear Him and put their hope in His unfailing love. This is an especially powerful Scripture for those of us afflicted with Alzheimer's. Hope is one of the first things many people give up after hearing the diagnosis of Alzheimer's. But not me! I don't place my hope in a miraculous cure, my doctors, clinical trials, or multiple medications. Don't get me wrong when I make this statement because I do keep all my doctor's appointments, participate in clinical trials, and take my medications as prescribed. I just don't place my hope in these things. Instead, my hope rests in the unfailing love of Jesus Christ since only He can guide me safely through my ordeal. So who or what have you placed your hope in today? If it is the Lord, then He is delighted!

Prayer: Lord, help us to truly place our hope in You and Your unfailing love. Amen

Saturday: A Future Hope

Do not let your heart envy sinners, but always be zealous for the fear of the Lord. There is surely a future hope for you, and your hope will not be cut off. Proverbs 23:17–18

Have you ever read something in the Bible that simply amazed you? Today's passage from Proverbs caught me completely off guard. I had to read it twice to fully grasp the promise of the passage. First, let me set the record straight regarding the whole "envying sinners" phrase. At this stage in my life, I'm not jealous or desirous of anything sinners may accumulate in their flashy lifetime. They may have wicked wealth, fabulous fame, awesome automobiles, huge houses, and spectacular spouses. Good for them because I don't need what they've got! I have all I want and need right here in the little town of Hodgenville. Second, my heart doesn't belong to worldly possessions nor does it beat only to accumulate what others say I need. My heart belongs to the Lord and I am His!

This is exactly what Solomon was trying to express in today's passage. Don't be heart set on possessing what someone else possesses, especially sinners, whom we often think have it all. Solomon also advises us to be zealous for the Lord and as a result we will have two important items we can count on; a future hope and a hope that won't be cut off. When I read those two promises I was amazed! All I need do is delight myself in the Lord and desire Him above all things, including what sinners possess, and my future hope in Christ is secured. As I deal with the day-to-day struggles Alzheimer's brings, this Scripture helps me realize I still have a viable future and it won't be cut off. Christ will make sure of that!

Prayer: Lord of Hope, thank You for providing us a future hope in You that can never be cut off if we will only desire You above all things. Amen

Sunday: Be Still and Find Hope in God

*Be still, and know that I am God; I will be exalted among the
nations, I will be exalted in the earth. The Lord Almighty is with us;
the God of Jacob is our fortress. Psalms 46:10–11*

This week has been particularly hot in the heartland of
Kentucky with temperatures surpassing 100 degrees. Today the
temperatures have cooled and remind me fall is lurking just around
the corner. Of course, with the change of season comes the hope of
much cooler weather. This week we have focused on the idea of
hope. The recurring theme in the Scripture we explored centered on
the Lord being the beacon of hope we all desperately desire. Now it
is time to be still and find hope in God through the passages we've
studied. As we meander back through the many passages we read
this week, here are some of the more memorable lines:

- "Find rest, O my soul, in God alone; my hope comes from
him."
- "There is surely a future hope for you, and your hope will not
be cut off."
- "The Lord delights in those who fear him, who put their hope
in his unfailing love."
- "Put your hope in God."
- "Blessed is he whose help is the God of Jacob, whose hope is
in the Lord his God."

These particularly powerful passages of hope gently remind us
the Lord is always with us and He cares immensely about our future.
These blessed words bring me tremendous comfort when the effects
of Alzheimer's disease wear down my spirit. It is my prayer these
wonderful words of hope will lift up your spirit so you can be a
messenger of hope to others.

*Prayer: Lord of All, may Your blessed name bring hope and
help to all of us facing the daily challenges of Alzheimer's disease.
Amen*

Mike Norton © 123RF.com

HIS DAILY MAJESTY

Devotions to help you breathe in the majesty of each new day as
you live with Alzheimer's disease.

Monday: Morning Expectations

In the morning, O Lord, you hear my voice; in the morning I lay my requests before you and wait in expectation. Psalm 5:3

One of Benjamin Franklin's famous sayings is, "Early to bed, early to rise, makes a man healthy, wealthy, and wise." One thing is for sure, Ben must have been an early riser! There is certainly something special about rising early in the morning to watch the majesty of a new day unfold. Mornings are the perfect time for prayer and Bible reading.

Today's passage from Psalms indicates King David enjoyed the mornings as well. This was the time he purposely prayed and laid out his requests before God. I find it comforting David wasn't afraid to ask God for help for the challenges he faced. The remarkable thing was David waited in <u>expectation</u> for the Lord to answer his prayers.

Mornings are absolutely the perfect time to wait expectantly for the Lord to respond. The new day has begun, the fears of the night are past, and the promise of something spectacular from God awaits. As I struggle with the daily challenges of Alzheimer's, I am reminded each morning of God's never failing promise to unfold a new day. His divine order for each day brings an opportunity to rekindle my relationship with Him through prayer. These prayers may be uttered silently in bed, hastily spoken while preparing breakfast, or mumbled quietly during a morning walk but God hears every word I utter. Like King David, I lay my requests before Him and wait expectantly for His reply!

Prayer: O Lord, hear our requests each morning as we begin our day and help us to wait expectantly for Your reply. Amen

Tuesday: Rejoice in Each Day

The stone the builders rejected has become the capstone; the Lord has done this, and it is marvelous in our eyes. This is the day the Lord has made; let us rejoice and be glad in it. Psalm 118:22–24

Today's passage from Psalms contains one of my favorite verses from the Bible, "This is the day the Lord has made, let us rejoice and be glad in it." I quoted this verse many times when I was having a bad day at work. It became a cornerstone verse after being diagnosed with Alzheimer's disease. When I spoke the words it reminded me each new day is a gift from God so I should be glad and rejoice!

Now I know this may seem a bit strange to anyone who has been diagnosed with Alzheimer's but you really have only two choices. You can give up on life and throw in the towel or you can savor life and try your best to rejoice in each new day. The easy way is to simply throw up your hands and give in to the temptation of negativity, depression, and woe is me. Of course, this is exactly what Satan desires; the opportunity to take a bad event and use it to ruin the life and witness of a long time Christian. Rather than do this, I choose to continue to savor each new day, rejoice in the opportunities before me, and wait expectantly for new blessings from the Lord. Each day brings an opportunity for God's promises to manifest themselves in ways I have yet to realize or even understand.

God's never ending love, grace, and mercies always find a way to break through the fog of my Alzheimer's disease and remind me He is right there beside me every step of the way. So why shouldn't I rejoice? How about you? Rejoice in each new day remembering He is in complete control!

Prayer: Lord, gently remind us each new day is a glorious gift from You so we might truly rejoice and be glad in it. Amen

Wednesday: Renewed Day by Day

Therefore we do not lose heart. Though outwardly we are wasting away, yet inwardly we are being renewed day by day. 2 Corinthians 4:16

As a child I couldn't wait for my birthday so I'd get another year older and hopefully reach a new milestone like:
- Five when I started school
- Eight when I rode my bike alone in the neighborhood
- Ten when I started cutting grass with the power mower
- Thirteen when I became a teenager
- Sixteen when I received my driver's license.

All along my body was growing stronger and my spirit was growing more mature. Somewhere along the way my body reached its prime and the downward spiral slowly began. Then tragedy struck at fifty-five when I was diagnosed with early-onset Alzheimer's disease. Like Paul describes in today's passage, my mind and body started wasting away in such a manner it was outwardly noticeable.

But what about my inward spirit? How was it fairing? Luckily, it was growing closer to Christ and being renewed daily even after the diagnosis of Alzheimer's disease. You see, your spirit can remain healthy, continue maturing, and be renewed daily no matter what is happening to your earthly body. Each new day brings an opportunity for spiritual revival if you abide in Christ. Of course, this spiritual renewal isn't guaranteed if you succumb to the worries of this life, the deceitfulness of wealth, and the desires for other things that choke out His Holy Spirit.

So how is your spirit today? Is it being renewed or choked out? Abide in Christ, pray, and read His word every day. Then anticipate His blessings and you won't lose heart!

Prayer: Holy Spirit, renew our inward spirits each day as we desperately try to abide in Christ and read His holy word. Amen

Thursday: Wait Daily at His Doorway

Blessed is the man who listens to me, watching daily at my doors, waiting at my doorway. For whoever finds me finds life and receives favor from the Lord. Proverbs 8:34

As a young child I can remember waiting at the door for my father to return home from work. It seemed like hours but I'm sure it was only minutes I waited impatiently for him to enter the house and give me a welcome hug. Today's passage from Proverbs reminds us even as adults we are to wait daily at the doorway of our Father's house and listen closely for Him. Of course, this doesn't mean we have to be standing at the church door waiting for the Lord to appear. Instead, we are to pray daily and expectantly wait for His reply to our prayers.

Every morning I read Scripture and spend time in prayer. By doing this I know my day will be blessed because my mind has been set on heavenly thoughts. Each day holds another opportunity to see how wonderfully God moves in His new and mysterious ways. A beautifully colored sunrise, a cool crisp morning, a fog gently rising from the nearby woods, or even a gentle morning rain remind me how wonderfully blessed I am as a new day unfolds. Perhaps Alzheimer's has made me focus on the simple pleasures I enjoy at daybreak rather than the technical complexities that used to populate my mornings at work. Enjoying the mornings has been a blessing brought on by Alzheimer's disease. It has allowed me more time to soak in the beauty of God's glorious creation here at the Hornback Homestead. It also allowed me an opportunity to read His word. Alzheimer's has brought many challenges into my life but it has strengthened my daily walk with the Lord and provided blessings beyond belief.

Prayer: Lord Jesus, help us start each new day prayerfully waiting at Your doorway in expectation of Your bountiful blessings. Amen

Friday: Examine the Scriptures Daily

*Now the Bereans were of more noble character than the
Thessalonians, for they received the message with great eagerness
and examined the Scriptures every day to see if what Paul said was
true. Acts 17:13*

I recently had a visit with my neurologist where he examined
me closely to see how Alzheimer's was impacting me physically. He
conducted all the normal checks to include reflexes, pupil light
response, nerve sensation, balance, and hand to eye coordination.
However, he didn't stop his examination at just the physical. He
continued on by talking with me about any new symptoms and how I
was progressing since the clinical trial ended. I suppose he wanted to
fully examine my physical, mental, and emotional health to
determine the impacts at this particular stage of the disease.

Today's passage from Acts reminds us, like the Bereans, we
need to thoroughly examine the Scriptures daily to make sure we are
in step with the word of God. However, Luke goes even further we
he says we are to "eagerly" receive the message contained in the
Scriptures. I have to admit, there are days I don't quite measure up to
the "eagerness" criterion when I read the Scriptures. Even on those
"not-so-good" days I still read the Bible because I need the
encouragement just to make it through the day. Alzheimer's
challenges your daily routine but it doesn't have to stifle your daily
Bible reading.

On days when reading is more arduous; I just push through the
difficulty and read the words over and over again until I can
understand them. By being persistent, God's word provides me daily
inspiration. How about you? Don't give up! Read the Bible daily
because in Christ you will have noble character.

*Prayer: Father, help us be eager to read Your word daily so we
might gain hope, inspiration, and encouragement for our struggles.
Amen*

Saturday: Belong to the Day

But since we belong to the day, let us be self-controlled, putting on faith and love as a breastplate, and the hope of salvation as a helmet. 1 Thessalonians 5:8

There is something majestic about the dawning of a new day. The sky goes from complete darkness to the faint glow of dawn in just a matter of minutes. Soon the faint glow gently transforms into a cascade of beautiful colors as the sun slowly approaches the horizon. As you can imagine, I love mornings because I can watch the controlled majesty of God transforming night's darkness into the brilliant light of a new day.

Today's passage penned by Paul reminds us since we belong to the day, we are also a controlled majesty of God. That is to say "self-controlled" as we practice faith, love, and hope in order to shine brilliantly as Christ's light on earth. Even though we struggle with the impacts of Alzheimer's disease, we can still be sons and daughters of light rather than children of darkness. All it takes is a little more effort on our part to consciously put on faith, love, and hope like we would put on an article of clothing or armor as Paul puts it.

Each morning I remind myself who I am in Christ and make a conscious effort to clothe myself with the characteristics Paul references in Thessalonians:

- Faith God is still in control despite my disease
- Hope He has specific plans for my life
- Love enough to cover my many shortcomings.

Now that is something to shine brilliantly about as you belong to the day. So go light it up!

Prayer: Lord of Light, help us shine brilliantly for You as we practice faith, love, and hope throughout the day. Amen

Sunday: Be Still and Seize the Day

Be still, and know that I am God; I will be exalted among the nations, I will be exalted in the earth. The Lord Almighty is with us; the God of Jacob is our fortress. Psalms 46:10–11

This week has been especially delightful for me to write about because I am a morning person who always looks forward to a new day. Each day is a chance to start anew, wait on an anticipated blessing from the Lord, delight in the marvels of God's creation, or enjoy the fellowship of other Christians. Every sunrise marks an opportunity to seize the day so God can be exalted in our lives, families, communities, and country. It all starts with the dawn of a new day and the eagerness to be still before the Lord.

Take time this morning to quietly read your Bible and spend some time mediating on the words you've read. Spend a few moments praising Him for His great works in your life, for the many blessings He has bestowed upon you, and for the plans He has for your life. Thank Him for the forgiveness of your sins and the right to be called a child of God. He is the Lord Almighty and is worthy of all our praise. If you will do these few things, your day will go unbelievably better and be filled with the joy that only comes from knowing Christ.

It won't matter you have Alzheimer's disease because you will be basking in the warmth, comfort, and safety of the Lord Almighty! He alone understands everything you are going through. He alone wants to be your guide along the unfamiliar Alzheimer's path. He is the only one who can provide the hope you need to continue forward. So be still before Him today and ask Him to help you seize the day!

Prayer: Heavenly Father, we need You more than ever and we praise You for helping us as we walk the Alzheimer's path. Amen

Songquan Deng © 123RF.com

GOD'S PROMISES

Devotions to help you hold on to God's promises as you deal
daily with Alzheimer's disease.

Monday: Generations of Mercy

His mercy extends to those who fear him, from generation to generation. He has performed mighty deeds with his arm; he has scattered those who are proud in their inmost thoughts. He has brought down rulers from their thrones but has lifted up the humble.
Luke 1:50–52

Today's passage comes from Luke and it is a small portion of Mary's Hymn of Praise (also known as the Magnificat which means glorifies). This hymn of praise from the Virgin Mary reminds us how wonderful the Lord has been and continues to be for those who live in harmony with Him. I especially love the beginning words, "His mercy extends to those who fear him, from generation to generation." How precious is this promise from the mother of our Lord Jesus especially for those with Alzheimer's disease?

Mercy is a marvelous gift when you need compassion, kindness, understanding, and leniency. Alzheimer's can seem like a prison sentence requiring years of "hard time" leading up to a slow arduous execution. However, it doesn't have to be that way! God's glorious mercy can extend even to those of us afflicted with Alzheimer's disease. His compassion fills your life with the simple joy of living in His grace, His kindness brings caring people into your life, His understanding allows you to vent your frustrations without fear of reprisal, and His leniency ultimately makes the difficult years easier to handle. Our Lord has done this in the past and He plans to stay the course in the future. Trust only in Jesus and understand you can do all things through Him who gives you strength. So sing a song of praise to the Lord today. Thank Him for His great works just as Mary praised Him in today's Scripture.

Prayer: Lord, extend Your marvelous mercies to us today. Amen

Tuesday: According to His Promise

You are my portion, O Lord; I have promised to obey your words. I have sought your face with all my heart; be gracious to me according to your promise. Psalm 119:57–58

My friends and I love to go hiking in mountainous areas filled with flowing streams of water. These areas naturally hold the promise of beautifully flowing waterfalls. We have hiked in many of the state parks in Kentucky, Tennessee, North Carolina, Virginia, West Virginia, and Ohio and been blessed with breathtaking views of waterfalls. Of course, reaching the best waterfalls requires miles of difficult hiking in rough terrain, up steep hillsides, over poorly marked trails, and across water filled streams. You must be willing to seek the prize!

Today's passage reminds us if we want to enjoy the promises of God we must seek Him with all our heart. The Psalmist states he has promised to obey God's words and has "sought" Him with all his heart. Seeking God with all one's heart is not an easy task because it requires solid perseverance and true dedication. For many, these spiritual muscles may have grown weak and we wonder why God's promises are not being fulfilled in our lives. For those of us with Alzheimer's, we may even blame the disease for our spiritual weakness but that is certainly not the case!

God's promises hold true no matter what is going on in our lives. His promises are linked to our spiritual well-being rather than our physical well-being. If you think you are missing out on His promises, then maybe your spiritual muscles need more flexing. Spend some time seeking His face, obeying His word, honoring Him, and walking in His ways. The "spiritual hike" will do you good!

Prayer: Gracious Lord, may Your promises fill our lives. Amen

Paul M. Hornback

Wednesday: His Promises Preserve Life

My eyes stay open through the watches of the night that I may meditate on your promises. Hear my voice in accordance with your love, preserve my life, O Lord, according to your laws. Psalm 119:148–149

Alzheimer's disease affects people in unique ways. The traditional effects include loss of memory, confusion, experiencing foggy days, getting lost in familiar places, and difficulty finding words during conversations. These are normal occurrences in the lives of Alzheimer's patients. But there are other impacts that don't necessarily happen to everyone diagnosed with the disease. For instance, I have trouble falling asleep. For some reason, I cannot turn off my mind at night so I have difficulty relaxing and falling into a deep sleep. In order to calm my mind from the day's activities, I try to recite familiar Scripture and meditate on the words and promises of God. Then I am able to relax and rest in the peace of God which transcends all understanding.

Today's passage from Psalms assures us reciting Scripture and meditating on His promises were common practices for God's people throughout history. Of course, in this particular verse the Psalmist alludes to using this practice to stay awake and to calm his fears. I use it to calm my soul, to feel God's continual presence, and to remind me of His precious promise to preserve my life. God's word has a remarkably calming effect on the troubled soul especially at night when fears rise up to begin their frenzied feeding. If you struggle with restlessness at night, practice what the Psalmist did in the watches of the night. God will ease your fears, calm your soul, bring reassurance of His love, and give you peace.

Prayer: Lord of Life, calm our fears and help us meditate on Your precious promises so we might have life more abundantly. Amen

Thursday: Precious Promises

Through these he has given us his very great and precious promises, so that through them you may participate in the divine nature and escape the corruption in the world caused by evil desires.
2 Peter 1:4

Peter was a dynamic disciple who often "stepped out of the boat" in his attempt to follow Christ wholeheartedly. Christ recognized Peter's unbridled enthusiasm and encouraged him to step out in faith in an effort to teach him how great God's power can be in one's life. In today's passage, Peter reminds us God has given us some very great and precious promises allowing us to participate in His divine nature while on earth.

Perhaps you have participated in God's glorious work in the past but now you wonder how much you can still accomplish given your daily battle with Alzheimer's. I struggle as well but remind myself having Alzheimer's doesn't permanently block my participation in His work. I must remember I can do all things through Him who gives me strength if I will simply step out in faith and try.

The other day I was asked if I could read a part in a skit for a Sunday morning worship service. Initially, I was afraid I'd mess up the words, not be able to think clearly, or get stuck if someone else messed up their lines. However, everyone in the church knows my condition and if I did mess up they'd be forgiving. If I didn't mess up, it would be a great testimony to God's perfect power to conquer the impacts of Alzheimer's disease. So I agreed to do it and the skit went marvelously. Like Peter, we must remain enthusiastic to serve, faithfully ready to rely on His perfect power, and cognizant of His precious promises which still hold true for all of us today!

Prayer: Lord, may we hold tightly to Your precious promises so we may participate in Your divine nature here on earth. Amen

Friday: Sweet Aroma of His Promises

Let us hold unswervingly to the hope we profess, for he who promised is faithful. Hebrews 10:23

Yesterday my wife bought an air freshener that plugs into the wall socket and uses heat to disperse the fragrant liquid contained in the replaceable bottle. She pushed the disposable bottle into the plug-in freshener and plugged it into the wall. In the evening she commented the air freshener didn't seem to be dispensing its aroma very well. I asked her to unplug it and hand to me so I could examine the mechanism to make sure it was working properly. To my surprise, she had failed to take the cap off the bottle thus preventing the "white linen" aroma from filling the air. We both had a pretty good chuckle out of the air freshener fiasco. I even commented I was the one with the brain disorder so what was her excuse!

Today's passage reminds us we need to hold unswervingly to our hope in God because He is faithful in all He has promised. How often do we forget to read about His promises so we can "uncap" the power of God's faithfulness in our lives? Just because we are dealing with Alzheimer's disease doesn't mean our hope in the fulfillment of God's promises in our lives has been squelched. In fact, we should hold unswervingly onto the hope we profess so His promises may rest on each of us. Of course, if you don't know what His promises entail, how can you hold onto them? That's why I make it a habit to read His word every day and prayerfully ask His promises be made manifest in the lives of me and my family. Why not choose this day to uncap God's powerful promises and smell the sweet aroma of His faithfulness.

Prayer: Faithful Lord, Your word reminds us how faithful You have been in fulfilling Your promises. Help us hold on to Your hope. Amen

Saturday: Promises Require Perseverance

You need to persevere so that when you have done the will of God, you will receive what he has promised. Hebrews 10:36

In the movie *The Outlaw Jose Wales*, Clint Eastwood gets the drop on Chief Dan George who is trying to capture him for the large reward placed on his head. Once Clint realizes the great Indian chief is not a threat, he ignores the ramblings of the old Indian. Chief Dan pontificates about his trip to Washington D.C. to meet with the Secretary of the Interior. The Secretary told the Chief and his tribe to "endeavor to persevere." This particular scene from the movie was pretty humorous but it brings to light perseverance may require more effort than most of us are willing to put forth.

We often use this term incorrectly and in a pretty cavalier manner. The dictionary defines persevere as "to persist steadily in an action or belief, usually over a long period and especially despite problems or difficulties." For those folks dealing with the daily struggles of Alzheimer's disease, we fully comprehend the meaning of persevere and understand its longevity connotation. However, we don't persevere aimlessly. Today's passage purports those who persevere and do the will of God receive what He promised.

I don't know about you but I stand ready to receive what God has promised. One particular promise I cherish is the fact He will never forsake me. Ultimately, He has our back no matter what circumstance we face to include Alzheimer's. God continues to be my formidable fortress, source of strength, and constant comforter during my daily battles. I can't begin to imagine persevering without Him. The same can be true for you!

Prayer: Father God, help us persevere in a manner worthy of Your calling so we might please You as You stand with us. Amen

Sunday: Be Still and Reflect on His Perfect Promise

Be still, and know that I am God; I will be exalted among the nations, I will be exalted in the earth. The Lord Almighty is with us; the God of Jacob is our fortress. Psalms 46:10–11

God's promises are contained in the Scriptures we read every day. Many promises are easily understood since the words of the Scripture articulate God's intended purpose pretty clearly. However, some require a much deeper understanding of His word through the help of the Holy Spirit. This week we have discussed God's promises in a very general context with the understanding He is faithful in fulfilling His promises in our lives.

Now it is time to be still and truly know He is God Almighty! He is worthy to be praised, adored, exalted, and worshipped, not solely because of His precious promises but because He is the "One True God" who loved us so much He gave His only Son so we might have everlasting life. Everlasting life seems like such a far off concept as you struggle with the daily demands of Alzheimer's disease. But experiencing everlasting life is much closer for those of us afflicted with this disease. All we need do is choose where we want to spend our eternity. God has promised us a perfect place in heaven if we would only believe in Jesus Christ.

Securing our perfect place is pretty easy but it does require a lifetime commitment plus a willingness to maintain a relevant relationship with Christ. You see, God's perfect promise is true, relevant today, and only available to those who believe. Take some time today to be still before God. Then reflect on His perfect promise so you might hold unswervingly to the hope you have in Christ!

Prayer: Heavenly Father, thank You for loving us so much that You gave up Your precious Son so we might have everlasting life. Amen

Kitti Bowornphatnon © 123RF.com

THE RIGHT ROCKS

Devotions to help you find the right rocks to fight the
Alzheimer's Goliath in your life.

Monday: Family

Now Jesse said to his son David, "Take this ephah of roasted grain and these ten loaves of bread for your brothers and hurry to their camp. Take along these ten cheeses to the commander of their unit. See how your brothers are and bring back some assurance from them. 1 Samuel 17:17–18

We are all familiar with the story of David and Goliath either from Bible stories during our youth, selected sermons in church, or reading the inspiring passage from Samuel. Today's passage reminds us how extremely important family was to David's father, Jesse. It was so important he sent his youngest son David to the camp of the Israelites to deliver food for his brothers and bring back assurance they were well.

Jesse knew how vitally important family was in his life and in the lives of his children. In our fight with Alzheimer's disease, family is extremely important because they provide love, endless encouragement, and wise council. After the initial shock of my diagnosis, my three children have been a constant source of support and encouragement. They keep my spirits up by staying in touch by phone, writing notes, visiting, and praying for me. They provided wise counsel as we made tough decisions about finances, property, legal matters, and clinical trials. My children were a constant source of support and encouragement during the 18 month clinical trial in which I participated. After my youngest son Sam graduated from college, he put his life on hold so he could help us fix up and sell our rental properties. Family is the first of the five stones God has given us in our battle against Alzheimer's.

Prayer: Father, thank You for the tremendous gift of family for they are so important in our daily battle with Alzheimer's disease. Amen

Tuesday: Friends

After David had finished talking with Saul, Jonathan became one in spirit with David, and he loved him as himself. From that day Saul kept David with him and did not let him return to his father's house. And Jonathan made a covenant with David because he loved him as himself. 1 Samuel 18:1-3

After killing the giant Goliath, David talked at length with King Saul regarding his actions against Goliath which were attributed to his mighty faith. Jonathan, King Saul's son, may have overheard this conversation and became David's loyal friend. They were such good friends Jonathan made a covenant with David and sealed it by giving him his robe, tunic, sword, bow, and belt. This friendship lasted a lifetime.

Friendships are especially important during the difficult times we all face. One of the five stones in my battle against Alzheimer's disease is friends. My friends are a constant source of encouragement and support. Whenever I am feeling down, God sends a friend my way either to lift me up or to engage me in some type of activity which brightens my day. They take me hiking, camping, canoeing, and exploring throughout all four seasons of the year. We have hiked in the heat of the summer and the snow of the winter. The places we have seen are breathtaking.

My friends have helped me remain socially active which experts claim is critical to keeping the mind mentally sharp. Without the motivation of my friends, I would likely stay home and simply watch television which is the worst thing one can possibly do. So maintain your friendships and let your friends keep you active so you won't wither away!

Prayer: Loving Lord, thank You for Your beautiful gift of Christian friends who readily keep us active and socially engaged. Amen

Wednesday: Fitness

Jesse's three oldest sons had followed Saul to the war: The firstborn was Eliab; the second, Abinadab; and the third, Shammah. David was the youngest. The three oldest followed Saul, but David went back and forth from Saul to tend his father's sheep at Bethlehem. 1 Samuel 17:13-15

I have read the story of David and Goliath numerous times and never realized David traveled back and forth from Bethlehem, where his father's flocks were grazing, to the battlefield at the Valley of Elah where Saul and his brothers were located. The Valley of Elah was located approximately 15 miles west of Bethlehem and David traveled this distance by foot. Needless to say, David was in pretty good physical shape and probably covered this distance in a morning.

Being physically fit was important in David's time because the common mode of travel was walking. Maintaining a good level of physical fitness is extremely important when Alzheimer's disease strikes. As we exercise vigorously, we push more blood into our brains which helps slow the progress of the disease. Like young David, I try to walk as much as I can. I generally walk 2-4 miles every day and hike as often as my friends feel like hitting the trail. The exercise and fresh air of walking always brightens my day and rejuvenates my spirit.

Experts claim exercise causes the release of endorphins in the brain creating an overall feeling of well-being. Perhaps this is why experts advise Alzheimer's patients to get plenty of exercise. If you have never exercised, try taking a leisurely stroll and build the pace over time. Believe me, you will feel so much better as you take control of your fitness.

Prayer: Father, thank You for giving us the desire and opportunity to exercise so we might feel better every day. Amen

Thursday: Focus

But David said to Saul, "Your servant has been keeping his father's sheep. When a lion or a bear came and carried off a sheep from the flock, I went after it, struck it and rescued the sheep from its mouth. 1 Samuel 17:34–35

Today's passage reveals some interesting facts about David. Not only was he brave but he was pretty intelligent. It takes considerable focus and mental acuity to track down a predator that has snatched a sheep from the flock and strike it in such a manner as to avoid injury to the sheep in the process. It seems David had both physical and mental agility.

It is absolutely essential Alzheimer's patients exercise their brains. I do this by reading, writing, and working puzzles every day. I have to admit there are days when solving the crossword puzzle is overwhelming and I have to seek my brilliant wife's assistance. However, I still attempt to work the puzzle as far as I can before asking for help. These puzzles provide a challenge and remind me I can still think, reason, and remember word associations. I also enjoy reading which helps maintain mental focus and even though I don't always remember what I've read, it keeps my mind active.

My favorite mental activity is writing since it allows me to be creative, impels me to do research, stretches my vocabulary, and provides a constructive outlet for my frustrations. Writing has been a saving grace and I thank God for His great insight as I write. Staying mentally active has been beneficial to my brain and emotional health. Although I won't be killing any lions or bears, hopefully I'll be keeping Alzheimer's at bay!

Prayer: Lord, help us stay mentally active and emotionally well so we might continue to be of service to Your kingdom. Amen

Friday: Faith

Your servant has killed both the lion and the bear; this uncircumcised Philistine will be like one of them, because he has defied the armies of the living God. The Lord who delivered me from the paw of the lion and the paw of the bear will deliver me from the hand of this Philistine. 1 Samuel 17:36–37

You have to admire the courage and faith exhibited by David as he declares an "uncircumcised Philistine" is no match for him because the Lord will deliver him from the hand of this Philistine. The firm faith David shows in today's passage stands in sharp contrast with King Saul's loss of faith. Faith is the fifth smooth stone I use in my daily fight against Alzheimer's disease.

Like David, I remember all the times God has delivered me from the paw of some dreaded foe. I have faced screaming, chair-throwing general officers who I had to stand against and explain why they were wrong; young misguided men armed with knives in places I never should have been; or pastors who veered off the path and had to be enlightened. Somehow God delivered me through these unpleasant and fearful situations. Now I face a fiercer foe, Alzheimer's disease, but my faith stands firm for I know my God will stand with me and deliver me from this dreadful disease.

Perhaps as you face the same fierce foe you are worried you will have to go it alone. Rest assured God is standing with you and moving in ways you can't understand as He fights your battle. I know this to be true because He helps me every single day by utilizing family, friends, fitness, focus, and faith. These are the five smooth stones He has prepared for you and me. So pick them up and use them in your fight against the disease!

Prayer: Father, help us to stand tall and hold on to our faith. Amen

Saturday: A Sling

Then he took his staff in his hand, chose five smooth stones from the stream, put them in his shepherd's bag and, with his sling in his hand, approached the Philistine. 1 Samuel 17:40

I am amazed at the fearlessness, fortitude, and faith of young David as he removed King Saul's armor and picked up his staff, selected five smooth stones, and holding his sling in his hand, confidently approached Goliath. David believed the Lord was with him and had equipped him with exactly what he needed to slay Goliath. We know one of the five smooth stones selected from the stream was the projectile that killed this blasphemous uncircumcised Philistine. However, it was David's trusty sling that hurled the smooth stone at just the right trajectory and with enough force to sink into the giant's forehead to kill him. David probably treasured his sling and took good care it because it was his most trusted weapon. Without the sling, David's battle with Goliath might have been much more difficult.

In our battle against Alzheimer's disease, we each need a "trusty sling" to hurl smooth stones accurately and powerfully into the forehead of our fierce foe. My "trusty sling" is my devoted wife of 38 years, Sarah. She engages my family when needed, will alert my friends as necessary, keeps me active and physically fit, helps me maintain mental focus, and reaffirms my faith when I falter. Where would I be without my trusty sling by my side? Just like David, we all need a sling in our hand as we face our daily battles. The sling may be a spouse, close relative, or trusted friend but remember to take good care of it just like David. Then it will be ready when you need it!

Prayer: Lord of Everything, thank You for providing us with a trusty sling as we face our daily battle with Alzheimer's disease. Amen

Paul M. Hornback

Sunday: Be Still and Know the Lord Is with You

Be still, and know that I am God; I will be exalted among the nations, I will be exalted in the earth. The Lord Almighty is with us; the God of Jacob is our fortress. Psalms 46:10–11

We have examined David's battle against Goliath from the perspective of the weapons the Lord provided for his memorable fight. However, we must not forget the most important aspect of the fight which was the presence of the Lord. It was God who ensured David's victory over the giant. David always knew the Lord was with him and acknowledged the Lord's presence before King Saul. David's past victories against lions and bears that attacked his sheep were successful because the Lord was with him. So when David stood before Goliath he knew he was not standing alone. The Lord was with him and would enable him to be victorious.

Perhaps David's relationship with the Lord was strengthened during the quiet times he spent talking with God while watching his father's sheep. In the stillness, David came to know and trust the Living Lord. Now it is time for us to be still before the Lord and talk with Him. Like David, we need to understand the Lord is always with us and He is our fortress against any foe we face. Alzheimer's can be an overwhelming foe just like the giant Goliath was to the Israelite army. However, with the Lord Almighty on our side, we can face the giant with confidence because the battle belongs to the Lord. He provides the stones we need to fight this foe. All we need do is reach down, pick them up, and use them in our fight against this "uncircumcised" disease. Just like Goliath, Alzheimer's can't be victorious against the Living Lord! So be still before the Lord today and remember He is with you.

Prayer: Living Lord, give us the courage and confidence to hurl the stones You have provided in our fight against Alzheimer's. Amen

Станислав Стельмахович © 123RF.com

DAILY EXERCISE

Devotions to help you maintain a daily exercise regime in your battle against the impacts of Alzheimer's disease.

Monday: Exercise

To this very hour we go hungry and thirsty, we are in rags, we are brutally treated, we are homeless. We work hard with our own hands. When we are cursed, we bless; when we are persecuted, we endure it; when we are slandered, we answer kindly. Up to this moment we have become the scum of the earth, the refuse of the world. 1 Cor. 4:11–13

The Apostle Paul certainly has a remarkable way with words. In today's passage, he graphically portrays his challenging conditions prior to writing his letter to the church at Corinth. As I close my eyes, I can see Paul in a tattered tunic, badly bruised, terribly thin, and despicably dirty as he takes pen in hand and begins a letter of love to his beloved brothers in Corinth. Pay particular attention to how he was cursed, persecuted, and slandered but he still managed to continue to act kindly toward others.

Even though I face the demands of Alzheimer's disease, it pales in comparison to what Paul faced as he spread the gospel of Christ during his lifetime. In spite of the horrid conditions, he continued to work with his own hands so as not to be a burden to his brothers and sisters in Christ. Exercise is a lot like work to many people. It is something you do every day and often something you don't look forward to, just like work! After you've been diagnosed with Alzheimer's you may feel like tossing in the towel but don't you dare! Exercise is a key ingredient necessary to continue independent living. Find an exercise you enjoy and make it an integral part of your daily routine. When you don't feel like exercising, remember how Paul worked with his own hands in horrid conditions as he spread the gospel. Then get up and get to it!

Prayer: Father, inspire us as You did Paul so we might continue to exercise so we might serve You more. Amen

Tuesday: Exercise Your Salvation

Therefore, my dear friends, as you have always obeyed – not only in my presence, but now much more in my absence – continue to work out your salvation with fear and trembling, for it is God who works in you to will and to act according to his good purpose.
Philippians 2:12–13

In Paul's letter to his beloved church in Philippi, he asks them to continue to "work out" their salvation. Paul did not mean their salvation was dependent on works. Rather, Paul wanted the Philippians to continue good works as evidence they were growing spiritually. This is certainly sound advice for us today! We need to "work out" or perhaps exercise our salvation by doing good works of service for our Lord. But we also need to "work out" and exercise our bodies so we will be able to continue doing acts of service and good works.

This is especially true for those of us with Alzheimer's disease. Exercising both our bodies and our salvation are absolutely essential for continued mental and spiritual development. My favorite exercise is walking in the park in our little town. As I walk, I often pray about the worries and illnesses of our church family. The walk exercises my physical body while the prayers exercise my spiritual body as I lift up the many concerns of our church. During my walk, I make a concerted effort to encourage the people I encounter along the way. Many of them are walking because of recent heart, knee, or back surgery and are eager for an encouraging word. Thus my daily exercise not only benefits me but also those with whom I come in contact. Perhaps that is why I walk and it explains what Paul meant when he wrote, "For it is God who works in you to will and to act according to his good purpose."

Prayer: Precious Savior, will in us the desire to work out our salvation and bodies so we might better serve You every day. Amen

Wednesday: Exercise for the Lord, Not for Men

Whatever you do, work at it with all your heart, as working for the Lord, not for men, since you know that you will receive an inheritance from the Lord as a reward. It is the Lord Christ you are serving. Col. 3:23–24

Today's Scripture comes from a rather perplexing part of Paul's letter to the Colossian Church. The passages leading up to today's passage deal with how Christian wives, husbands, children, fathers, and slaves are to act as they go about their daily duties. Paul reminds the Colossians they need to accomplish their work with their whole heart as if they were working for the Lord, not for mankind. Paul's perfectly penned words apply to us today in whatever we do.

Since this week has been devoted to exercise, I believe Paul's words apply to it as well. Let me ask you this; if you exercise, why do you do it? Perhaps you want to stay healthy, fit, and mentally alert because Alzheimer's experts claim exercise provides these particular benefits. This is all well and good but it isn't enough according to Paul. We need to exercise so we are healthy, fit, and mentally alert in order to serve the Lord.

After completing the harsh physical training of Officer Candidate and The Basic Schools in the Marine Corps, we were advised to maintain a rigorous exercise program not just to stay in shape but because it would enable us to serve the Corps more effectively. In essence, I was exercising to be of better service to the Marine Corps. As we struggle with Alzheimer's, we have to remember we are still servants of our Lord. Therefore, we must exercise to serve Him better. So, find a fitness program you can work and work at it as if working for the Lord and not just to offset Alzheimer's!

Prayer: Lord, help us exercise daily to better serve You. Amen

Thursday: Walking Through the Valley

Even though I walk through the valley of the shadow of death, I will fear no evil, for you are with me; your rod and your staff, they comfort me. Psalm 23:4

As I have already mentioned, I love walking. This particular form of exercise gently clears my confused mind, connects me with God's glorious creation, and maintains my physical fitness so I might better serve the Lord. In addition, walking always brightens my mood and improves my attitude toward everything. Scientists attribute this particular benefit to the release of endorphins in the brain. Endorphins are the body's natural feel-good chemicals, and when they are released through vigorous exercise, mood is boosted and a feeling of euphoria can occur. If you want to feel good, then exercise.

Today's passage implies the Psalmist walked through the valley of the shadow of death. He certainly didn't lie down and hibernate in the valley of death. Heaven forbid just because we have Alzheimer's disease, we all turn into sofa spuds eating fatty foods and watching hours of television!

Exercise helps fight depression while improving your overall health. When I participated in a clinical trial, I was required to answer a series of questions every two months. Many of the questions centered on my mood and attitude. I was able to respond optimistically because my daily exercise routine helped keep my outlook positive. The clinical trial team was pleasantly surprised by my continued positive responses to the attitude questions even though I was struggling with Alzheimer's. You see, although I walk through the valley of the shadow of Alzheimer's, my Lord comforts me, guides me, and keeps me exercising so I'll be a better witness for Him!

Prayer: Good Shepherd, keep us exercising so we might have positive attitudes truly reflecting Your grace in our lives. Amen

Friday: Get Up and Walk

"Which is easier: to say to the paralytic, 'Your sins are forgiven,' or to say, 'Get up, take your mat and walk'? But that you may know that the Son of Man has authority on earth to forgive sins..." He said to the paralytic, "I tell you, get up, take your mat and go home." Mark 2:9–10

Today's passage from Mark reminds us how important the actual act of walking was in Jesus' time. Walking was how the common man was able to work, get food, visit his friends, pay his taxes, get water, and live independently. If you were a paralytic and could not walk, you depended on others to take you everywhere. There were no wheelchairs or medical transit chariots the government provided to help paralytics. Walking was the only way the common man could travel. Jesus' healing of the paralytic was evidence to the teachers of the law that not only did He have authority to heal but He was also able to forgive sins. The interesting part was when Jesus healed the paralytic, He had him pick up his mat and walk home. Jesus gave this man an opportunity for independence.

Walking is very important to me now as I struggle with Alzheimer's disease. It keeps me healthy and allows me to remain independent because it helps fend off the fogginess in my brain. Walking pumps more blood into the brain, releases endorphins, and increases the oxygen level in the blood. All of these benefits of exercise help produce a feeling of well-being while reducing stress. Stress is especially damaging to Alzheimer patients as it worsens the effects of the disease. If you are struggling with the impacts of Alzheimer's, do what Jesus commanded of the paralytic; get up and walk!

Prayer: Son of Man, please keep us walking and exercising so we might continue to live independent lives in service to You. Amen

Saturday: Be Busy at Home

Then they can train the younger women to love their husbands and children, to be self-controlled and pure, to be busy at home, to be kind, and to be subject to their husbands, so that no one will malign the word of God. Titus 2:4–5

In Paul's pastoral letter to Titus, he instructs him to teach the older women to be reverent so they can teach what is good to the younger women. In this particular passage, Paul proposes the older women teach the younger ones to be busy at home.

My mother was a homemaker for most of her married life. She took a job outside the home only once prior to my dad retiring from the military to help save money for the down payment on a farm. As a homemaker, she busied herself by vacuuming, dusting, cleaning, cooking, baking, painting, and other chores that made our home inviting and comfortable. As she went about her tasks she did them vigorously and as a result, stayed fit well into her fifties. She taught me the joy of housework and the importance of doing a job right.

I still enjoy cleaning the house which also pleases my wife! When the impacts of Alzheimer's start to weigh on me, I pull out the vacuum and start sweeping. Like my mother, I sweep with vigor and it becomes a form of exercise. Not only do I start feeling better, I also end up with a clean house. As we used to say in the Marines, there's nothing like a "field day" to lift your spirits! You see, there are all types of things you can do to exercise if you don't enjoy walking, calisthenics, or aerobics. For example, I enjoy gardening, mowing, yard work, cleaning house, washing windows, and washing the car. All these activities, if done vigorously, are just as effective as exercising. So have an old fashioned field day and feel better!

Prayer: Father, guide each of us to some form of exercise that will lift our spirits, keep us active, and make us feel better. Amen

Sunday: Be Still

Be still, and know that I am God; I will be exalted among the nations, I will be exalted in the earth. The Lord Almighty is with us; the God of Jacob is our fortress. Psalms 46:10–11

This week we have focused on the importance of exercising every day in order to supply our brains with the necessary blood, nutrients, and oxygen to promote health. We've explored different types of exercise like walking, calisthenics, and vigorous housework. The type of exercise you choose isn't really important as long as you perform the exercise vigorously and make it a part of your daily routine.

If you've been routinely exercising, now is the time to be still before our Lord and thank Him for providing the physical ability, healthy body, and mental motivation to maintain your exercise regime. If you haven't started exercising yet, now is the time to be still before the Lord and ask Him to set the crucial conditions in your mind, body, and spirit to enable you to begin exercising. Remember the Lord Almighty is with you all the way. He wants you to stay active as long as possible so you might enjoy your life more abundantly.

Having Alzheimer's disease doesn't change who God is in your life. Nor does it change how much He loves you. God's deepest desire is you would love Him. Thank Him for loving you, for life, and for inspiring you. He alone deserves our thanks and praise because He is the one true God. Take time today to reflect on your relationship with our Lord for He is always with you in everything you attempt to do including exercising for health!

Prayer: Lord Almighty, thank You for Your inspiration to live life more abundantly. Help us to do our part by exercising daily so we might remain healthy, happy, and humble before You. Amen

Dean Fikar © 123RF.com

GOOD TIMES REMAIN

Devotions to help you discover God still has good times in store as you live with Alzheimer's disease.

Monday: Don't Worry about Your Life

*Then Jesus said to his disciples; "Therefore I tell you, do not
worry about your life, what you will eat; or about your body, what
you will wear. Life is more than food, and the body more than
clothes." Luke 12:22–23*

Jesus often talked to His disciples about what was truly
important in life. Today's passage reminds us not to worry about our
lives, body, clothing, or food. This is good advice for those of us
afflicted with Alzheimer's disease because we can easily get
wrapped around the axle about the future. It is pretty easy to think
our lives are over and the good times have passed us by. Nothing
could be further from the truth. We still have lots of living left
because the Lord remains in control. He will ensure we still have a
life worth living.

The caveat to all the promises in Luke is to seek first God's
kingdom and then all these things will be given to you. Are you
seeking God's kingdom even though you are struggling with
Alzheimer's? I have found myself being more and more concerned
with God's kingdom since my diagnosis. Not so much regarding my
place in the kingdom but more so with whether or not my family,
friends, and acquaintances will be there. I still teach a young adult
Sunday school class and want these young men and women to grow
into a rich relationship with Christ so their lives will be filled with
Christ's blessings.

As a result of putting His kingdom first, my life is fulfilling. It
has also been peaceful and my needs have been met, just like Jesus
promised! So don't worry about your life, body, clothes or food but
seek first His kingdom and everything else will fall into place. It's a
perfect promise from Jesus!

*Prayer: Help us seek first Your kingdom in everything we do.
Amen*

Tuesday: Life Doesn't Consist of Possessions

Then he said to them, "Watch out! Be on your guard against all kinds of greed; a man's life does not consist in the abundance of his possessions." Luke 12:15

I received a diagnosis of early-onset Alzheimer disease after over a year of medical tests, scans, exams, and clinic visits. One of my first decisions was to transfer all of my real estate property and major possessions into my wife's name. The amazing thing was I had no hesitation in making this decision. Like Jesus said in today's passage, our lives aren't about owning an abundance of possessions! Personally owning property or things won't change a diagnosis of Alzheimer's.

I've read today's Scripture many times but until I was diagnosed with Alzheimer's disease and relinquished my major possessions, I didn't fully understand what Jesus was talking about. I always tied my happiness in life to the things I acquired. For example, I was happy and fulfilled when I bought a new car, a lovely new house, or a beautiful small farm. Unfortunately, my happiness was short lived because my joy in these newly acquired possessions wore off long before the monthly payments were completed. I should have heeded the words of today's passage so my happiness would not have been tied to an "abundance of possessions."

Now my joy is tied to living the Christian life, serving God, and enjoying the pleasures of a beautiful sunrise, a colorful sunset, playing with my dogs, and spending time with my family and friends. I am at peace with my disease not because I've given up my property and major possessions but because Christ lives in my heart. The same can be true for you!

Prayer: Father, help us to be happy in life by serving You rather than by accumulating an abundance of possessions. Amen

Wednesday: Life to the Full

The thief comes only to steal and kill and destroy; I have come that they may have life, and have it to the full." John 10:10

Today's passage from John is a very familiar one. It comes right on the heels of Jesus' miraculous healing of the blind man and the blind man's encounter with the Pharisees after his healing. Christ gave this man much more than just his sight, He also gave him the opportunity for a full life because the man believed in the Son of Man.

"Life to the full" may seem impossible after you receive a diagnosis of Alzheimer's disease but nothing can be further from the truth. Christ's promise of a full life did not exclude those with Alzheimer's. We can still have a full life if we abide in Christ. Does it mean our lives will be the same as before? Most certainly not! Our lives will be different as we experience the changes the disease brings.

The fullness of my life has certainly changed as I've grown closer to Christ. He has enriched my life by allowing me to enjoy the simple pleasures I once took for granted or had little time to enjoy. My life is full with writing, reading, gardening, hiking, walking, exercising, praying, studying the word, working puzzles, spending time with friends, helping others, sending notes, participating in ministries at church, playing with the dogs, cleaning house, and feeding and watching the birds in my yard. These are but a few of the many things making my life rich. The routine of these activities bring comfort and contentment into my life. Life to the full is still possible with Alzheimer's if you don't give in to the disease. So live your life to the full as you abide in Christ!

Prayer: Lord Jesus, You have promised us life to the full so help us to live our lives accordingly as we abide in You. Amen

Thursday: Make the Most of Every Opportunity

Be very careful, then, how you live – not as unwise but as wise, making the most of every opportunity, because the days are evil.
Ephesians 5:15

This morning started like any typical morning as my wife and I got ready for the day. Just before we sat down to eat, the phone rang with the news a friend and colleague of my wife had been killed in a tragic car accident earlier in the morning. She was the principal of a local elementary school and she left behind a teenage son and a ten year old daughter. We were both devastated as were the rest of folks in our small town. She was a vibrant and caring woman who had experienced unbelievable tragedy over her short lifetime but remarkably rebounded from every blow that came her way.

After hearing the news, today's passage seemed especially fitting to remind us to make the most of every opportunity because we never know what the day may hold. Paul was explaining how to live according to God's will rather than in direct disobedience to Him. However, his words go much deeper and imply every day is a generous gift from God.

Even though we live with Alzheimer's disease, each day is a glorious gift. As such, God requires us to take advantage of every opportunity to live lives worthy of His calling. The day may contain evil, Alzheimer's may impair our thinking, and tragic events may occur but they are opportunities to show God's love and grace. Therefore, try to live life to the fullest in spite of evil, tragedy, and even Alzheimer's disease. You can do this if you remember God's grace is sufficient if you will only lean on Him!

Prayer: Father, no matter what our condition, let us lean on Your grace so we might make the most of every opportunity. Amen

Paul M. Hornback

Friday: Have Life in His Name

Jesus did many other miraculous signs in the presence of his disciples, which are not recorded in this book. But these are written that you may believe that Jesus is the Christ, the Son of God, and that believing you may have life in his name. John 20:30–31

Everyone probably knows the Gospel of John was written so we might believe Jesus was truly the Christ, the Son of the living God. Today's passage reminds us Jesus did many other miraculous signs than those recorded in John's gospel as a witness to the truth of Him being the Christ. But John goes even further in this Scripture by stating if we believe, we will have life in His name. So what did John mean by this solid Scripture? Obviously, by believing in Jesus we may have eternal life as spoken by Him many times in the New Testament. But does it just end at eternal life? I would have to shout a resounding NO to that question! I believe Jesus and John were also talking about our earthly lives as well.

Before I truly believed, my life lacked focus and I felt as if I was going through the motions of living while eking out an existence. Now I have a purpose driven life filled with focus and fullness in spite of having Alzheimer's. This disease is but a blip on my radar screen as I continue to live life in His name. Christ brings joy to my life as I read His word, talk with Him, and share my story with others. You see, we are all strangers who share the same spectacular story of a shepherd savior who offered "life to the full" if only we believe. We can have "Life to the full" now and eternal life later with no other stipulations but you believe. Alzheimer's may be the disease impacting my earthly life but I can still live a full life through the One who gave me eternal life. So can you!

Prayer: Son of God, thanks so very much for Your precious gift of eternal life with the Father and for a full life here on earth. Amen

Saturday: Persevere in Your Life

Watch your life and doctrine closely. Persevere in them, because if you do, you will save both yourself and your hearers.
1 Timothy 4:16

In the Apostle Paul's pastoral letter to Timothy, he instructs him in supervising the affairs of the growing Ephesus Church. In today's passage, Paul reminds his young assistant to watch his life and doctrine closely because he will be under the scrutiny of both believers and non-believers. Paul's wise instruction is not just for pastors but also for lay people who must live their lives under the scrutiny of Christians and non-Christians alike. We are to live full lives guided by the principles and teachings of Jesus Christ so others might see Christ through our thoughts, words, and actions.

This is especially true for Christians diagnosed with Alzheimer's disease. We simply don't get a bye because we are sick. We are still in the "sweet sixteen" and have to play the game worthy of the calling of Christ. Our faith must remain strong and be evident in the way we live our lives. The things we do, joy we project, doctrine we follow, servant life we practice, and thankfulness we express all pay tribute to the Lord. I realize this is a hard row to hoe as my father used to say when I embarked on a seemingly difficult undertaking. But Paul reminds us we must persevere if we are to save ourselves and others! Don't let this disease steal your full life, faith, service, or love for the Lord.

He is with you always even with the limitations this disease brings. He will help you maintain a life worthy of His calling. Be diligent and give your life fully to Him. He'll do the rest.

Prayer: Lord Jesus, help us persevere in our lives so we might live according to Your perfect will. Amen

Paul M. Hornback

Sunday: Be Still and Ask for Life to the Full

*Be still, and know that I am God; I will be exalted among the
nations, I will be exalted in the earth. The Lord Almighty is with us;
the God of Jacob is our fortress. Psalms 46:10–11*

This week we have lingered on living full lives in spite of
having Alzheimer's disease. I hope you have discovered it is
possible to have a full life but also that God's desire we live our lives
in a manner worthy of His Son's calling. Now it is time to be still
before the Lord and recognize we can only do this if we abide in
Him. He alone provides the power for life to the full now and an
eternal life later.

Spend some special time with the Lord today exalting Him for
who He is among the nations and throughout the earth. His name is
mighty, powerful, and full of hope and in His name we have life
abundantly. He provides a fortress in which we take refuge from the
worries of life, deceitfulness of wealth, desire for possessions, and
ravages of Alzheimer's, all trying to eat away at having a full life
with the Lord. He alone can protect you from the one who steals
your joy for living.

Call on His name this very moment and quietly wait for His
reply. It may come through beautiful thoughts, overwhelming peace,
feelings of immense gratitude, or some other unique way. Be still
and allow Him to fill you with His presence as you pour your heart
out to Him. Living a full life in spite of Alzheimer's requires special
time with the Lord. If you do this you will be refreshed, refocused,
and revitalized for serving Him and living according to His will.

*Prayer: Lord of Heaven and Earth, let us be still before You
today so You might fill our lives with Your spirit and grant us a full
life as we continue to serve You in whatever manner You desire.
Amen*

Dean Fikar © 123RF.com

GOD'S GRAND CREATION

Devotions to help you enjoy the beauty of God's grand creation as you live with Alzheimer's disease.

Monday: Morning Has Broken

In the beginning God created the heavens and the earth. Now the earth was formless and empty, darkness was over the surface of the deep, and the Spirit of God was hovering over the waters. And God said, "Let there be light," and there was light. God saw that the light was good, and he separated the light from the darkness. God called the light "day" and the darkness he called "night." And there was evening, and there was morning-the first day. Genesis 1:1–3

Cat Stevens has a stunning song entitled *Morning Has Broken*. The wonderful words from the first verse are:
Morning has broken, like the first morning
Blackbird has spoken, like the first bird
Praise for the singing, praise for the morning
Praise for the springing, fresh from the word.
Each time I sing these words I am reminded of the creation story from the first chapter of Genesis. It is impossible to imagine how absolutely phenomenal the first morning and evening were as God unfolded the day. Perhaps this helps explain why I am fascinated with watching the morning sunrise and the evening sunset. It is as close as I can come to experiencing the first day of creation. I am simply amazed at how God orchestrated light to shape the day and darkness to frame the night. Then He repeats the process over and over as a reminder of His spectacular creation. I cannot fathom all that took place on the first day, but I do understand God loved us enough to continually repeat this perfect process as a living testimony of His greatness. So sit and watch a sunrise or sunset today. Then remember God did it all for you because He loves you!

Prayer: God of Creation, thank You for Your glorious creation and the beautiful reminder we can see every daybreak and dusk. Amen

Tuesday: Stars in the Heavens

When I consider your heavens, the work of your fingers, the moon and the stars, which you have set in place, what is man that you are mindful of him, the son of man that you care for him?
Psalm 8:3-4

Last night, I went outside with the dogs before bedding them down for the evening. It was a wonderfully cool evening without a cloud in the sky. The moon was dark and the stars were spectacular. I stood in amazement as I observed the stars, constellations, and planets. Today's passage came to mind as I took in the magnificent beauty of the night sky.

Perhaps King David was looking at a similarly spectacular sky when he wrote the words of today's Scripture. Like David, I thought how wonderful the works of God's hand truly were and how small I was in comparison. It made me remember how God is still in complete control of the universe including everything happening in my life! Sometimes, the impacts of Alzheimer's weigh heavily on my soul and gnaw at my faith. Such was the case the other night but when I saw the majesty of the night sky, I knew God was in control.

If God had a plan for the creation of the heavens, stars, moon, planets, and earth, then surely He has a plan for my life with Alzheimer's disease. I need to trust Him and step outside occasionally to take in the magnificence of His glorious creation. If you are struggling with the impacts of Alzheimer's disease, take a moment, step outside, and allow God to remind you He is in complete control of all of creation. Then remember His creation definitely includes you!

Prayer: Father, thank You for the wonderful reminder You are in complete control of all creation to include each of us. Amen

Paul M. Hornback

Wednesday: Take a Hike

He has made everything beautiful in its time. He has also set eternity in the hearts of men; yet they cannot fathom what God has done from beginning to end. Ecclesiastes 4:11

I love to go hiking especially in the winter when snow covers the ground. Recently, a few friends from church and I went to Hocking Hills, Ohio and hiked during some pretty frigid weather. There's nothing like a winter hike to lift your spirits. The air was brisk and the ground was covered with snow and ice. The outside air temperature one morning was 8 degrees Fahrenheit which is pretty darn cold! However, it was perfect weather to explore the gorge in Hocking Hills as many of the waterfalls and small streams were frozen. Large icicles hung from the gorge walls and the scenery was breathtaking. Like today's Scripture says, "He has made everything beautiful in its time." This was especially true for the gorge in wintertime as it was simply spectacular.

The hike through the gorge lifted my spirits and for just a few hours I forgot I had Alzheimer's disease. God used the splendid scenery of this winter wonderland to whisk me away from the burdens I carry each day. What a joy it is to be free for even a few hours and not think about this disease! Perhaps that is why I love to be outdoors for at least part of the day. God ministers to me through the majesty of His creation and I am so very thankful for His glorious gift. Whenever the burdens of Alzheimer's weigh heavily on your mind, step outside and take in the beauty of God's magnificent creation. You can't help but feel better as you partake of the wonderful works He so caringly created. So, go take a hike today!

Prayer: Father God, thank You for the wonderful works of Your creation which bring spectacular beauty at just the right time. Help each of us to breathe in the majesty of Your creation. Amen

Thursday: Still the Roaring Seas

You answer us with awesome deeds of righteousness, O God our Savior, the hope of all the ends of the earth and of the farthest seas, who formed the mountains by your power, having armed yourself with strength, who stilled the roaring of the seas, the roaring of their waves, and the turmoil of the nations. Psalm 64:5–7

I love to go to the beach! It doesn't matter what coast it is on as long as there is a plethora of seashells. I especially love early mornings on the beach. I sit on the sand with a cup of coffee and listen to the waves rolling methodically onto shore. It is so perfectly peaceful. I can easily lose myself in the soft slapping of the surf against the sand. I often pray on the beach as I walk along the shore. I imagine I'm with Jesus strolling along the Sea of Galilee as He listens carefully to my concerns. The sea is peaceful but my troubles are tumultuous within me. As Jesus gently strolls by my side, He reminds me how He stilled the seas and calmed the crashing waves.

Today's Scripture from Psalms reinforces how God is the hope for all humanity because He alone framed the mountains and stilled the waters. Somehow, walking on the beach brings everything into perspective like the Alzheimer's disease I struggle with daily, my love for my wife and children, and the faith that promises me a place in eternity. The constant churning of the water against the shore assures me God is in complete control and He has a perfect plan for my life. Even though I may be physically alone on the beach in the morning, I know I'm never spiritually alone. Next time you go to the beach, spend a few peaceful moments early in the morning walking and talking with Jesus along the shore.

Prayer: Lord Jesus, thank You for the beauty of the beach and the gentle reminder of how You quieted the Sea of Galilee. Amen

Friday: Waterfall of Blessings

Deep calls to deep in the roar of your waterfalls; all your waves and breakers have swept over me. Psalm 42:7

Everyone seems to be fascinated with waterfalls and I am no exception. My hiking trips are focused on finding unique waterfalls so I can photograph these grand creations. Today's passage from the Psalms uses a literary allusion to waterfalls but the true nature of the Scripture has a deeper meaning. The Psalmist uses the waterfall metaphor to illustrate God's boundless storehouse of blessings falling like water and surrounding us with blessings that constantly flow in our lives.

Every time I encounter a waterfall, I am gently reminded of God's tremendous storehouse of blessing awaiting those who are willing to plunge into the water to feel the refreshing spray of God's love as it pours over them. I remember one trip on the scenic Skyline Drive when my son and I hiked down a gorge on an especially hot July day. The hike back up the gorge held the promise of three beautiful cascading waterfalls. As we reached the final waterfall, we were thirsty, hot, and exhausted. No other hikers were on the trail so we stripped down to our underwear and dove into the cool water. We swam to base of the waterfall and treaded water directly under the falls. It was amazingly refreshing!

God's love and blessings are just as refreshing to those whose lives are dry, empty, and exhausting. All you need do is jump into the living water and be refreshed. Alzheimer's disease can be especially exhausting if you don't bath in the cool water of God's storehouse of blessing. Next time you see a waterfall, thank God for the countless blessings in your life.

Prayer: Father, thank You for the waterfall of blessings You constantly provide to each of us every day of our lives. Amen

Saturday: Everything God Created Is Good

For everything God created is good, and nothing is to be rejected if it is received with thanksgiving, because it is consecrated by the word of God and prayer. 1 Timothy 4:4–5

In today's text from 1 Timothy, the Apostle Paul reminds us everything God created is good and should be received with thanksgiving. These are powerful words as we think about the wonderful creation God has provided in which we live, work, and play. We have God to thank for His bounty of precious resources set aside in our national and state park systems. These parks provide thousands of acres of stunning scenery for our personal enjoyment.

Every time I go hiking in one of these parks, I am amazed at how stunningly spectacular our Creator made the earth. The beauty draws me closer to God as I imagine how pleased He is I am gratefully enjoying His creation. Since my diagnosis of early-onset Alzheimer's disease, I have begun to treasure the beauty of everything God created. I stand in awe of the majestic forests, cliffs, gorges, rock formations, waterfalls, streams, lakes, and mountains in which I hike. God's fingerprints not only touch the landscape, but they touch the fabric of my spirit as I see the majesty of His creation.

Being outdoors and seeing the spectacular scenery of our parks brings the creation story of Genesis closer to my heart. I am humbled as I realize God created and sculpted this beauty so all generations might see a mere glimpse of His majesty here on this earth. Everything He created is good so get outside and connect with the Creator of the universe. It will help you as you realize He is still in complete control of His creation. Everything He created is good, including you!

Prayer: God of Creation, thanks for Your great handiwork! Amen

Paul M. Hornback

Sunday: Be Still and Praise His Creation

Be still, and know that I am God; I will be exalted among the nations, I will be exalted in the earth. The Lord Almighty is with us; the God of Jacob is our fortress. Psalms 46:10–11

I slept late this morning as my wife was out of town for a training seminar. When I arose I happened to open the curtains in our bedroom window and saw the start of an incredibly beautiful sunrise. I immediately threw on some clothes, grabbed a jacket, stepped into my gum boots, called for the dogs, and raced outside where I was overwhelmed by the morning sky. There were just enough clouds in the sky to capture the vivid colors of this spectacular sunrise. I was humbled as the morning unfolded in front of my eyes.

All I could do was take in the delicious dawning of the day and utter insufficient words of praise to God for this incredible scene. I was tremendously thankful I woke up early enough to enjoy this simple blessing from God. I stood silently still as the colors changed steadily before my eyes. At that moment, I understood again that God is an awesome God and He must be exalted in all the earth.

This week we have focused on the incredible beauty of God's magnificent creation. To enjoy it all we need do is simply slow down, step outside, and be still with the Lord. Then you will know the Lord is with you, loves you, and has a perfect plan for your life just like His perfect plan for creation. Take time today to be still before the Lord, thank Him for His magnificent creation, and praise Him for loving you more than anything. Humble yourself before the Lord, exalt Him above all things, and thank Him for all He does in your life. He is the Lord Almighty and He is worthy of all your praise!

Prayer: Lord of All Creation, thank You for Your incredible creation giving us life and reminding us of Your marvelous majesty. Amen

Gary718 © 123RF.com

A SMALLER WORLD

Devotions to help you recognize it is perfectly okay for your world to close in a little as you deal with the daily demands of Alzheimer's disease.

Monday: Withdraw to Pray

Yet the news about him spread all the more, so that crowds of people came to hear him and to be healed of their sicknesses. But Jesus often withdrew to lonely places and prayed. Luke 5:15–16

As the news about Jesus' ministry and miracles spread, Luke tells us crowds of people came to hear him speak and be healed of their sicknesses. Of course, there was no evening news broadcast complete with live video to digitally record His healings. Instead, news of His miracles spread by word of mouth from those who heard or witnessed His life changing miracles. Yet Luke records in his gospel how Jesus often withdrew to lonely places and prayed. Jesus needed this time alone with His Father to focus His ministry and gain wisdom for the rigorous road ahead.

As you struggle with the impacts of Alzheimer's disease, you may feel a strong urge to withdraw from the crowds and find a quiet place to reflect in prayer as well. In my daily battle with Alzheimer's, I've discovered my capacity for crowds has dwindled immensely. I become anxious, edgy, and uncomfortable in large groups. Although I still go out with my wife to areas like the local mall or Wal-Mart, I prefer to stay at home where I feel less anxious and more comfortable.

Like Jesus, I especially enjoy time alone with my Father to quietly pray, read, and reflect on His holy word. I realize my world is closing in a little bit but it is okay because I've learned to be content no matter what the circumstance. How about you? If you are having trouble adjusting, spend some time in prayer and ask our Lord to help bring you peace.

Prayer: Heavenly Father, help us adjust to a new way of living as we withdraw a little bit more to spend some quiet time with You. Amen

Tuesday: A House with Many Rooms

"Do not let your hearts be troubled. Trust in God, trust also in me. In my Father's house are many rooms; if it were not so, I would have told you. I am going there to prepare a place for you.
John 14:1–3

My wife and I built a new house about thirteen years ago. This was to be our retirement home as it was built on her parents' farm. The two-story house has a master bedroom, four bedrooms upstairs, living room, dining nook, family room, kitchen, utility room, study, three baths, and basement. The floor plan was laid out so we could live on the first floor while reserving the second story for our children, grandchildren, or friends who come to visit or vacation at our homestead.

When we built the house we had no idea I would have Alzheimer's disease. Fortunately, the house is perfectly designed for someone who may need assistance because of dementia. Since we live on a farm in the country, we don't have to worry about traffic or wandering off since the house has fences all around it. There are lovely gardens and plenty to keep me entertained during the day. As Alzheimer's disease continues to limit my daily activities, I'm more comfortable staying at home and enjoying the many rooms of our house.

Today's passage says our heavenly Father has a perfect place for our retirement as well. It was designed with many rooms and our Lord is going there to prepare a place for us. I imagine it will be very comfortable and none of us will want to leave. Alzheimer's disease gradually closes in your world so you feel more comfortable staying at home. If this happens, it's okay because your Lord is just preparing you for heaven's bliss!

Prayer: Lord, help us to remain comfortable and content as we begin to linger at home more and more. Amen

Paul M. Hornback

Wednesday: Shelter of Home

For in the day of trouble he will keep me safe in his dwelling; he will hide me in the shelter of his tabernacle and set me high upon a rock. Psalm 27:5

As a young boy I often got in trouble because of my devilish nature. Afterwards, I would run and hide in my room where I always felt safe. My room contained all my earthly treasures. The bed was warm and comfortable and the only window looked out onto the neighborhood street where my father parked his car after work. Unfortunately, my parents soon learned if I was hiding in my room before bedtime, I had probably done something wrong. It's funny how we feel safe in the comfort of our humble homes.

Today's passage from Psalms reminds us even King David felt safe in the shelter of God's tabernacle, His holy dwelling. Perhaps you are struggling with the difficulties stemming from Alzheimer's disease. As the troubling days of Alzheimer's continue to take their toll on me, I find myself acting like a little boy as I hide in the shelter, safety, and security of the family room of our home. When foggy days significantly impair my thinking, I'll curl up on the couch with a Sudoku book or the daily crossword puzzle and attempt to work through the confusion.

On troubling days, I know my world has closed in significantly and I'm content to stay in the shelter of my house. I seek the comfort of the Lord and ask Him to shelter me so I do nothing to bring me harm. When the difficult days of Alzheimer's strike, do like David and call on the name of the Lord for safety, contentment, and shelter from the troubles you face.

Prayer: Lord on High, shelter us from the troubles we face as we struggle with the difficult days of Alzheimer's disease. Amen

Thursday: Refuge at Home

For you have been my refuge, a strong tower against the foe. I long to dwell in your tent forever and take refuge in the shelter of your wings. Psalm 61:3–4

Our house has three dormer windows on the second floor looking out over the front lawn and adjoining 40 acre field. I love to sit in one of the dormer windows and look out over the landscape. Since our house sits atop a small hill, the view is simply incredible, especially after a fresh winter snow or when fall brings its brilliant color to the woods on the horizon. On days I don't feel comfortable going out because of bad weather or the frightful fogginess of Alzheimer's disease, I often sit in a window box enjoying the scenic beauty of the landscape as I read or pray.

I believe the Lord's hand was upon us when we built our retirement home. Only He knew I would face the fierce foe of Alzheimer's and would require a comfortable place to live safely. As such, I take refuge in our home, my strong tower, which the Lord has provided as I struggle with my daily battles. Like King David wrote in today's passage from Psalms, I also long to dwell in His tent while I take refuge under the shelter of His wings. I know my home is but an earthly tent to shelter me from the confusion of the outside world. It is also a sacred place where I call upon the Lord. Surely He is in this place because I feel so calm and content inside its walls.

Perhaps you have a special place in your house, apartment, or quarters where you feel safe under His wings of love. Go to it during your difficult days and bask in the warmth of His love. He will safely shelter you from harm if you will come to Him!

Prayer: Lord, thank You for the special places You provide where we feel the shelter of Your holy presence. Amen

Friday: Safety at Home

The angel of the Lord encamps around those who fear him, and he delivers them. Taste and see that the Lord is good; blessed is the man who takes refuge in him. Psalm 34:7–8

King David had an unfathomable faith in the Lord's protection no matter what circumstances came his way. He knew the Lord was with him and would deliver him from the world's ever present evil. Today's passage provides David's view of how the Lord protected His loyal servants by encamping His angels nearby. I don't know what you believe about angels of the Lord, but it is clear King David understood their purpose and welcomed their presence.

I also believe in the Lord's angels and welcome their presence in my life as I struggle with Alzheimer's disease. The other day while I was in the yard playing with the dogs and enjoying the wonderful warm sunshine, I noticed a dead possum in the road in front of our large yard. I meandered down to the road and noticed two cars approaching on the opposite side of the road. I walked a little further so I could step into the road to grab the dead possum. Before I stepped in the road, something made me stop and look back toward the approaching cars. Thankfully I did look because one of the cars had decided to pass and if I had stepped into the road I would have been hit by a car going approximately 65 mph! An angel of the Lord must have been encamped around my home protecting me from deadly harm.

Although I was having a difficult day, the Lord was with me while I stayed at home in order to be safe. I thanked the Lord for His protection and deliverance from harm. Trust in Him and His angels. They will protect you as well!

Prayer: Lord, thank You for the angels encamping around us. Amen

Saturday: His Home Is in You

But Christ is faithful as a son over God's house. And we are his house, if we hold on to our courage and the hope of which we boast.
Hebrews 3:6

There is a wonderful worship song entitled *Blessed Be Your Name*. The words of the song that touch me deeply are:
When the darkness closes in, Lord, still I will say
Blessed be the name of the Lord
Blessed be your name
Blessed be the name of the Lord
Blessed be your glorious name.
Does the darkness of Alzheimer's disease ever close in on you? When the darkness comes, I stay at home where I feel safe and secure from the confusion of the world. On these days, Alzheimer's narrows my world quite a bit; however, it doesn't steal my faith and hope in Christ. Today's passage reminds us we are His house and He lives in us thereby providing hope and courage.

Christ told us to be in this world but not to be a part of this world. Alzheimer's has made me understand more fully what Christ meant by this perplexing phrase. Obviously, I must be in the world to live but I must not gain strength, joy, success, self-worth, purpose, or hope from what the world has to offer. All of these qualities must be grounded in Jesus Christ. There was a time when my status, accomplishments, and possessions seemed to supply my strength, joy, purpose, and hope. All those worldly things have been stripped away but I still have joy, purpose, and hope because they rest in the Lord. When the darkness closes in, He is with you so blessed be His name!

Prayer: Christ, come live in us so we might gain our strength, joy, hope, courage, purpose, worth, and success from You. Amen

Sunday: Be Still at Home

*Be still, and know that I am God; I will be exalted among the
nations, I will be exalted in the earth. The Lord Almighty is with us;
the God of Jacob is our fortress. Psalms 46:10–11*

This week we have discussed how Alzheimer's disease causes
our world to close in. As such, you may feel more comfortable
remaining at home where you have a sense of safety and security.
We've examined Scripture focused on Christ dwelling in us, Christ
being present in our homes, and Christ's angels encamping around
us. Now it is time to be still before the Lord and acknowledge His
holiness.

Invite Him into your house. Allow Him to take up residence in
your home. Place your hope and courage in Him. He will tenderly
abide in you. His angels will encamp around your home. They will
keep you safe when the darkness and confusion of Alzheimer's
foggy days fall upon you. Don't be afraid for He is most certainly
with you when the difficult days narrow your world. Continually
praise Him, worship Him, thank Him, exalt Him, and acknowledge
Him in your home. He will always remain there because He is
faithful and honorable in all things.

Spend some time today being still before Him. Acknowledge He
is God and worthy of praise. He alone is your fortress and He defines
who you are in Christ. Even though the darkness may come you can
still say, *"Blessed be the name of the Lord, blessed be His glorious
name."* Although Alzheimer's may close your world in, it shouldn't
weaken your faith. Why? Because your faith rests in Christ and not
in this world!

*Prayer: Lord Almighty, please be our fortress, reside in our
homes, and abide in our hearts as we faithfully trust in You. Please
mature our faith, and strengthen our relationship with You. Amen*

Aliaksei Skreidzeleu © 123RF.com

PRAISEFUL MUSIC

Devotions to encourage you to use spiritual music to calm your soul on the foggy days brought on by Alzheimer's.

Monday: Sing for Joy

But let all who take refuge in you be glad; let them ever sing for joy. Spread your protection over them, that those who love your name may rejoice in you. Psalms 5:11

There are so many beautiful old church hymns, magnificent contemporary Christian melodies, and glorious gospel songs to wondrously move our hearts and souls. They bring back joyful memories of special times when Christ was stirring in our lives. If you have ever been on a Christian retreat you probably agree the music stirs your heart. Every time you hear a special song you remember a particular aspect of the retreat.

Christian music helps us joyfully sing praises to the one in whom we take refuge like today's passage from the Psalms purports. King David had a joyous heart and a love for music through which he worshipped the Lord. Music allowed him to express his joy and love for the Lord. It moved his spirit, freed his mind, and gladdened his heart.

As I struggle with Alzheimer's disease, I've found music plays a very important role for me during the worship service. I struggle during the pastoral prayer and can't concentrate or comprehend all the words. The same thing occurs during the sermon but the music somehow frees my mind and allows me to express my praise freely. Perhaps you also struggle in a similar fashion during the worship service. If so, use the music to help express your joy for the Lord. It doesn't matter if you sing off key for the Lord only hears what flows from your heart! Sing loud and praise the One who protects and strengthens you every day.

Prayer: Joyful Lord, let the words of our songs and the joy in our hearts fill us with adoration and praise for You are awesome. Amen

Tuesday: Sing to the Lord

Then my head will be exalted above the enemies who surround me; at his tabernacle will I sacrifice with shouts of joy; I will sing and make music to the Lord. Psalms 27:6

Do you have a special worship song or hymn that moves your spirit when you sing it? The words flow effortlessly from your heart to your tongue and the sweet sound is lifted to the Lord who joyfully listens to your song of praise. It really doesn't matter how well you sing, whether or not you're on key, or if you mess up a word or two just as long as you sing with all your heart, all your spirit, and all your soul!

One of my absolute favorite praise songs is "As the Deer Pants for the Water." The first verse goes like this:
As the deer pants for the water,
So my soul longs after You.
You alone are my heart's desire,
And I long to worship You.

These words stir my soul and bring sweet tears to my eyes. The thirst of a small helpless deer as it longs for a cool crisp drink of clear creek water seems a fitting metaphor for the longing of the soul as it seeks to worship our Lord and Savior. As I struggle with the daily pains of Alzheimer's disease, I feel just like the deer panting for water. Singing this sweet song puts me in touch with my Lord. The words soften my confusion and center me on what is important. I worship and praise Him rather than feel sorry for myself.

Do you struggle during your difficult days as well? Maybe this praise song will help you forget your misfortune and allow you to focus on worshipping our Savior! So sing to the Lord with all your heart and He will quench your thirsty soul!

Prayer: Soothe our panting souls as we worship You. Amen

Paul M. Hornback

Wednesday: Sing Joyfully to the Lord

Sing joyfully to the Lord, you righteous; it is fitting for the upright to praise him. Praise the Lord with harp; make music to him on the ten-string lyre. Sing to him a new song; play skillfully, and shout for joy. Psalms 33:1–3

Do you ever have days when joy just jumps in and overtakes your spirit? Today was one of those days. We were under a severe thunderstorm and tornado watch for the entire morning. Tornadoes had touched down all around our county and my four Chihuahuas were acting unusually strange. While I was outside watching the stormy sky, I saw a funnel cloud form in the air about 5 miles from our home. I called my son out to make sure what I saw was a tornado. He got real excited as he raced me inside and rushed me and the dogs into the basement. Fortunately, the tornado stayed east of our home and we received no damage from its high winds.

After the tornado threat passed, I was filled with such joy all I could do was offer praise and thanks to the Lord. The song *"You Are God Alone"* by Philips, Craig, and Dean filled my mind. Although I could not remember all the words, I sang what I could remember. Finally, I got on the internet to find the music and words so I could sing them all. My heart and soul were filled with joy as I sang aloud my praises to Him who sheltered me through the storm!

Perhaps that is how King David felt when he wrote, *"Sing to him a new song...and shout for joy."* Whenever you feel joy overtaking you, take time to praise the Lord in song so you can worship him in the moment. Whatever you do, don't let Alzheimer's disease steal your praise and joy for Him!

Prayer: Lord, let us sing aloud precious praises to You. Amen

Thursday: Sing Praises to Him

Again, it says, "Rejoice, O Gentiles, with his people." And again, "Praise the Lord, all you Gentiles, and sing praises to him, all you peoples." Romans 15:10–11

Experts agree music has a way of connecting Alzheimer's patients to the past. You see, Alzheimer's robs people of their short-term memory but their long-term memory often remains unaffected. It is funny how I may not be able to remember the words to a song; however, when the music plays, the words magically begin to flow from my lips. Perhaps the Apostle Paul knew how important music was when he wrote today's passage in Romans.

Music is important in worship but also in preserving our memory of spiritual things. "It appears the words to a song get encoded in a different place in the brain than the words we use in speech, and it appears that people with Alzheimer's actually preserve the music, and the words that go to music, long after much of the rest of the brain is not functioning well," says Elaine Bearer, a neuroscience professor at the University of New Mexico. Music provides a comforting connection to past spiritual experiences and allows us to rejoice in memories of our fervent faith. By singing worship songs, you remain mentally active and joyfully content in your connection to the Lord.

Alzheimer's robs us of many things but it needn't rob us of the joy of praiseful worship in song. Just as Paul declared to his brothers and sisters in the church at Rome, rejoice and sing praises to Him. Besides, singing will connect you to His people and minister to your heart and soul.

Prayer: Father, fill our hearts with the joyful songs that gently flow from a life lived loving You. Amen

Paul M. Hornback

Friday: Sing to Awaken the Dawn

*My heart is steadfast, O God, my heart is steadfast; I will sing
and make music. Awake, my soul! Awake, harp and lyre! I will
awaken the dawn. I will praise you, O Lord, among the nations; I
will sing of you among the peoples. For great is your love, reaching
to the heavens; your faithfulness reaches to the skies. Psalm 57:7–10*

Have you ever awoken in such a great mood you just had to sing
something? I love to wake up in this frame of mind so I can turn on
the CD player, pop in a WOW hit collection, and sing to my heart's
content. Unfortunately, my wife is just not a perky morning person.
She has no trouble getting up for work but she prefers no loud music
or singing as she endures the silent solitude of her morning. Since
I'm retired and she is still working, I honor her desires. While she
spends her time in the master bathroom getting ready for the day, I
fix breakfast and turn the radio to KLOV in hopes of hearing a
familiar song to sing along quietly. After she leaves for work the
volume is cranked up and I sing loud enough to wake the dead!

Today's passage from Psalms reminds us if our hearts are
steadfast in the Lord, we will praise Him with music and song
among all the world. Do you ever wonder what King David would
do with the technology we have today? Would he record songs and
music so others could praise the Lord? Would he stream live praise
services with lots of singing so nations of the world could share his
love for the Lord? I think he would have done all these things and
more because his love for the Lord could not be contained. If
Alzheimer's disease is pulling you down today, follow David's lead
and sing your praises aloud to the Lord!

*Prayer: Lord, You are God alone and worthy of all our praise.
Amen*

Saturday: A New Song in My Mouth

He put a new song in my mouth, a hymn of praise to our God.
Many will see and fear and put their trust in the Lord. Psalm 40:3

Music has a way of mellowing the pains experienced as you face the adversities of living in an imperfect world. The Psalmist experienced adversity in his life but through it all he was able to praise his Lord in song. Today's passage reminds us not only did God put a new song in his mouth but he used his praise hymn to allow others to place their trust in the Lord.

Is there a hymn that has enabled you to see the Lord in a different light so you could place your trust in Him? For me it is the praise song, "How Great Is Our God" sung by Chris Tomlin. The wonderful words to the chorus seem to echo the Psalmist's tribute:

How great is our God, sing with me
How great is our God, and all will see
How great, how great is our God.

These words remind me no matter what is going on in my life, no matter what the trial may be, no matter what adversity may fall my way, our God is great and all must see His greatness!

As you struggle with the limitations brought on by Alzheimer's disease, don't forget how great God is in your life. He is concerned about your wellbeing, your living life to the full, and your unwavering faith in Him. He has not abandoned you nor has He forsaken you. He remains faithful and yearns for your praiseful worship. If you are struggling, find a great Christian CD and sing along to the music. You'll begin to feel better and like the Psalmist, you'll be praising the Lord for who He is in your life.

Prayer: Lord of Life, place a new song in our hearts so the entire world might see You and place their trust in You alone. Amen

Paul M. Hornback

Sunday: Be Still and Listen to the Music

*Be still, and know that I am God; I will be exalted among the
nations, I will be exalted in the earth. The Lord Almighty is with us;
the God of Jacob is our fortress. Psalms 46:10–11*

Today we had a healing service during the Sunday morning
worship. This was a unique service since there wasn't a sermon, just
lots of congregation praise music; specific prayers for physical,
emotional, and spiritual healing; special contemporary music sung
by a trio, quartet, and soloist; communion; and an anointing of oil for
those seeking healing. The service was absolutely amazing and His
precious presence was felt by everyone who participated. The
congregational music we sang included *He is Jehovah, Mighty to
Save, Amazing Grace My Chains are Gone, My Faith Looks Up to
Thee, and Trading My Sorrows* which are all popular praise and
worship songs that simply stir one's spirit.

Since this week's series of devotions focused on music, I was
elated to experience a Sunday morning worship service with more
congregational singing and special music. The Lord was certainly
exalted in His house as we praised His name in song. Like the
Psalmist said, the Lord Almighty is with us and He is our fortress.
We left the service knowing He is a God who really cares for our
needs.

If you haven't been able to worship Him today, be still right
now and exalt His holy name. Sing aloud your favorite hymn
knowing He lovingly listens to your musical offering. He loves and
adores you and understands fully all the struggles you face with
Alzheimer's disease. But be aware of this: when you exalt Him in
spite of your struggles, it adorns His heavenly throne room with an
especially sweet aroma of grateful praise!

*Prayer: Lord Jehovah, may we always love, praise and worship
You no matter how Alzheimer's disease impacts our daily lives.
Amen*

Foottoo © 123RF.com

TRUST HIM

Devotions to help you learn how to totally trust God in your battle with Alzheimer's disease.

Monday: Sheltered by His Wings

He will cover you with his feathers. He will shelter you with his wings. His faithful promises are your armor and protection.
Psalm 91:4

I just finished watching an episode of *In Plain Sight* where a successful doctor's family gave up all their major possessions, changed their identities, and moved because their daughter witnessed the murder of her boyfriend by a notorious street gang. The family placed their trust in the U.S. Marshall Service and changed their lives so they could continue living a reasonably safe and normal life.

I'm not sure if the episode was based on a true story but it sounds similar to being sidelined by Alzheimer's disease. You see, I have had to place all my trust in the Lord since there is no known cure for this dreadful disease. I still take my medicine daily, eat a healthy Mediterranean diet, exercise, and reduce stress in my life; however, my life and identity have changed dramatically just like the family from *In Plain Sight*. I sold all my major possessions (or signed them over), my identity changed from an independent and intelligent analyst to a dependent retiree, and I know at some point I'll be moving to an assisted living facility. The big difference is I have placed my trust in the Lord rather than the U.S. Marshall Service.

Today's passage promises He will cover and shelter you from all harm, His faithfulness will be your armor and protection. As Alzheimer's continues to change your life be assured His wings will protect you. Trust in Him for He is forever faithful!

Prayer: Heavenly Father, spread Your wings around us and shelter us from harm as we walk through the Alzheimer's valley. Amen

Tuesday: May Your Trust Be in the Lord

Pay attention and listen to the sayings of the wise; apply your heart to what I teach, for it is pleasing when you keep them in your heart and have all of them ready on your lips. So that your trust may be in the Lord, I teach you today, even you. Proverbs 22:17–19

When I was going through flight training as a young officer in the United States Marine Corps, I had to learn to trust my instruments when flying in zero visibility. If I relied on the aircraft's instruments I could maintain level flight, a specific altitude, and a set speed fairly easily. However, if I tried to fly by the seat of my pants, I could end up in a deadly downward spiral. The flight instructor, generally a very seasoned pilot, would demonstrate this fact by turning off my instruments while I was under the hood and allowed me to fly by what 'felt' right. Once I told him I was straight and level he would have me open the hood and I saw I was anything but straight and level! Trusting the instruments rather than my instincts is a paradigm preached by flight instructors so pilots don't crash and burn when flying in zero visibility!

Today's passage reminds us to pay attention to the teachings of the Lord so our trust will be in Him. When Alzheimer's disease strikes, it is like flying in zero visibility and you realize you have to place your trust in something. You cannot fly solo by your instincts or you will crash and burn. I've learned from prayer, Bible reading, and a personal relationship with Christ to put my trust in the Lord. He is my "set of instruments" and I'll follow Him closely! As you deal with the disease, trust in Him and you fly straight and level.

Prayer: Faithful Father, keep us safe, straight, and level as we endure the difficult and uncertain days of Alzheimer's disease. Amen

Wednesday: Blessed Is He Who Trusts in the Lord

"But blessed is the man who trusts in the Lord, whose confidence is in him. He will be like a tree planted by the water that sends out its roots by the stream. It does not fear when heat comes; its leaves are always green. It has no worries in a year of drought and never fails to bear fruit." Jeremiah 17:7–8

We planted a weeping willow tree in our back yard next to the pond on our homestead in rural Kentucky. The tree flourished despite the dry weather we have experienced in the summers since its planting. All the other trees planted in various places away from the pond have died in spite of my feeble attempts at watering and nurturing them. Now, we plant any tree we want to flourish on the banks of the pond. Today's passage reminds us the tree's roots will grow toward the stream and when drought come the trees will flourish and bear fruit.

The prophet Jeremiah compares a man who trusts and places his confidence in the Lord to a tree planted by the water. The comfort of this Scripture is found in the depth of its meaning. You see, the passage doesn't imply we won't have times of drought or heat. Instead, it states when these tough times come we will have no worries because we will bear fruit and stay green. The key is to be planted firmly by the Living Water, our Lord Jesus Christ. As long as we stay close to Him we will flourish despite difficult conditions.

You could correctly say Alzheimer's disease is my drought but I placed my confidence in the Lord decades before the drought hit. Therefore, my roots are deep! They are firmly established in the Lord so my life is green and filled with fruit. Place your trust and confidence in the Lord today. He will help you flourish throughout the drought you are facing.

Prayer: Lord, helps us flourish in the drought of Alzheimer's. Amen

Thursday: Trust and Faith

Now faith is being sure of what we hope for and certain of what we do not see. This is what the ancients were commended for.
Hebrews 11:1–2

Today's passage starts the beautiful faith chapter in Hebrews. The author of Hebrews was addressing Jewish converts who were familiar with the Old Testament but were struggling with Judaizing the gospel or reverting to Judaism. This particular passage reminds them how important faith was to the Old Testament heroes. It also gives the biblical definition of faith.

I use the terms faith and trust interchangeably because they are linked indelibly. After being diagnosed with Alzheimer's disease I had to "throw off everything that hindered" me and "run with perseverance" the new race laid out before me. I had no idea what particular course this race was going to take. My faith and trust in the Lord were certainly going to be put to the test! However, my God is faithful to His promises just like He was to the heroes of the Old Testament. All I need do is trust Him and not let my faith waiver as I continue to run my race.

Perhaps you are struggling with your faith and trust in the Lord after being diagnosed with Alzheimer's disease. Be assured God has not forsaken you. Read Chapters 11 and 12 of Hebrews and surround yourself with the cloud of witnesses who maintained their faith in spite of what lay ahead. Dealing with the daily debilitating demands of Alzheimer's disease may be the faith-defining event in your life. It is easy to trust the Lord in good times but like the faithful, the difficult times define who we are in Christ! Trust in Him and have faith like our Old Testament heroes.

Prayer: Father, our trust is in You alone. Help our faith be steadfast as we struggle with the daily demands of this disease. Amen

Paul M. Hornback

Friday: My Heart Trusts in Him

The Lord is my strength and my shield; my heart trusts in him, and I am helped. My heart leaps for joy and I will give thanks to him in song. Psalm 28:7

Prior to Marine Corps Officer Candidate School, I attended the Army's Parachute Training School more commonly called Jump School. Soldiers are taught to jump out of perfectly good airplanes to land in strategic locations in hopes of surprising the enemy. The key to successfully completing Jump School is learning how to land safely without breaking any bones. You must learn to trust your equipment and have confidence your parachute will open when you step out of the airplane.

The Jump School cadre do an excellent job of training soldiers how to execute parachute landing falls or PLFs. You practice this skill over and over during Ground Week. Next is Tower Week where everyone practices exiting a mock aircraft door, adjusting to the jerk of the chute, and more PLFs. Finally Jump Week arrives and you prepare to make your first jump. Nothing compares to standing in the door and taking that initial leap into thin air. You step out of the plane, feel the jerk of the static line pulling the chute open, and float gently to the ground where you execute a perfect PLF!

Living with Alzheimer's is like stepping out of a perfectly good airplane with a parachute on your back. If you trust your spiritual training and rely on the Lord, you need not fear the future for He will help you land safely. Take a leap of faith today and put your trust in the Lord as you face a future filled with Alzheimer's. I did and my PLFs are still great!

Prayer: Lord on High, You are our parachute as we leap out into the unknown world of Alzheimer's disease. Keep us free from harm, fully functional, and faithfully alert as we face the fall. Amen

Saturday: Trust in the Shadow of His Wings

Keep me as the apple of your eye; hide me in the shadow of your wings from the wicked who assail me, from my mortal enemies who surround me. Psalm 17:8–9

The Resurrection Fern is a plant I discovered while in Florida on vacation. This fern thrives in moist conditions but as the weather turns hot and dry, the plant turns brown, shrivels up, and looks dead. However, it is only in a dormant state. After an afternoon shower, the plant springs to life as the leaves turn green again. For this reason it is called the Resurrection Fern.

I feel much like the Resurrection Fern as I live in the early stages of Alzheimer's disease. During the good days I appear to be my old self. I am lively, mentally sound, active, and rather clearheaded. However, when the foggy days arrive, I am like the fern that hasn't had a rain shower in days. I am dormant since my mental abilities are drastically reduced, I'm lethargic, and I move around in a stupor. But then, like a spring shower, the foggy days are gone as I have resurrected to an active state where I'm more mentally and emotionally sound. Hallelujah for good days following foggy days. Thankfully, I'm only dormant for a short duration.

Like the Psalmist praised in today's passage, I trust the Lord to keep me in the shadow of His wings during the foggy days. Then when the good days return, we rejoice together as He prepares me for the next set of foggy days on the horizon. It is great to be alive in Christ, to trust in Him alone, and to stay in the shadow of His wonderful wings! Trust in Him and you won't be high and dry for long.

Prayer: Lord, thank You for keeping us in the shadow of your wings when Alzheimer's eats away at our mental abilities. You are our protector and Savior who loves us dearly. Amen

Sunday: Be Still and Worship Him

Be still, and know that I am God; I will be exalted among the nations, I will be exalted in the earth. The Lord Almighty is with us; the God of Jacob is our fortress. Psalms 46:10–11

Sunday mornings are a joyous occasion for me. I seldom have trouble getting out of bed on Sunday. It is the day I have set aside to worship the Lord, spend time with family and friends, and breathe in the sweet breath of peace. I understand why God intended for mankind to rest and relax on one day out of the seven. Not only do our bodies need a break from the toil of working but our minds and spirits need a break from the world's stress. When we take a break from the toil of the work week, we are encouraged, inspired, and spiritually prepared for the coming week through our worship experience. Our faith is solidified through the worship service as we join with others in praising our Lord and Savior, Jesus Christ.

My daily struggles with Alzheimer's disease take a terrible toll on me during the week. Sundays are a welcome reprieve from the daily battles because I am re-energized as I am still before the Lord with my family of faith. I am once again reminded the Lord Almighty is with me and He alone is my fortress! My trust in the Lord is deepened through the faithful presence of others as we worship together.

Spend time today in worship with your family and friends as you collectively praise and honor the Father of your faith. Be still before Him today and breathe in His breath of peace. It will make your daily struggles with Alzheimer's so much easier to bear. Take time today to trust in Him alone!

Prayer: Father of Faith, thank You for Your holy presence and for the opportunity to worship with family and friends this day. Amen

Foottoo © 123RF.com

LOVING CHRIST

Devotions to help you find new ways to stay in love with Christ as you deal with the demands of Alzheimer's disease.

Monday: Seek His Face Always

Glory in his holy name; let the hearts of those who seek the Lord rejoice. Look to the Lord and his strength; seek his face always.
Psalm 105:3–4

I have always loved waking up in the morning next to my wife so I can see her first thing. She has natural beauty and her radiance always fills me with joy. This is one of the things I cherish about our marriage and I pray I'll never lose this beautiful blessing. While serving in the Marines, I was deployed away from home more than I wanted. I had my wife's college picture above my rack so I could see her first thing in the morning. It wasn't the same as waking up next to the welcomed radiance of her face but it helped me endure the separations imposed by flying helicopters in the Marine Corps.

Today's passage reminds us we are to seek the Lord's face and rejoice in His holy name. I like to seek Him in the morning when I read Scripture and talk with Him about my day. I often visualize Him just listening intently to my conversations with Him as He smiles radiantly as if I'm His only concern. This morning ritual helps me stay focused on living a Christ-like life and ensures my love for Him is rekindled each day. If I miss these precious morning dialogues, I lose sight of Christ and am more apt to stray off the narrow path He's laid out for me to follow.

Staying in love with Christ takes special effort, especially as you struggle with the difficult days Alzheimer's disease brings your way. Being intentional with a daily devotion time helps you stay focused on Christ. If you do this He will bring you joy in the midst of confusion.

Prayer: Lord Jesus, welcome us into Your presence each morning so we might see Your face and bask in Your love all day long. Amen

Tuesday: Love by the Holy Spirit

However, as it is written: "No eye has seen, no ear has heard, no mind has conceived what God has prepared for those who love him" – but God has revealed it to us by his Spirit.
1 Corinthians 2:9–10

There is a lovely elderly couple who have been active members of our congregation for as long as I can remember. James and Jean Flowers are both in their nineties and attend worship services regularly. They love the Lord immensely as exemplified by their smiling faces, genuine faith, and sincere service to others. James taught the senior adult Sunday school class for over 25 years and Jean mentored my daughter after she sponsored her during her confirmation class 20 years ago. This Christian couple is the epitome of how Christ shines in the lives of those who love and serve Him. I am confident the Holy Spirit lives and thrives within James and Jean because of their faithful love of Christ.

Today's passage from Paul's letter to the Corinthians reminds us we cannot conceive what God has in store for those who love Him but His Spirit will reveal it. Staying in love with the Lord is made so much easier when we invite the Holy Spirit into our lives so He might thrive within us. His Spirit guides our lives, helps us understand the Scriptures, reveals God's perfect plan for our lives, and comforts us in times of despair.

As you deal with Alzheimer's disease, the Holy Spirit tempers the struggles you face by guiding your daily activities, comforting you on foggy days, and reminding you to pray daily. God's Holy Spirit keeps you in love with Christ while softening the debilitating impacts of this dreadful disease. Invite Him into your life and you'll live much better!

Prayer: Heavenly Father, thank You for Your precious Holy Spirit who thrives in the lives of those who love the Lord. Amen

Wednesday: Anticipate Surprises

However, as it is written: "No eye has seen, nor ear has heard, no mind has conceived what God has prepared for those who love him." 1 Corinthians 2:9

My wife's birthday fell on Mother's day this year so my daughter, Katy, and I decided to surprise her. Katy secretly flew in from Florida and I picked her up at the airport. We devised an incredible scheme to surprise her on this special day. Since my wife and I usually walk in the park after work, we decided I should go straight to the park and walk with her just like normal. Katy would sneak down to the park and sit disguised on one of the park benches. She put on big sunglasses, pulled one of my ball caps down over her face, and opened a book as if reading it. We hoped my wife would walk right by without noticing her. The plan worked perfectly. My wife was so engrossed telling me about her day she walked right past Katy! After she passed Katy quietly said, "Mom" but my wife thought this strange lady was talking to someone else. Katy said much louder, "MOM" and my wife turned around, hugged her, and was completely surprised!

To nurture our love for Christ, we must be hopeful for the surprise moments Christ has prepared for those who love Him just like today's Scripture says. They often creep into our lives in the most marvelous ways like an unexpected visit, a beautiful sunset, a powerful prayer time, a special Scripture, an angelic encounter, or the whisper of the Holy Spirit.

Even with Alzheimer's disease, Christ continues to surprise me as I trust Him. Stay open to the precious surprises Christ has in store because He hasn't forgotten you and He still loves you dearly. Trust in Him and stand ready to be surprised!

Prayer: Lord and Savior, thank You for the surprises You bring into our lives simply to remind us of Your precious love for us. Amen

Thursday: Fix His Word on Your Heart and Mind

Fix these words of mine in your hearts and minds; tie them as symbols on your hands and bind them on your foreheads.
Deuteronomy 11:18

I have to make a confession about an unmanly characteristic I have developed. I love to read novels written by Nicholas Sparks. *Nights in Rodale, The Notebook, A Walk to Remember* and *The Lucky One* all paint a perfect picture of romance growing from the heartaches of living in an imperfect world. Sparks is a gifted writer and I am simply amazed at how he weaves each story around the day to day struggles we face. By reading his enchanting novels, the lasting love I have for my wife is enriched in a way I cannot fully explain.

The same is true for our love relationship with Christ. As we read the Bible, the Scriptures nurture and enrich the love we have for Him. As I struggle with the daily limitations brought on by Alzheimer's disease, I've found reading the Scriptures aloud reinforces the words in my mind and on my heart. As I read the words aloud, I can almost hear Christ speaking to me as if He is right beside me. It's like we are having a conversation but mine is the only audible voice. I know He is with me as He moves my spirit in sweet serenity by speaking the Scriptures. What a joy this brings to my heart.

By reading the Scriptures aloud the words become fixed in my mind and on my heart like today's passage from Deuteronomy instructs. Alzheimer's can certainly play havoc on your memory but the spoken word of God breaks through the grip it has on the brain. By reading His word aloud my love for Christ is strengthened and I'm assured He is with me. The same can be true for you if you will read the Scriptures aloud.

Prayer: Lord Jesus, thank You for the power of Your Holy Scripture enriching our lives and strengthening our love for You. Amen

Paul M. Hornback

Friday: Talking Together with Jesus

Now that same day two of them were going to a village called Emmaus, about seven miles from Jerusalem. They were talking with each other about everything that had happened. As they talked and discussed these things with each other, Jesus himself came up and walked along with them.... Luke 24: 13–15

Today's Scripture from the Gospel of Luke is a well-known passage often entitled "The Road to Emmaus." It is the theme passage for the Emmaus Walk. If you have been on an Emmaus Walk you will certainly remember this precious passage! If you haven't been on an Emmaus Walk, I implore you to find an Emmaus Community and go on an Emmaus Walk. It will deepen your spiritual relationship with the Lord.

After attending an Emmaus Walk you will be encouraged to participate in a Reunion Group. My group meets on Wednesday morning at 6:30 am. I have to admit, my daily struggles with Alzheimer's sometimes hamper my focus and conversations during the meeting but my Christian brothers lovingly accommodate my moments. This group keeps me accountable to my daily walk, prayer time, and Bible reading. We discuss our closest moments, where we acted as the His hands and feet, and where we failed Christ over the past week. It is often a humbling experience to share our failures but what a joy to share our closest moments.

Through this Emmaus Reunion Group, my love for Christ is renewed by sharing with other men. Although I struggle with Alzheimer's disease, I am spiritually encouraged every week by their testimonies, faithfulness, and failures. In fact, my love for Christ has deepened because of these men. I pray you can find a group in which you can share and grow close to Christ.

Prayer: Lord, thank You for strong, loving Christian brothers. Amen

Saturday: In Remembrance of Me

And he took bread, gave thanks and broke it, and gave it to them, saying, "This is my body given for you; do this in remembrance of me." Luke 22:19

On my daughter Katy's thirtieth birthday, my wife and I mailed her thirty unique gifts to open on her birthday. Since she lives in Jacksonville Florida, we could not be present with her on this special occasion. However, we were able to "Skype" with her using my wife's new Galaxy tablet and my daughter's laptop computer. If you aren't familiar with the technology of Skyping, it entails using computers to teleconference over the internet. In our case, my daughter could see and talk with us while we watched her open the thirty presents we sent her the week before her birthday. It was truly amazing to Skype with Katy as it made us feel like we were right there with her.

Being able to share memorable occasions together reinforces the love we feel for the members of our family. The same is true for our loving relationship with the Lord. The Lord's Supper, or Holy Communion, is a very memorable occasion in the spiritual life of any Christian. When we gather together to participate in Holy Communion, we remember the loving sacrifice Jesus made so we might experience true forgiveness. In Holy Communion we draw closer to Him by partaking of the communal elements. We do this in remembrance of Him as depicted in today's passage from Luke. The Passover Meal Jesus shared with His disciples was an occasion drawing them closer together. As we partake of Holy Communion our love of Christ is reinforced and even Alzheimer's disease cannot break the bond we share with Him!

Prayer: Lord and Savior, thank You for sharing the Last Supper with the disciples so we might remember Your love for us. Amen

Paul M. Hornback

Sunday: Be Still and Love the Lord

Be still, and know that I am God; I will be exalted among the nations, I will be exalted in the earth. The Lord Almighty is with us; the God of Jacob is our fortress. Psalms 46:10–11

This week our focus has been on nurturing our love for Christ and maintaining a close personal relationship with the Lord. Even though we struggle with Alzheimer's disease, we can still foster our love for Christ in simple ways like:

- Joyously seeking His face daily
- Allowing the Holy Spirit to thrive in us
- Anticipating the surprises Christ brings
- Fixing His word in our hearts and minds
- Talking with Christ every day
- Remembering His love by partaking of Communion.

Today's passage from Psalms reminds us to take time to be still before God, acknowledge Him, and exalt Him above everything else. Sounds pretty simple doesn't it? Yet we often fail to pause long enough to express our love and appreciation to God the Father, Christ the Son, and the Holy Spirit. If we truly love Christ, we'd have a deep desire to spend time with the Father, His Son, and the Holy Spirit in prayer.

No matter how much you've struggled this week with the limitations of Alzheimer's disease, pause for a few minutes and exalt our Father, give thanks to His Son, and invite the Holy Spirit into your life. The holy Trinity will never let you down, will encourage you through struggles, and will enable you to continue the fight in an honorable manner. Remember, God is our fortress from which we fight the foe of Alzheimer's. Be still and rest assured God is with you!

Prayer: Holy Trinity, encourage and enable us to fight the battles we face as we struggle with Alzheimer's disease. Amen

Daniel Prudek © 123RF.com

FIGHTING FEAR

Devotions to help you learn how to stifle the spirit of fear brought on by Alzheimer's disease.

Monday: A Righteous Man Will Have No Fear

Surely he will never be shaken; a righteous man will be remembered forever. He will have no fear of bad news; his heart is steadfast, trusting the Lord. His heart is secure, he will have no fear; in the end he will look in triumph on his foes. Psalm 112:6–8

Today's passage from Psalms talks about a righteous man who can never be shaken. He has no fear of bad news because his heart is strong, secure, and steadfast in the Lord. In the end, this man will look in triumph over his foes because he has no fear for his faith rests in the Lord. Does such a man or woman exist in the world today? What faith does he possess so there is no spirit of fear in his life?

This week I helped teach vacation Bible school. The theme was trusting God no matter what happens because with God all things are possible. A young child in my class shared she was always being picked on, bullied, and scoffed at during school. I told her it takes real courage to continue to go to school every day even when you have to endure the constant barrage of ridicule. Although this young girl was hurt, she was not shaken. In the end she will look in triumph over her foes!

It takes courage to face bad news, difficult times, and even sickness especially when the situation may never change. Perhaps you are staring Alzheimer's disease in the face and it's been a battleground in your life for quite a while. Today's passage reminds us a righteous man will never be shaken because his trust is in the Lord and not in earthly things. Keep a secure, strong, and steadfast heart. God has not forsaken you and He will help you through your difficult days!

Prayer: Lord, help us not to be shaken and to have no fear for our trust rests in You alone for You are our Lord and Savior. Amen

Tuesday: A Spirit of Power, Love, and Self-Discipline

For this reason I remind you to fan into flame the gift of God, which is in you through the laying on of my hands. For God has not given us a spirit of fear and timidity, but of power, love, and self-discipline. 2 Timothy 1:6–7

I can remember a competition my father and I participated in when I was a young Boy Scout. Twelve father and son teams were spread out underneath a three foot high cotton string and given one match. The first team to build a fire high enough to burn through the string won. Each team had to gather wood and kindling but the key to winning was to start the fire with small twigs and then fan the flames while the other guy sought out larger fuel. We lost the contest but the idea of starting a fire by fanning the flames stuck with me my entire life.

In Paul's second letter to Timothy, he reminds him to fan into flame God's gift of power, love and self-discipline. Paul knew Timothy struggled with a lack of confidence bordering on fear. Paul reminded Timothy God did not give him a spirit of fear and timidity but one of power, love, and self-discipline. Perhaps you struggle with a spirit of fear knowing you or a loved one has been dealing with the demon of Alzheimer's disease. Fear not, for the Lord has empowered you with a spirit of power, love, and self-discipline thereby enabling you to persevere through your struggles. Just remember you will not fight the battle alone, the Lord will not forsake you, and His angels will watch over you no matter what!

Am I afraid of what I may face? Not as long as I trust in the God who loved me and sent His only Son to die for me! Fan the flames of faith and you will push fear far away from you.

Prayer: Father, empower each of us with a spirit of power, love, and self-discipline so we may face our daily struggles courageously. Amen

Wednesday: No Slave to Fear

For you did not receive a spirit that makes you a slave again to fear, but you received the Spirit of sonship. And by him we cry, "Abba, Father." The Spirit himself testifies with our spirit that we are God's children. Romans 8:15–16

Two of my prize guineas share a chicken coop with my ten laying hens. Recently, these rascal guineas started eating the chicken eggs. As a result, I've had to catch the guineas in the morning and put them outside the chicken pen to stop the on-going egg slaughter. Catching a guinea in the coop is quite an ordeal. After I caught one, the smallest hen in my flock started to attack me. She was fierce and no matter what I did she would not let up until I let the guinea go. For some reason, she had adopted the guineas when they were young and nothing was going to harm one of her adopted chicks!

Today's passage from Romans reminds us we are all children of God and we can cry, "Abba, Father" anytime we are afraid. Because we are sons and daughters of the living God, just like Christ, we no longer have to be a slave to fear. Perhaps you have been recently diagnosed with Alzheimer's disease or are already struggling in an early stage of this disease. Maybe you're afraid of what lies ahead as your memory fades. There is no need to be afraid because your adopted Father will watch out for you just like my little red hen did for the guineas.

I can testify our Father has made me fearless of the future, sent His angels to watch over me, and comforts me in ways simple words cannot express. As I continue to serve Him in some manner, He assures me all will be well and I have nothing to fear. So if you're afraid, simply cry out, "Abba, Father" and His peace will permeate your spirit. Don't be a slave to fear!

Prayer: Abba Father, keep us from being slaves to fear as we strengthen our faith by relying on You alone. Amen

Thursday: Godly Knowledge Defeats Fear

For this reason, since the day we heard about you, we have not stopped praying for you and asking God to fill you with the knowledge of his will through all spiritual wisdom and understanding. Colossians 1:9

The Apostle Paul penned a purposeful letter to the church in Colossae to describe the complete adequacy of Christ in stark contrast to the barren emptiness of philosophy. Today's passage reminds us God can fill us with the knowledge of His will through all spiritual wisdom and understanding. So what does knowledge about God's will have to do with squelching the spirit of fear in our lives? Fear exists because we lack knowledge and understanding of the situation we are facing.

After learning I might have early-onset Alzheimer's disease, I was afraid because I didn't know what was ahead. Rather than struggle with worrisome fear, I read all I could about the symptoms, prognosis, and stages of the disease. Although I wasn't happy, I was no longer afraid of being diagnosed with the disease. Of course, it wasn't the best day of my life when my neurologist told me I had Alzheimer's disease but at least I knew what to expect.

In spite of my diagnosis, I knew God was going to continue His perfect will for me even though I had this terrible disease. I could still live a life worthy of His calling, continue to bear fruit, and press on toward the goal of glorifying His name. What do I need to fear if God is planning on using me in spite of my illness? Absolutely nothing because He will be with me! So trust God and allow Him to fill you with the knowledge of His love and abolish your fears.

Prayer: Gracious Lord, give us the strength and wisdom to continue to serve You in spite of our infirmities. Amen

Friday: Fear Not, I Have Summoned You by Name

But now, this is what the Lord says – he who created you, O Jacob, he who formed you, O Israel: "fear not, for I have redeemed you; I have summoned you by name; you are mine. When you pass through the waters, I will be with you; and when you pass through the rivers, they will not sweep over you. When you walk through the fire, you will not be burned; the flames will not set you ablaze.
Isaiah 43:1–2

I love to work outside in the yard and flowers. Unfortunately, since I battle Alzheimer's disease, I tire out pretty easily especially when it is hot and humid. When I get tired I usually go inside and rest. I've noticed I tire more easily and fear overwhelms me as I wonder how long I can continue to work. I've always enjoyed hard manual labor since it gives me a feeling of manly accomplishment. Therefore, when I can no longer work, I'm afraid I won't be much of a man anymore.

Today's Scripture reminds me I need not be afraid because the Lord has summoned me by name and I am His! Isaiah said even if I pass through the river or walk through the fire I will not be overcome because He is with me. I certainly won't be walking through fire or passing through rivers anymore but I will be working in the heat and humidity of the day. As such, the Lord will be with me and not allow me to be overcome by the conditions I face. He has summoned me and I will always be able to work in some manner until He calls me home.

What do I need to fear? Absolutely nothing! He is always with me and He is surely with you. Alzheimer's disease pales in comparison to drowning or being burned by fire. Since He overcame these extremes, He can overcome the impacts of Alzheimer's disease as well!

Prayer: Lord of Israel, protect us from the extremes and squelch our fears of the future as You are with us always. Amen

Saturday: Demolishing the Stronghold of Fear

For though we live in the world, we do not wage war as the world does. The weapons we fight with are not the weapons of the world. On the contrary, they have divine power to demolish strongholds. 2 Corinthians 10:3–4

Marine second lieutenants are trained as infantry officers prior to learning their particular field of specialization. During initial infantry training, officers are required to learn and become proficient in rifle platoon tactical maneuvers. One particularly difficult exercise is attacking a reinforced enemy machine gun emplacement. It is impossible to defeat this type of stronghold head on. You must split your forces and flank the position while still maintaining frontal cover fire. Using only a frontal assault will certainly result in failure and loss of life.

In today's passage, Paul says in order to defeat strongholds in our lives we must rely on divine power instead of worldly weapons. Using only worldly weapons would be like attacking a machine gun emplacement head on. The fear of what might happen in the future when diagnosed with Alzheimer's disease is a significant stronghold in the life of one facing this disease. In order to defeat this fear, it is absolutely essential to employ divine power and all the spiritual weapons you can muster.

For me, daily prayer, Bible reading, encouragement from the Holy Spirit, and good Christian counsel all work together to flank the stronghold of fear and defeat it when it flares up! Do I still have skirmishes with fear from time to time? The simple answer is yes. But by engaging divine power and employing spiritual weapons, it no longer has a stronghold in my life. Try using divine power and you can demolish fear's stronghold as well!

Prayer: Lord, help us to use divine power in our daily fight. Amen

Sunday: Be Still and Cast Your Fear Away

Be still, and know that I am God; I will be exalted among the nations, I will be exalted in the earth. The Lord Almighty is with us; the God of Jacob is our fortress. Psalms 46:10–11

There is something special about Sundays separating it from the rest of the week. Perhaps it is the expectation of enjoying a wonderful day of worship, praise, and fellowship with my brothers and sisters in Christ. Since we have focused on squelching the spirit of fear during this week's devotions, it is important to note how fear doesn't seem to raise its ugly head on Sunday. I'm just guessing but I believe Satan doesn't have a prayer of penetrating our Sunday service if we worship the Lord wholeheartedly.

The interesting twist to this theory is why can't we have this spiritual sense of worship every day of the week? If we could do this, fear would never develop a stronghold in our lives! By being still before the Lord, our fears, anxieties, and worries are washed away like dust on a sidewalk during a summer rain.

Take time today to be still before the Lord. Praise Him for the many joys and blessings in your life. Lay your worries, fears, and anxieties at His throne. Take His yoke upon you for He is gentle and humble in heart and you will surely find rest for your weary and fearsome soul. Remember, His strength is far greater than yours alone. Allow the Lord Almighty to take your fears upon Him so you might trust and serve Him with all your heart, soul, mind and strength!

Prayer: Lord Almighty, Your yoke is easy so allow us to cast our fears, worries, and anxieties at Your throne so we might take Your yoke upon us. Help us not give in to the spirit of fear but instead rely on the spirit of faith You have so generously given us. Amen

Scott Prokop © 123RF.com

HIS CALMING WORD

Devotions to help you discover how calming the Scriptures can be for your daily battle with Alzheimer's disease.

Monday: Trapped in the Fowler's Snare

Surely he will save you from the fowler's snare and from the deadly pestilence. Psalm 91:3

Today a young female cardinal got trapped in my chicken pen. She frantically flew around to avoid getting pecked by my flock of chickens. However, she kept flying into the wire mesh and finally got trapped between one of the corner posts and the wire mesh. Her head was sticking through the wire mesh and her body was trapped against the wooden corner post. The chickens were nipping at her tail feathers while the dogs were snapping at her head. Needless to say the poor cardinal was terrified. She was stuck and surrounded by things that would certainly do her harm.

Perhaps that is how you feel right now as you struggle with a diagnosis of Alzheimer's and the daily demands of living with the disease. Feeling trapped is probably a pretty good analogy for living with Alzheimer's. But, as Paul Harvey would say, here's the rest of the story. The young cardinal was at her wit's end. Hearing the commotion, I ran to the chicken coop and saw the cardinal catastrophe. I went inside the coop and after she calmed down, gently pulled on her body and with my finger pushed her head back through the wire mesh. I got her out and held her in my hand as her heart throbbed rapidly. I gently laid her down so she could fly away.

God is just like this when you feel trapped. If you can calm down and yield to His gentle hand, you will be saved from the fowler's snare. If Alzheimer's is getting you down and making you fearful, trust in the Lord and He will surely rescue you.

Prayer: Lord of heaven and earth, save us from the debilitating effects of Alzheimer's disease so we might serve You more. Amen

Tuesday: Calm the Storm

They cried out to the Lord in their trouble, and he brought them out of their distress. He stilled the storm to a whisper; the waves of the sea were hushed. They were glad when it grew calm, and he guided them to their desired haven. Psalm 107:28–30

I spent many days at sea in my six short years as a pilot in the Marine Corps. The majority of the days were fairly smooth with calm seas. However, there were some harsh winter days in the North Atlantic with high seas and extremely rough weather. Flying during those conditions was strenuous but landing on a ship during rough weather and high seas was not only strenuous but dangerous. The key to weathering the storm was to remain calm especially when landing. Panicking, putting a death grip on the controls, ignoring your co-pilot, and becoming over-anxious because of the rough conditions usually resulted in a hard, unsafe landing. However, remaining calm, remembering the training, relying on the co-pilot's assistance, and maintaining a firm but relaxed grip on the controls generally resulted in a safe, gentle landing.

The same is true in life when we encounter storms in our lives. Alzheimer's disease is indeed a terribly rough storm to survive. If we can remain calm, remember our spiritual training, and rely on our Lord, then we will weather the storm and be guided to safe harbor. The Psalmist knew God could quiet the storm and waves so they could find safe haven. This is exactly what the Lord has done for me. He has quieted the storm of Alzheimer's so I can remain functional, safe, joyful, fulfilled, and of service to Him. He can do the same for you if you will only call on His name.

Prayer: Lord, calm the Alzheimer's storm in our lives and quiet the waves of confusion tossing us about. Amen

Wednesday: From Storm to Calm

The disciples went and woke him, saying, "Master, Master, we're going to drown!" He got up and rebuked the wind and the raging waters; the storm subsided, and all was calm. "Where is your faith?" he asked his disciples. In fear and amazement they asked one another, "Who is this? He commands even the winds and water, and they obey him." Luke 8:24–25

If you've ever been caught outdoors in a sudden violent flash flood, you can identify with how the disciples felt as their boat was about to be swamped. I'm sure some of the disciples were good swimmers since they were fishermen. Nonetheless, a squall generally implies violent weather where even a good swimmer has trouble staying afloat and out of danger.

Life has a tendency to stir up violent storms in our lives. When this happens we often cry out in fear and agonize about what the future holds. Alzheimer's disease is like being on a lake with little hope of making it to the other side. The disease will flare up from time to time like a violent storm. Confusion sets in, disorientation defines your day, and communication often becomes difficult

During these foggy days, I try to stay at home and maintain my daily routine. I also read Scripture reminding me of how the Lord calmed the sea, rebuked the wind, and caused the storms to subside by simply speaking. Reading these wonderful words calms my spirit and energizes my faith. I realize He is with me and will safely watch over me no matter what storm comes my way. If He can settle the waves, stop the wind, and cause the storm to subside, He can surely handle something like Alzheimer's in my brain. Trust in Him today and He will calm your storms and fears.

Lord of Peace, calm the storms flaring up inside of us as we fight the daily battles which Alzheimer's brings into our lives. Amen

Thursday: His Word Is Flawless

As for God, his way is perfect; the word of the Lord is flawless. He is a shield for all who take refuge in him. For who is God besides the Lord? And who is the Rock except our God? It is God who arms me with strength and makes my way perfect. Psalm 18:30–32

Anyone struggling with the impacts of Alzheimer's disease understands how easily fear and anxiety can overtake the foggy days littering the landscape of your life. To temper the fear and anxiousness accompanying these particular days I slow my pace down, stay at home, relax outside, talk with the Lord, and read Psalms. There is something wonderful about the calming affect the Psalms have on an anxious spirit. Perhaps this is why the Psalms were written so we might enjoy comfort during difficult and trying times.

Today's passage reminds us God's word is flawless and His way is perfect. Because of these two triumphant truths, I know His promises prevail, He makes my path perfect, He shields me from all harm, and His strength is sufficient for all I face in life. Alzheimer's is by no means an easy foe to subdue; however, my God, my rock and my fortress will protect me from all Alzheimer's hurls my way. Will I be different because of the disease? Perhaps my outward actions will be but my inward spirit belongs to the Lord and He will make sure it never changes! So what do I have to fear from this disease? Absolutely nothing for God is my shield and Alzheimer's will have to yield to His awesome power.

The Psalms are comforting, His promises are perfect, and His Holy Spirit will help you during your difficult days. Remember, His word is flawless and life is much better with His help!

Prayer: Rock of Ages, calm our spirits and shield us daily. Amen

Paul M. Hornback

Friday: Righteousness Brings Peace and Security

The fruit of righteousness will be peace; the effect of righteousness will be quietness and confidence forever. My people will live in peaceful dwelling places, in secure homes, in undisturbed places of rest. Isaiah 32:17–18

I ran across today's passage from Isaiah and thought it was from King David's Psalms. I had to take a double look at the top of the page of my Bible to make sure I was in fact reading from Isaiah. This passage provided such a profound promise I paused and read it over a couple of times. What a blessing it is to truly know the Lord Almighty promises if we live our lives for Him in a righteous manner, we will find peace, quietness, and confidence forever.

Wow, what a perfect promise for someone struggling with Alzheimer's disease! Love the Lord with all your heart, soul, mind, and strength; live a righteous life; honor God; and serve Him and your reward will be peace, quietness, and confidence God is with you. Therefore, as long as I stay focused on righteousness, my life will be filled with peace, security and confidence. However, when I lose my daily connection with the Lord, fear and anxiety will begin to find a foothold in my life.

Today's incredible passage from Isaiah holds tremendous hope for anyone suffering from Alzheimer's disease. Does it mean we won't suffer the effects of the disease? No, but it does promise we can live in peaceful dwelling places, secure homes, and undisturbed places of rest. I'm holding on to His perfect promise! How about you?

Prayer: Lord of Peace, please reign in our hearts so we might live righteously and thereby find peace, safety, quietness, confidence, and undisturbed rest in Your loving care all the days of our lives no matter what Alzheimer's may do to our brains. Amen

Saturday: God's Living and Active Word

For the word of God is living and active. Sharper than any double-edged sword, it penetrates even to dividing soul and spirit, joints and marrow; it judges the thoughts and attitudes of the heart. Nothing in all creation is hidden from God's sight. Everything is uncovered and laid bare before the eyes of him to whom we must give account. Hebrews 4:12–13

I love today's passage from Hebrews because it reminds me God's word is living and active. I'm taking some liberty with this passage as I step off into deep water for those dealing with the daily struggles of Alzheimer's disease. We all have foggy days when we are confused, slow to speak, not thinking clearly, or having difficulty making conversation. On these days, I try to spend time reading the Bible. I generally have to read it aloud and often have to read the passage over a couple of times. But when I make a conscious effort to read God's holy word I find the fogginess, confusion, and dullness of spirit begin to lift from within my brain.

I believe the "living and active" word of God is piercing the tangles of my Alzheimer's stricken brain. This is something akin to microscopic brain surgery by the Great Physician. I am convinced as long as I continue to read His word, live my life for Him, and praise Him for His great works, then my struggles with Alzheimer's disease will be tempered by His healing touch.

Today's passage assures me His word is more powerful than anything I can take. Do I still take medication? Absolutely! I believe He has made these drugs available to me. They all work for my good but are made more effective because of His "living and active" word. Therefore, I urge you to read from His word today and you will find peace!

Prayer: Lord, thank You for Your living and active word. Amen

Paul M. Hornback

Sunday: Be Still and Find Peace

Be still, and know that I am God; I will be exalted among the nations, I will be exalted in the earth. The Lord Almighty is with us; the God of Jacob is our fortress. Psalms 46:10–11

This morning was remarkably peaceful here at our homestead. During my morning walk in the gardens, I spied a yellow swallowtail butterfly that appeared out of nowhere and meandered to the butterfly bush outside my kitchen window. This butterfly didn't have a care in the world as it gently moved from one blue flower to another. It made me consider how peaceful and calm my life could stay if I continually placed my worries, fears, and anxieties at the feet of our Lord's mighty throne.

This week we have concentrated on learning ways to stay calm and peaceful while focusing on God's holy word. There is an amazing connection between the word of God and a calm and peaceful spirit. Now it is time to be still before God and realize He truly is the Lord Almighty. It is in the quiet moments of the morning, as I stroll through the gardens and breathe in the majesty of the day, I realize how precious my relationship is with Him.

The quiet mornings remind me of how Adam must have strolled along communing with God without a care in the world. How absolutely incredible it must have been! Perhaps it was similar to the yellow swallowtail butterfly I had the privilege of watching this morning as it flitted around the butterfly bush's blossoms.

I hope you take time this morning to be still before the Lord. Talk with Him about your troubles and allow His peace to fill your heart as you trust in Him. You won't be disappointed!

Prayer: Precious Savior, help us to be still before You each morning so we might fill our lives with Your peace and confidence. Amen

Dmitry Rukhlenko © 123RF.com

DEALING WITH SIN

Devotions to help you seek new ways to overcome sin in your life as you struggle with Alzheimer's disease.

Paul M. Hornback

Monday: Cleanse Us from Sin

...let us draw near to God with a sincere heart in full assurance
of faith, having our hearts sprinkled to cleanse us from a guilty
conscience and having our bodies washed with pure water.
Hebrews 10:22

If you have ever spent an extended amount of time in the desert, you understand how precious water is in this environment. It is an absolutely wonderful thing when you can take a shower in the desert. The dirt, grime, and sweat accumulate on your body in this parched environment making you feel filthy all the time. A refreshing shower cleanses your body and rejuvenates your spirit.

Perhaps the writer of Hebrews understood this concept as he wrote today's passage. Of course, he isn't concerned with washing the filth off of our bodies. He uses this analogy to demonstrate how filthy our souls become when covered with sin and how the blood of the new covenant cleanses us. Sin accumulates just like dirt, grime, and sweat accumulate on our bodies. As sin builds up, our spirits become downtrodden and we are pulled further away from Christ. To become clean again we must confess our sins and ask forgiveness. The act of confession draws us nearer to God and He cleanses our souls just like taking a shower with soap and clean water.

I have noticed one interesting thing about having Alzheimer's; I don't struggle with sin. Don't get me wrong, I still sin but not nearly as much. Maybe I'm more focused on Christ which enables me to keep sin at bay. It is a spiritual benefit from the disease for which I am amazingly thankful!

Prayer: Sweet Savior, cleanse us from the filthy sin in our lives as we desperately need help keeping Satan at bay so we might avoid the sinful desires he deliberately sends our way. Amen

Tuesday: Acknowledge the Sin in Your Life

*But among you there must not be even a hint of sexual
immorality, or of any kind of impurity, or of greed, because these are
improper for God's holy people. Nor should there be obscenity,
foolish talk or coarse joking, which are out of place, but rather
thanksgiving. Ephesians 5:3–4*

My wife and I live in a white vinyl-sided house on a small hill
in the middle of a 240 acre farm. Over time, the white siding gets
covered with a layer of grime which builds up from dust thrown in
the air while mowing the lawn, baling hay, and tending farm crops.
From a distance, our house still appears white since the annual
collection of filth is barely noticeable. However, up close, the dingy
layer of dirt is quite visible. Unfortunately, I become accustomed to
the gradual build-up of grime and don't even notice it.

This morning I decided to clean part of the siding since the
weather was nice. I cleaned for an hour before exhaustion set in. I
was surprised the difference the hour of hard work made as I
compared the washed and unwashed siding. It started me thinking
how sin can gradually build up in our lives and we don't even notice
it. Today's passage from Ephesians reminds us sin easily
accumulates on our Christian character. We must first recognize the
sin in our lives before we can deal with it.

Since I was diagnosed with early-onset Alzheimer's, I've
noticed many of Paul's listed items griming up my image. Perhaps
they've become apparent since I've had more time to read the Bible,
reflect on it, and talk with God. As part of God's holy people, we
must examine our lives, acknowledge our sins, and allow God to
cleanse us. Then we can be bright shining houses on a hill reflecting
the image of Christ!

*Prayer: Precious Lord, clean our sins away so we might shine
brightly for You. Amen*

Wednesday: Repent and Live

Therefore, O house of Israel, I will judge you, each one according to his ways, declares the Sovereign Lord. Repent! Turn away from all your offenses; then sin will not be your downfall. Rid yourselves of all the offenses you have committed, and get a new heart and a new spirit. Why will you die, O house of Israel? For I take no pleasure in the death of anyone, declares the Sovereign Lord. Repent and live! Ezekiel 18:30–32

In our young adult Sunday school class we discussed sin one morning. We could collectively remember the sins from the Ten Commandments and were pretty sure we were doing well on most of them. However, the study we were using led us into the "gray sins" which we listed on the dry erase board. We listed things like stirring up stuff, talking trash about others, telling white lies, ignoring the needy, not living up to our full potential, and being two-faced. Our list of thirty "gray sins" remained on the board for a month and members of the church were both intrigued and convicted by the list.

As I read today's passage from Ezekiel, I understood why God was disappointed with the House of Israel. Perhaps they were doing somewhat okay on most of the Ten Commandments but their hearts were not as pure as God had hoped. Apparently, the gray sins had surfaced in horrendous ways.

Since I've retired because of Alzheimer's disease, I've had lots of time to reflect on my life. I suppose I'm as guilty as anyone, to include the House of Israel, of not having my heart right with God. I've engaged in many of the gray sins. All I can do is repent, forget the past, and press on to live a life pleasing to Him. I hope you can reflect, repent, and live a worthy life because Alzheimer's doesn't give us a free pass!

Prayer: Sovereign Lord, help us to repent so we might live. Amen

Thursday: Encourage Others in Their Faith

We sent Timothy, who is our brother and God's fellow worker in spreading the gospel of Christ, to strengthen and encourage you in your faith, so that no one would be unsettled by these trials. You know quite well that we were destined for them.
1 Thessalonians 3:2–3

The other morning as I was finishing my two mile walk, I heard the happy honking of a gaggle of geese as they flew from a nearby field. As I listened, I remembered someone telling me geese honk to encourage the lead bird as it has the difficult job of breaking the wind for the "V" formation. It made me wonder why we often fail to encourage our fellow Christians as they break through the wind of sin engulfing their lives. What a blessing it is to receive the encouragement of loving Christians as you push through the greediness, gossiping, lustfulness, slothfulness, false witness, foul language, coarse joking, womanizing, and drunkenness we find littering the landscape of our lives. Unfortunately, we are prone to point out the sinful acts we see rather than encourage the change in behavior brought on by repentance.

Today's Scripture reminds us how Paul sent his trusted friend and fellow worker, Timothy, to the Ephesians to strengthen and encourage them as they endured all types of tempting trials. Perhaps Timothy was the lead layman in a gaggle of laity with the primary purpose of breaking through the wind of dissention and discouragement for the church at Ephesus. Anyone can be an encourager, even someone with Alzheimer's disease. When I can, I write encouraging notes to fellow Christians who are having a particularly rough time. I encourage you to use your gifts to encourage others because the gaggle of Christ could use some positive honking today!

Prayer: Lord, help us to encourage someone struggling in sin. Amen

Friday: Throw Off Sin

Therefore, since we are surrounded by such a great cloud of witnesses, let us throw off everything that hinders and the sin that so easily entangles, and let us run with perseverance the race marked out for us. Hebrews 12:1

We built our home on top of a hill so we could have a walk-out basement. The basement opens onto a patio leading to my raised-bed gardens and chicken coop. In the morning, I walk out the basement door to feed the chickens and run right into a huge spider web. No matter how often I remove the web, the next morning it reappears. Yesterday morning I fed the chickens later than usual and to my surprise I found the notorious spider on her web. I gently wrapped the web around her and moved the huge garden spider to another location. This morning there was no web for me to walk into as I exited the patio door. Hallelujah!

Today's Scripture from Hebrews reminds us to throw off everything that hinders and the sin that entangles our lives. To do this we must take deliberate action to throw off sin. Sometimes our actions work and other times they don't. Like the spider's web, there is a solution if we keep on trying. Just because we have Alzheimer's disease we can't expect a pass on the sin issue. In fact, it may even be harder as we struggle with foggy days, confusion, and uncertainty.

Perhaps you become more easily frustrated and lash out at others because they don't understand your situation. When this happens I ask the Holy Spirit to help me by allowing the "Fruit of the Spirit" to flow through me to put sin at bay. It is a small step I take to throw off the sin that so easily entangles. Try asking the Holy Spirit for help as you struggle with sin in your life.

Prayer: Father, help us throw off the sin entangling us. Amen

Saturday: Defender of Those Who Sin

My dear children, I write this to you so that you will not sin. But if anybody does sin, we have one who speaks to the Father in our defense – Jesus Christ, the Righteous One. He is the atoning sacrifice for our sins, and not only ours but also for the sins of the whole world. 1 John 2:1–2

I love to watch movies about the law. One of my favorites is "A Few Good Men" since it deals with a legal issue in the Marine Corps. This movie centers around two young Marines accused of murdering a "slacker" Marine. Tom Cruise stars as their Navy JAG Corps attorney whose modus operandi has been plea bargaining cases to avoid court. Through the course of the movie, Tom Cruise realizes how important honor and duty are to his defendants. He discovers there are issues worth trying in the military court system for the sake of justice.

Today's passage reminds us we have someone who speaks in our defense, understands our sinful case, and is willing to plead our case before our heavenly Father. I believe this applies to our sins as well as the difficult situations we face in life. Since I struggle with Alzheimer's disease, I believe Jesus is pleading my case before the Father. I know I sin like any normal human but also because my brain isn't working exactly right.

Jesus is ready to speak on our behalf since He understands our situation. He pleads for our forgiveness, healing, protection, and wellbeing but ultimately understands His Father's purpose and obeys Him above all else. As you struggle with sin and the issues of living with Alzheimer's disease, remember you have an advocate with the Father who personally pleads your case. Don't be afraid to ask for help. He loves you unconditionally and you have a right to Christ's counsel as a child of God!

Prayer: Righteous One, plead our case as we need Your help. Amen

Sunday: Be Still and Deal with Sin

Be still, and know that I am God; I will be exalted among the nations, I will be exalted in the earth. The Lord Almighty is with us; the God of Jacob is our fortress. Psalms 46:10–11

This morning I sat on the patio outside our family room. I often drink coffee there in the morning so I can see the flower gardens and the recently added small stream flowing to our fish pond. Yesterday we rearranged the end of the stream and created a small waterfall that cascades into the fish pond. This morning I could hear the water gently trickling down the rock lined stream before it fell into the pond.

It is amazing the sounds you hear when you are quietly still for a few moments. Perhaps the Psalmist understood how important stillness is as we come before the Lord. In the stillness we can confess our sins, ask forgiveness, and repent knowing God hears our petition and gently replies, "You are forgiven so go and sin no more." During these quiet moments I know He is with me, He cares for me, and He will never forsake me. The stillness reassures me His perfect peace, which surpasses all understanding, will remain with me as long as I take time to tarry with Him.

As I struggle with Alzheimer's disease, I find the quiet moments are important to my emotional health. Being still before the Lord reminds me He has a plan for my life. Living with Alzheimer's while under His care works to the good of His plan for my life. It is only through the stillness He can calm my soul and assure me His strength is sufficient. Be still before the Lord, talk with Him, repent of your sins, and He will give you the peace that surpasses all understanding!

Prayer: Lord, forgive us of our sins as we are still before You. Amen

Dean Fikar © 123RF.com

PLEASING GOD

Devotions to help you find ways to please God as you continue
to battle Alzheimer's disease.

Monday: Pleasing God through Faithfulness

By faith Enoch was taken from this life, so that he did not experience death; he could not be found, because God had taken him away, he was commended as one who pleased God. And without faith it is impossible to please God, because anyone who comes to him must believe that he exists and that he rewards those who earnestly seek him. Hebrews 11:5–6

One of the things I remember most about my father was he was an avid reader. He loved the condensed versions of books from the Readers Digest Book Club. He favored the condensed versions of books because it allowed him to get the pertinent information without having to read all the fluff.

I love the faith chapter of Hebrews because it provides the "Readers Digest" condensed version of the faithful fathers of our faith without all the fluff. Now before you burn me at the stake for heresy, let me say I have read the entire Bible! I just love this chapter of Hebrews because it summarizes how the forefathers of our faith did great things for God. Today's passage points out how critical faith is to our heavenly Father and without faith it is impossible to please Him. Keep in mind none of the fathers of our faith had an especially easy life. Many of them failed to see the full fruit of their faith yet they remained steadfast in their dedication to God.

As you struggle with Alzheimer's disease, I urge you to remain steadfast in your faith. God has not forgotten you during this tedious time of testing. He runs right alongside as He coaches you in your race of perseverance. All you need do is fix your eyes on Jesus, maintain your faith, and don't lose heart. Remember, by being faithful you please God greatly!

Prayer: Lord, may we always please You by being faithful. Amen

Tuesday: Ask What You Can Do for God

Will the Lord be pleased with thousands of rams, with ten thousand rivers of oil? Shall I offer my firstborn for my transgression, the fruit of my body for the sin of my soul? He has showed you, O man, what is good. And what does the Lord require of you? To act justly and to love mercy and to walk humbly with your God. Micah 6:7–8

One of my favorite quotations from President John Kennedy is, "Ask not what your country can do for you, ask what you can do for your country." I suppose it stems from the fact my father loved this quotation as well. He would often come home from instructing at the U.S. Army Intelligence School at Fort Hollabird and ask me what I had done for God and country today. If I didn't answer readily, he would laugh and say President Kennedy would not be very pleased with my patriotism.

Today's Scripture from Micah reminds us God also has daily demands for each of us. Our actions of justice, mercy, and humbleness are far more pleasing to Him than the offerings we lay at His feet. I often have to remind myself of the tenets of today's passage during the foggy days brought on Alzheimer's disease. On these days, I pay particular attention to walking humbly and acting mercifully to those I encounter. Otherwise, I have a tendency to become irritable and inconsiderate which is not pleasing to God.

It takes considerable effort but I find it is easier if I read the Bible, pray aloud, and write about my feelings. As I make a conscious effort to do these things, God pierces my fogginess and uses me in some small way. Try to act justly, love mercy, and walk humbly so you do something for God today that pleases Him!

Prayer: Lord, help us do something that pleases You today. Amen

Wednesday: Pray for Those in Authority

I urge, then, first of all, that requests, prayers, intercession and thanksgiving be made for everyone – for kings and all those in authority, that we may live peaceful and quiet lives in all godliness and holiness. This is good and pleases God our Savior, who wants all men to be saved and to come to a knowledge of the truth.
1 Timothy 2:1–4

One of my favorite pictures of the American Revolution is "The Prayer at Valley Forge" painted by Arnold Friberg. This painting depicts General Washington kneeling in prayer beside his horse in a snowy field at Valley Forge in the winter of 1777-78. It was a harsh winter and a difficult campaign for the Americans. There's no doubt General Washington spent many hours praying about the fate of the nation. He was a devout man who had a deep and humble dependence on the "all wise and powerful being" on whom the fledging nation depended.

I am humbled by the faith of General Washington as he kneels in prayer. I'm reminded how significant it was for him to pray for the nation, troops, and leaders. Today's passage reinforces we should all pray and lift up thanks for our nation's leaders and those in authority. The Apostle Paul provides these instructions so all men might live peaceful and quiet lives in godliness and holiness.

I often pray for our nation's leaders but I also pray for my wife, who has the burden of caring for me, keeping me safe, ordering my medicine, driving me to the doctors, and checking up on me while she's at work. She has authority over all my affairs as I struggle with Alzheimer's. I believe the prayers for her, and others in authority, are helpful and pleasing to God. I hope you will pray for those in authority as well.

Prayer: Father, give our nation's leaders wisdom and knowledge to handle the difficult decisions they must make every day. Amen

Thursday: Live to Please God

Finally, brothers, we instructed you how to live in order to please God, as in fact you are living. Now we ask you and urge you in the Lord Jesus to do this more and more. For you know what instructions we gave you by the authority of the Lord Jesus.
1 Thessalonians 4:1–2

After being diagnosed with early-onset Alzheimer's disease, I tried to continue my work as an analyst with the Department of the Army. Unfortunately, my brain was no longer working like before so my analytical abilities were severely impacted and my work suffered. The command I worked for didn't want me to retire because they felt they could use my well established analytical record and good name to possibly push through shoddy work. After screwing up some assignments, I knew in my heart I could not allow my exemplary record to become tarnished so I retired early.

I wonder how often our good Christian names are tarnished because of the way we live our lives. Today's Scripture reminds us to live our lives in a manner pleasing to God. The Apostle Paul desired the Thessalonians to live holy lives free from sexual impurity. He wanted his brothers to lead quiet lives, mind their own business, and work with their hands to ensure their daily lives would win the respect of others. Living under these holy guidelines is certainly pleasing to God.

As I struggle with Alzheimer's, I continue to work with my hands in service to others, live a peaceful life, mind my own business, spend time with the Lord, and avoid unrighteous activities. In fact, Alzheimer's has enabled me to slow down; spend more time in prayer, reading, and study; and live more simply. I pray my life is pleasing to God. How about you?

Father: Help us live our lives in ways pleasing to You. Keep us holy, quiet, humble and willing to serve others. Amen

Friday: Love and Obedience Pleases God

For you were once darkness, but now you are light in the Lord. Live as children of light (for the fruit of the light consists in all goodness, righteousness and truth) and find out what pleases the Lord. Have nothing to do with the fruitless deeds of darkness, but rather expose them. Ephesians 5:8–10

Growing up as the son of an Army staff non-commissioned officer was interesting to say the least. My father survived two wars; served as a drill instructor; served in the Infantry, Armor, and Intelligence branches; spoke Russian; and did numerous tours overseas in his 22 year career. He was a gentle man with a strong sense of honor and commitment to our nation. I loved and respected him greatly and always tried to please him. I excelled at school, sports, and debate because it brought him great joy when I'd bring home various accolades of achievement. I especially worked hard to please my dad whenever we worked together in the immaculate yard he maintained on our family farm.

Today's passage urges us to find out what pleases the gracious Lord we serve. The fact is, what pleases God is pretty straight forward but accomplishing the task is far more difficult. As I reflect back on my life under my earthly father's tutelage, the things that pleased him most were my love for him and my obedience to his instructions. The same is true for our heavenly Father; He desires first our love followed closely by obedience to His instructions.

As you struggle with Alzheimer's disease, it's refreshing to know pleasing God only requires love and obedience. You don't have to build churches, erect statues, or build wealth to hand over to Him. Love and obedience are more than enough!

Prayer: Lord, let our love be evident as we obey You today. Amen

Saturday: Righteousness Pleases God

The Lord detests the sacrifice of the wicked, but the prayer of the upright pleases him. The Lord detests the way of the wicked, but he loves those who pursue righteousness. Proverbs 15:8–9

They say a picture is worth a thousand words but I think a few carefully chosen words can paint a pretty precise picture in the mind of a reader. Perhaps this is why I love Proverbs so much. Today's passage paints a picture of what is pleasing to the Lord and what is detestable in His sight. The pleasing part is simple: all we need do is remain righteous, upright, and prayerful. On the other hand, walk the way of the wicked and even your offerings, sacrificial giving, and acts of mercy will be detestable in His sight. That is a lot to digest in two biblical bites from Proverbs but sometimes the truth is difficult to swallow!

After being diagnosed with early-onset Alzheimer's disease, I have to admit I struggled with thoughts of going the way of the wicked. I rationalized this by thinking if I had lived a righteous life and was stricken with Alzheimer's disease, what good was my righteousness? The fact of the matter is no matter what my health, wealth, or status may be in life, God still desires me to live righteously. You see, past behavior does not necessarily guarantee future health and prosperity. God isn't concerned with our status but rather our character.

Remaining righteous in difficult and complicated conditions is especially pleasing to the Lord because it exemplifies the character of Christ in your life. Perhaps you have struggled with remaining righteous after your diagnosis of Alzheimer's. Stay the righteous course and you will definitely please God!

Prayer: Help us remain righteous in the midst of turmoil. Amen

Sunday: Be Still and Please Him

Be still, and know that I am God; I will be exalted among the nations, I will be exalted in the earth. The Lord Almighty is with us; the God of Jacob is our fortress. Psalms 46:10–11

This week we have focused on the concept of pleasing God. We explored Scripture depicting ways to please God. These included:

- Faithfulness
- Acting justly, loving mercy, and walking humbly
- Praying for those in authority
- Living according to His law
- Loving and obeying Him
- Living righteously.

The easiest way to bring God pleasure is found in today's passage. It is perhaps the prime reason God felt David was a man after His own heart. David spent time being still before God and exalting Him above all things. He did this even as a small boy watching over his father's sheep. He walked with God daily and sang joyfully before Him. He stood in awe of all God created and thanked Him for the beauty and wonder of His marvelous creation.

Because of my dealings with Alzheimer's disease, I have learned to slow down, spend time being still before the Lord, take in the majesty of each new day, and be truly thankful for God's glorious creation in which we live. It isn't at all hard to do. Take time today to be still before the Lord and exalt Him with your prayerful presence. Perhaps God will call you a man after His own heart!

Prayer: Lord, may we be still before You and may our actions on this earth please You today. Amen

Randy Hines © 123RF.com

FEATS OF FAITH

Paul M. Hornback

Monday: Leave the Game Better

...that we have put our hope in the living God, who is the Savior of all men, and especially of those who believe. Command and teach these things. Don't let anyone look down on you because you are young, but set an example for the believers in speech, in life, in love, in faith, and in purity. 1 Timothy 4:10–12

Deacon Jones, the infamous defensive tight end for the Los Angeles Rams football team from 1961-71 was known for his clean but hard hitting play which specialized in quarterback "sacks", a term he invented. He was inducted into the Pro Football Hall of Fame in the first year of his eligibility. Throughout his career he was a positive influence on young rookie football players. He encouraged them to "leave the game better than you found it." Wow, what a wonderful message for Christians today! We should all want to leave the game Christ called us to play much better than we found it.

In Paul's letter, he reminds us to set an example for other Christian believers in speech, life, love, faith, and purity. By placing our hope in God, remaining attached to Christ's vine, serving our Savior, and soaking in the Scriptures, we move toward perfection in all five areas Paul references in his letter. The example we set allows us to leave the game better than we found it and encourage the same in other Christians.

The interesting thing about Paul's instructions to Timothy is even though we struggle with Alzheimer's disease, we can still strive to perfect these areas of Christian growth. Deacon Jones strove to perfect the way he played his game. In so doing, he established a clean, hard hitting style of football none have surpassed. How will you leave God's game?

Prayer: Lord, may the lives we live be worthy of Your Heavenly Hall of Fame. Amen

Tuesday: Allow God to Do Amazing Things

Joshua told the people, "Consecrate yourselves, for tomorrow the Lord will do amazing things among you." Joshua 3:5

In June 2012, Spencer West climbed Mount Kilimanjaro in an effort to raise money and awareness for Free the Children's sustainable water initiative in Kenya, Africa. Spencer raised in excess of $500,000 when he scaled the summit. Although climbing Mount Kilimanjaro had been done by many people who are expert climbers, they all pale in comparison to Spencer West who had his legs amputated at age 5 because of a rare genetic spinal disorder called Sacral Agenesis. To scale the summit he walked, climbed, and moved using only his hands and arms. The fact he climbed Mount Kilimanjaro in this condition is in itself simply amazing; however, to do it with the intent of raising resources and attention to help others in need is mind boggling!

Today's passage reminds us if we consecrate ourselves before Almighty God, the Lord will do amazing things among us. This is a pretty tough nut to crack if you are struggling with Alzheimer's disease in your life because you are somewhat impaired. How can God use someone with this disease? There are countless ways God can use you even though you are struggling with Alzheimer's! The key is to ask God what He wants you to accomplish for His kingdom today.

Every morning I get up and wonder what act of service I can do today. It can be as simple as writing a note to someone having a rough time or as exhaustive as mowing the church lawn. One thing is for sure, it won't be climbing Mount Kilimanjaro using only my hands and arms! Consecrate yourself today and let Him do amazing things through you.

Prayer: Father, use us in some manner to better serve Your kingdom today. Amen

Paul M. Hornback

Wednesday: Persevere and Receive the Crown of Life

Blessed is the man who perseveres under trial, because when he has stood the test, he will receive the crown of life that God has promised to those who love him. James 1:12

Can you guess who has won more NCAA basketball games than any other coach? Maybe you think its Mike Krzyzewki (Duke), John Wooden (UCLA), Adolf Rupp (UK), or Jim Calhoun (UConn) but you would be wrong. It is the University of Tennessee's Pat Summit who coached the Lady Volunteers. This Hall of Famer ended her 39 year career with a 1,098–208 record, 16 SEC regular season championships, 16 SEC titles, and 8 NCAA crowns. If anyone mentions the Lady Volunteers one immediately thinks of Pat Summit. She is a legend in women's basketball and now serves as coach emeritus for the program she built at Tennessee. This amazing coach retired in 2012 at age 59 just 8 months after being diagnosed with early-onset Alzheimer's disease. She coached one last season before realizing the stress and strain of coaching was taking an additional toll on her health. Her iconic career, perseverance in the midst of strife, and can-do spirit made her a legend on and off the court.

Today's passage asserts if we persevere under trial, we will also receive a crown. It is the crown of life which is far more glorious and lasts longer than a NCAA crown. Perhaps you are wondering what you are persevering. Well nothing holds a candle to persevering through Alzheimer's disease. Each day brings a new twist to the game of living as another play has been defeated by the Alzheimer's defense. However, through perseverance and a loving Lord, you are able to adjust your offense so as not to be defeated. Stand firm, persevere, and receive a crown. You deserve it!

Prayer: Father, help us stand the test and play the game of life in such a manner as to receive Your crown. Amen

Thursday: Press On to What God Is Calling You to Do

Not that I have already obtained all this, or have already been made perfect, but I press on to take hold of that for which Christ Jesus took hold of me. Philippians 4:12

While living in Baltimore, I was a huge fan of the Baltimore Colts. I loved to watch them play on television but was never able to see a game in person. When the Colts franchise was moved to Indianapolis I was heartbroken. I did, however, remain a Colts fan. I especially enjoyed watching the team under the tutelage of Coach Tony Dungy. It wasn't until after his 2007 NFL Super Bowl Championship win did I understand what a powerful influence he was on the team and players. Tony Dungy was a strong and committed Christian who not only practiced his faith but lived it on and off the field. He has been quoted many times saying, "It's about the journey--mine and yours--and the lives we can touch, the legacy we can leave, and the world we can change for the better."

Today's passage from Paul's letter to the Philippians reminds us we are to press on to take hold of Christ's goal for us. Perhaps you are wondering how you can "press on" as you struggle with Alzheimer's disease. It is an excellent question that deserves some thought. First, don't press on using only your own power. You must rely on Christ's help to strengthen you. Second, don't press on toward a goal that hasn't been established by Christ. Therefore, continue inviting Christ into your daily struggles and ask Him what to do from this point forward. For me, it is to encourage others who are struggling with this awful disease. One thing is for sure, Christ has a goal in mind for you. If Christ can lead Tony Dungy to a Super Bowl win with a struggling franchise, then He can surely lead you to His goal for your life as well!

Prayer: Lord, help us press on toward Your goal for our life. Amen

Friday: Seek First His Kingdom

So do not worry, saying, "What shall we eat?" or "What shall we wear?" For the pagans run after all these things, and your heavenly Father knows that you need them. But seek first his kingdom and his righteousness, and all these things will be given to you as well. Matthew 6:31–33

Kurt Warner, quarterback of the St Louis Rams, led his team to an amazing Super Bowl victory in 1999 and astonishingly piloted the Arizona Cardinals to their first ever Super Bowl appearance in 2008. Kurt's "rags to riches" tale is both heartwarming and inspirational because he wasn't a first round NFL draft pick. His rise to stardom started rather humbly as a free agent and a third string quarterback. The most amazing part of his story is his faith in Jesus Christ and the undeniable faith of his wife Brenda. Through their faith they established the "First Things First Foundation" dedicated to impacting the lives of people by promoting Christian values, sharing experiences, and providing opportunities to encourage people. All things are possible when you put 'first things first'.

Today's passage reminds us to seek God's kingdom first and then all these other things will be given to us. This is a pretty powerful statement but it is true and can be trusted! So, what does it mean to put "first things first" for someone struggling with Alzheimer's disease? Well the answer is the same for an Alzheimer's patient, a quarterback, or anyone else. Seek first the Kingdom of God and His righteousness. If we continue to put God and our relationship with Him first, our needs will be met through the grace of our heavenly Father. As one with Alzheimer's disease, I fully understand the struggles but I can attest to God's grace in meeting all my needs. Put Him first and He will handle the rest!

Prayer: Father, thank You for graciously meeting our needs. Amen

Saturday: Know the Father through the Son

All things have been committed to me by my Father. No one knows the Son except the Father, and no one knows the Father except the Son and those whom the Son chooses to reveal him.
Matthew 11:27

If you were to make a list of the most influential Christians in the 20th century, your list would have to include the Reverend Billy Graham. For over six decades this Christian evangelist has worked tirelessly to lead hundreds of thousands of people to faith in Jesus Christ. His worldwide evangelistic crusades have touched the lives of millions of people around the globe by allowing the grace and power of the Living Lord to work through his ministry. He has been an advisor to numerous American presidents and is regularly listed as one of the "Ten Most Admired Men in the World."

It amazes me to think it all started when, at the age of 16, Billy Graham made a lifetime commitment to Christ during a revival meeting near his home in Charlotte, North Carolina. Like today's Scripture states, the Son of God revealed to Billy Graham the knowledge of the heavenly Father so he might know and serve Him fully. As you struggle in your daily dealings with Alzheimer's disease, stop and ask yourself if you truly "know" our heavenly Father. If your answer is no, then ask His son Jesus to reveal Him to you.

It is the knowledge of the Father through the Son that changes the heart, life, and ministry of people no matter what their circumstances. I believe even with Alzheimer's disease I will continue to "know" my Lord and He will continually reveal the Father to me in new ways every day. The same can be true for you if you will only ask the Lord for His help.

Prayer: Lord, reveal to us the knowledge of the Father so we might better serve Him with our whole heart. Amen

Sunday: Be Still and Know Your Lord

Be still, and know that I am God; I will be exalted among the nations, I will be exalted in the earth. The Lord Almighty is with us; the God of Jacob is our fortress. Psalms 46:10–11

This week we explored the lives of two coaches, two athletes, a mountain climber, and an evangelist who were able to do great things not only for themselves but for others through the grace of our heavenly Father. Many of these courageous individuals gave credit to their Lord and Savior, Jesus Christ, who propelled them to stardom in their careers. Some of these individuals rose up from humble beginnings while others came from "well-to-do" families. I am sure most of them spent time being still before the Lord. In this stillness, they came to know the Lord Almighty and exalted Him through their public professions of faith. Their rise to public acclaim took decades to accomplish and the Lord was most certainly with them as they struggled to perfect their chosen profession.

I often wonder how they pushed through periods of disastrous defeat, painful bodies, troublesome thoughts, sheer exhaustion, and unbelievable disappointments. How many hours of prayer did it take to reinforce the fact that the Lord was with them and He alone was their fortress? As I think of each of their stories, I am encouraged to remain confident in the awesome power, grace, love, and mercy of our heavenly Father. Alzheimer's may play havoc on my brain, cause my body to decline, and eat away at my strength but one thing is for sure; it cannot touch the confidence I have in Jesus Christ. He alone controls the future of the faithful so Alzheimer's will always pale in comparison to the hold He has on our lives!

Prayer: Jesus, let us be still before You today so we might truly know You are Lord of all. Amen

Chaoss © 123RF.com

STUDYING GOD'S WORD

Devotions to help you study the Bible and make it a strong weapon in your daily fight against Alzheimer's disease.

Monday: A Studying Servant

*Through these he has given us his very great and precious
promises, so that through them you may participate in the divine
nature and escape the corruption in the world caused by evil desires.
For this very reason, make every effort to add to your faith
goodness; and to goodness, knowledge; and to knowledge, self-
control; and to self-control, perseverance; and to perseverance,
godliness; and to godliness, brotherly kindness; and to brotherly
kindness, love. For if you possess these qualities in increasing
measure, they will keep you from being ineffective and unproductive
in your knowledge of our lord Jesus Christ. 2 Peter 1:4–7*

Today's passage is a rather lengthy excerpt from Peter's second
letter to the church at large. I chose this passage to begin our
devotions on studying God's word because Peter provides some
excellent reasons for increasing our knowledge. By understanding
and accepting the precious promises God reveals in Scripture, we
can escape the corruption in the world caused by evil desires. This is
important because as my rational thinking diminishes due to
Alzheimer's disease, I must avoid falling into the trap of desiring
evil things. To prevent this I study His word daily. By renewing my
mind and spirit with God's precious promises and wonderful words,
I can focus on Him rather than the world.

By increasing my knowledge of Him I will remain effective and
productive in His kingdom. As we deal daily with the demands of
Alzheimer's disease, it is important to remember we are still servants
of the Savior. As a studying servant, I serve a loving Lord who
wants only the best for me regardless of my circumstances. The
same is true for you.

*Prayer: Lord, allow the study of the word to refresh us daily and
keep us humble before You. Amen*

Tuesday: Treasures of Wisdom and Knowledge

My purpose is that they may be encouraged in heart and united in love, so that they may have the full riches of complete understanding, in order that they may know the mystery of God, namely, Christ, in whom are hidden the treasures of wisdom and knowledge. Colossians 2:2–3

As a young boy, I can remember exploring my grandfather's farm during the summers when my family visited Kentucky. It was during one memorable summer I decided to look for Indian treasures after studying in school how Indians buried their dead in mounds filled with artifacts from their life. I can still picture the place on my grandfather's farm with small mounds I thought were ancient burial sites. I took a shovel from the tool shed and announced I was going in search of Indian artifacts. Needless to say, I didn't find any ancient treasure. All I came home with were blisters on my hands from digging in the hard red clay of my grandfather's farm.

Today's passage penned by Paul to the Colossian church, reminds us in the fullness of Christ are hidden treasures of wisdom and knowledge to give us complete understanding of the mystery of God. In order to attain this understanding, we must study God's holy word which was in Christ from the beginning. Even with Alzheimer's disease, I find studying His word still reveals secrets I somehow missed in the past. Perhaps my mind was not focused on the Scripture I read because the worries of the world, deceitfulness of riches, and desires for other things choked out the word! These distractions no longer roam the corridors of my mind, thereby allowing the Holy Spirit to reveal treasures contained in His holy word. So spend some time in study today. You will find treasures beyond your imagination!

Prayer: Holy Spirit, reveal to us the treasures found in the holy word of God. Amen

Wednesday: Truth and Trust

This is good and pleases God our Savior, who wants all men to be saved and to come to a knowledge of the truth. For there is one God and one mediator between God and men, the man Christ Jesus, who gave himself as a ransom for all men- the testimony given in its proper time. 1 Timothy 2:3–6

Today's passage from Paul's letter to Timothy reveals this fundamental truth: God wants all men to be saved and to come to a knowledge and understanding of the "truth." As I read this passage and pondered on the meaning of "truth", I came to a realization the "truth" is not just a simple factoid of information you uncover in the Scriptures. Rather, "truth" comes as a deepened relationship develops with the Father and His son, Jesus Christ, as one studies the Scriptures. Gaining the knowledge, or understanding, of the "truth" results in a greater ability to "trust" in the promises of our Father.

As I struggle with the demands of Alzheimer's disease, it is the "truth" from the Scriptures and the resultant "trust" in my Lord that allow me to remain hopeful in His perfect promises. Understanding "truth" from years of study has developed a deepened "trust" which strengthens my spirit and prevents me from blaming God for my disease, severing my relationship with Him, and becoming totally disheartened. The knowledge of "truth" allows me to realize God is with me during this difficult period.

Remember, He still has plans for your life. Without Him, it will be hopeless! Seek salvation and study the Scriptures so "truth" will bring "trust" in the Almighty to you.

Prayer: Heavenly Father, we understand You want all of us to be saved and to come to a knowledge of the truth. Encourage us to seek a deeper relationship with You as we study Your word. Amen

Thursday: Teach Me Your Decrees

Do good to your servant according to your word, O Lord. Teach me knowledge and good judgment, for I believe in your commands. Before I was afflicted I went astray, but now I obey your word. You are good, and what you do is good; teach me your decrees.
Psalm 119:65–68

My nephew Joey is a very intelligent and disciplined young man whose good judgment has served him well during his teenage years. He studies hard, practices hard, and works hard at everything he undertakes. All his effort has made him a great success in high school band, speech, and academics as evidenced by all the accolades and trophies he's accumulated. It just goes to prove knowledge, discipline, and good judgment will always lead you to successful endeavors while keeping you out of trouble.

Today's passage from Psalms describes an incredible request from a lowly servant to his loving Savior. Simply put, the Psalmist wants to be taught knowledge and good judgment to keep him along the tight and narrow route of righteousness. The passage prompts us to learn everything we can from God's holy word so we will not go astray while serving Him. Learning the basics of God's word requires continual study, insight from the Holy Spirit, and even memorization of selected Bible passages.

It is amazing how much Scripture I can still quote even though I struggle with Alzheimer's disease. It was hard work and took practice to memorize these passages but in the end it was certainly worth it. These special Scriptures encourage me enormously and provide a firm footing for my faith in times of fogginess and confusion. Spend some time today studying God's word and learning His delightful decrees so you won't go astray!

Prayer: Father, teach us Your decrees contained in Your holy word so we won't go astray. Amen

Friday: Wisdom over Rubies

Choose my instruction instead of silver, knowledge rather than choice gold, for wisdom is more precious than rubies, and nothing you desire can compare with her. Proverbs 8:10–11

As a young "tween", my grandfather taught me how to operate his Western Auto riding lawn mower. For a kid who grew up in Baltimore where cutting grass with a push mower was the norm, driving his riding lawn mower was absolutely the most wonderful thing I ever did! He taught me the ins and outs of mowing along the side of the road, slowing down in tall grass, avoiding the wet areas, and how to blow the grass in long rows if the lawn had gotten too tall. My grandfather also taught me how to check the oil, clean the mower, and sharpen the blades.

Thus began my lifelong love affair with riding mowers and lawn care that remains with me today. A few years ago, my mother gave me one of my grandfather's rubies from India mounted on a tie clasp. Every time I put on the tie clasp, I remember his lessons about riding lawn mowers. I cherish those memories far more than the red ruby she gave me.

Today's passage reminds us how precious godly knowledge and wisdom are in comparison to silver, gold, and even rubies. Studying the Scriptures to gain wisdom is by far more important than accumulating wealth and precious stones. Having struggled with early-onset Alzheimer's disease for the past six years, I've come to realize worldly wealth does little to provide lasting peace and contentment in my life. On the other hand, studying the Scriptures, reading the word, and memorizing certain passages have brought me perfect peace and extraordinary contentment. His word is far more precious than anything silver, gold, or even rubies can provide!

Prayer: Lord, thanks for the wisdom contained in Your word. Amen

Saturday: Grow in the Knowledge of Christ

Dear friends, since you already know this, be on your guard so that you may not be carried away by the error of lawless men and fall from your secure position. But grow in the grace and knowledge of our Lord and Savior Jesus Christ. To him be glory both now and forever. 2 Peter 3:17–18

The disciple Peter penned today's passage in the closing of his second letter to the church at large. This letter had a threefold purpose: to spur Christian growth, to counter false teaching, and to implore watchfulness for the Lord's return. It provides a profound purpose for studying the Scriptures; to grow in the knowledge of our Lord and Savior so we might not be carried away by the "error of lawless men" and fall from our secure position in Christ. In more simple terms, don't get carried away by the false teaching of wayward witnesses!

Alzheimer's disease has impacted my brain in such a way I'm much more gullible than before. I have to balance what I hear with what the Scriptures actually say. I constantly have to look up Scripture, study it, and seek the counsel of the Holy Spirit to make sure I understand what God wants me to learn from a particular passage. As such, I don't necessarily rely on how a minister might interpret a particular Scripture. I also seek the counsel of godly men and women who I know have a firm grasp of the Scriptures.

The last thing any of us would ever want to happen is to be led astray by false teachers because of Alzheimer's impairments. Peter's passage reminds us to be on our guard and to continue to grow in the grace and knowledge of Jesus Christ. Peter's advice is certainly sound advice especially for those of us with Alzheimer's disease!

Prayer: Lord, keep us from going astray by false teachers. Amen

Paul M. Hornback

Sunday: Be Still and Study

Be still, and know that I am God; I will be exalted among the nations, I will be exalted in the earth. The Lord Almighty is with us; the God of Jacob is our fortress. Psalms 46:10–11

This week we have focused on the importance of not only reading the word but also studying and scrutinizing the Scriptures. It is through a concentrated study of the Scriptures God's word becomes real in your life. By studying the word we are able to understand not only what was happening at the time God inspired the writing but also how these wonderfully whispered words apply to our lives today.

Through careful study and reflection on God's holy word, I've found these precious passages provide perfect peace even during times of strenuous struggle and deep despair. This week has been filled with Scriptures about:

- Studying the precious promises of the word
- Gaining the full richness of complete understanding so we may know the mystery of God
- Achieving a knowledge of the truth
- Learning good judgment through His decrees
- Understanding the true value of God's holy word which is worth far more than gold, silver, or even rubies
- Growing in the grace and knowledge of God.

Now it is time to be still before the Lord. Reflect on who He is; the creator of everything, daily director of the righteous, infinite fortress for those who love Him, and incarnate inspiration for the holy word. Take time today to praise Him for His lavish love, peaceful presence, and continual compassion in your life. He loves you so very much so praise Him today!

Prayer: Heavenly Father, let us be still before You so we might grow in grace and knowledge of the one true God. Amen

Svetoslav Sokolov © 123RF.com

A NEW NORMAL

Devotions to help you discover the importance of accepting a "new normal" when Alzheimer's disease strikes.

Monday: A New Normal for Working

Make it your ambition to lead a quiet life, to mind your own business and to work with your hands, just as we told you, so that your daily life may win the respect of outsiders and so that you will not be dependent on anybody. 1 Thessalonians 4:11–12

Perhaps one of the most difficult things I've had to do since I was diagnosed with early-onset Alzheimer's disease is to live my life within the bounds of a "new normal" as I go about my daily activities. Throughout my life I have loved to work with my hands and do hard manual labor. I am not a skilled carpenter, artist, or craftsman but I have a lasting love of manual labor.

Today's passage from 1 Thessalonians underscores the biblical premise we are to work with our hands and lead quiet lives minding our own business. The Apostle Paul truly put forth a mouthful when he penned these words to the church at Thessalonica. I personally don't have a problem doing as Paul instructed, my problem is I still try to labor manually like I'm not afflicted with Alzheimer's. Unfortunately, I often work too hard, for too long, until I'm exhausted.

As a young healthy man I would bounce back pretty quickly after a long hard day. Now after working only a few hours of limited manual labor, I'm exhausted and it takes days to recover. My loving wife tries to remind me of my "new normal" condition but I often just forge ahead like a bull in a china shop when she leaves. Today's passage certainly says we should work with our hands but we must remember we are living under a "new normal" where shorter periods of work, with rest periods, are the norm!

Prayer: Lord, help us to remain productive with our hands as we enjoy the benefits of manual labor. Instill in our hearts and spirits the need to work a little slower and take more breaks. Amen

Tuesday: The Blame Game

And he said, "Who told you that you were naked? Have you eaten from the tree that I commanded you not to eat from?" The man said, "The woman you put here with me-she gave me some fruit from the tree, and I ate it. Genesis 3:11–12

From the very beginning, man has had difficulty taking responsibility for his actions. Today's passage reminds us even Adam, the man God created to rule His creation, failed to admit his sin and passed the blame to Eve. In his reply to God, Adam not only disappointed his Lord but also disappointed and hurt his God-given companion. How difficult would it have been for Adam to "man up" and say he ate the fruit from the tree on his own accord? It is always easier to pass the buck rather than accept responsibility for one's actions.

If you struggle with the daily impacts of Alzheimer's disease like I do, keep in mind this particular passage when you make mistakes. You see, I'm pretty prone to doing stupid things for which I'd like to blame someone else. For instance, I fell off an old school desk while putting up a shelf in the basement rather than using a step ladder. I "manned up" to my stupidity even though I was sure my wife would get upset and bar me from climbing. To my surprise, she took the news pretty well and was glad I confessed my sheer stupidity. She was only looking out for my best interests like God was with Adam.

Living under a "new normal" requires we not play the blame game. Therefore, confess the judgment errors you make and accept the consequences. It isn't easy but it is certainly the right thing to do. Besides, I doubt your spouse will throw you out of the garden or even the house!

Prayer: Father, help us confess our sins to You and our mistakes to others so we might live safer lives under Your care. Amen

Paul M. Hornback

Wednesday: Go with the Flow

Who cuts a channel for the torrents of rain, and a path for the thunderstorm, to water a land where no man lives, a desert with no one in it, to satisfy a desolate wasteland and make it sprout with grass? Job 38:25–27

I have been in the desert where no man lives and the ground is so dry it can barely sustain growth. On one trip, I remember traveling a side road to reach the interstate so I could get to the airport. On the road there were signs warning drivers not to attempt to cross particular places during raging thunderstorms due to flash flooding. The sign's location struck me as being rather odd in this part of the desert which probably had little rain; however, as I witnessed a thunderstorm raging far away to the north, I quickly grasped the gravity of the sign's warning.

Today's passage was God's terse response to Job's question of His "ways" which are truly beyond human understanding. As I read the passage I was humbled as if God was answering my prayer about why I had to endure Alzheimer's disease. I took the words as a loving reminder we often have to ride the rivers created by God's thunderstorms as they lead us to a desolate place dying for water. Going with the flow is all we can do as we adjust to the "new normal" which God is working in our lives.

Fighting against the current of the rain's raging river leaves you completely exhausted and spiritually depleted. Therefore, I choose to ride the river on God's rugged raft as He guides me through the rocky Alzheimer's canyon in which I'm trapped. He is my guide, He knows the water well, and He's prepared a destination ahead. Therefore, I'll go with His flow forever! Join me and God on the ride of a lifetime!

Prayer: Lord, help me flow safely in this raging river. Amen

Thursday: Communication in the New Normal

The Lord said, "If as one people speaking the same language they have begun to do this, then nothing they plan to do will be impossible for them. Come let us go down and confuse their language so they will not understand each other." Genesis 11:6–7

I have to admit there are days I have a small inkling of how the people building the Tower of Babel must have felt after God came down and confused their language. On "foggy days" I have more difficulty remembering words and the names of things. Thankfully, I still communicate using the same language as others so eventually I work out what I'm looking for or asking for help with.

The other day I was looking for the satellite television remote. I couldn't recall the word for remote or satellite but explained it changed the channels. My wife tried to hand me the TV remote when what I needed was the satellite remote. It was frustrating but thankfully I remembered I was operating under a set of "new normal" conditions. I explained I needed the device that changed the channels for the satellite antenna thing-a-ma-bob! Under the "new normal," communication becomes more difficult but it isn't impossible like for the people of Babel.

As God reminds us in today's passage, nothing is impossible for them nor is it impossible for those afflicted with Alzheimer's. We must work through our limitations and accept the "new normal" communication conditions we face. Referring to an item by using multiple words rather than its unique name is perfectly acceptable in our world. Calling it a thing-a-ma-bob, whirly-gig, or even a what-cha-ma-call-it is okay. At least we aren't having a "failure to communicate" like Cool Hand Luke did with the warden!

Prayer: Gracious Lord, help us communicate more clearly. Amen

Paul M. Hornback

Friday: Listening in the New Normal

He who answers before listening - that is his folly and his shame. Proverbs 18:13

When my youngest son Sam was in high school, he would often come to me to complain about something happening at school with his friends, the attitude of a teacher, or a problem he was facing. As a man, I often tried to solve his situation. I would usually come up with a perfect solution before he finished his lengthy explanation and had fully vented the situation. This continued for many months and I honestly thought I was taking the right approach as I provided my advice, years of worldly experience, and the solution to solve his problems. Unknown to me, my seemingly perfect responses had placed a huge strain on our relationship. Finally, during a particularly grueling gripe session with an exhaustive explanation of the very difficult situation he was facing, I interrupted him with the perfect plan of attack to address his dilemma. In a fit of rage, Sam stood up with tears in his eyes and said, "Dad, I don't want a solution to my problem, all I want is for you to listen to me."

Today's Scripture from Solomon is especially fitting as it reminds us if we answer before listening, we are foolish and shameful. I should have read Proverbs daily during my children's teenage years! Now I'm facing Alzheimer's disease and I find myself more willing to listen and less prone to blurting out solutions to my family's problems. Perhaps this is because it is difficult to take everything in, process it, work a plan of attack, and then find the right words to convey the perfect solution. But under the "new normal" condition this is all okay. Besides, I'm becoming a great listener which translates to a great father and an even better husband!

Prayer: Lord, help us listen more and jump to conclusions less. Amen

Saturday: Stay Active in the New Normal

As you know, it was because of an illness that I first preached the gospel to you. Galatians 4:13

This week has been especially difficult for me personally. Two months ago I received notification from the Office of Personnel Management (OPM) they erroneously overpaid me approximately $47,000 during the 28 months it took to finalize my disability retirement annuity. I appealed the decision asking for reconsideration or waiver of the overpayment due to OPM's gross negligence, delay in finalizing the annuity, failure to respond to my numerous attempts to question the interim payment, and because of my Alzheimer's disease situation.

This week I received the reply which stated OPM had denied my appeal because I had not proved my case; my argument lacked equity and good conscience; and their recovery of $47,000 was not an unconscionable act. OPM proposes to take over 40% of my take home retirement check for 99 months to settle the overpayment! All of this is very confusing to someone struggling with Alzheimer's disease so I tried to call someone to discuss the letter. It took me an entire day to finally get the phone number of the individual who wrote the denial letter and she was out of the office!

Today's passage reminds us even Paul had an illness in which he suffered yet he continued forward in his gospel activities. As we deal with Alzheimer's, we must remember to continue forward with life's activities, try not get discouraged, and hold the course. Keep remembering who you are in Christ as you adjust to a new normal and move forward with determination while holding on to the fruit of the spirit. If you do, you will shine forth through all your activities including any appearance before a judge!

Prayer: Lord, keep us active and holy in our new normal lives so we might show Your fruit of the spirit in all we do. Amen

Sunday: Be Still and Give Up Control

Be still, and know that I am God; I will be exalted among the nations, I will be exalted in the earth. The Lord Almighty is with us; the God of Jacob is our fortress. Psalms 46:10–11

Living under a "new normal" set of rules requires adjusting our lives to accommodate the limitations which arise as we struggle with Alzheimer's disease. This can be made easier if we fully surrender our lives, actions, and emotions to Christ. As Christians, we all agreed to take on a "new normal" set of rules when we decided to follow Christ as we gave up our old normal set of rules dictated by the world. Surrendering to Christ after a diagnosis of Alzheimer's simply allows us to accept the "new normal" life under His care.

Every new adjustment in my life with Alzheimer's disease over the past three years has been made easier by giving complete control to Christ. During my flight training, I remember whenever we passed control of the aircraft to our training pilot (or vice versa) the pilot giving up control would say, "You take control." The receiving pilot would say, "I have control" and the other pilot would let go of the controls saying, "You have control." As we accept our "new normal" conditions under Christ, we are saying, "Lord you take control" and He replies lovingly, "I have control, so trust me!"

Take time today to be still before the One who has complete control. Allow him to fly the best course for you under your "new normal" set of rules. You won't be disappointed because He knew you before you were even born, He etched the details of you in the womb, and He alone has your best interests at heart. Love Him, trust Him, turn it over to Him, and allow Him complete control. He is the Lord and can be trusted!

Prayer: Lord Almighty, giving up control is never easy for humans. Help us surrender control to You so our paths may be perfect. Amen

Natalia Bratslavsky© 123RF.com

A GODLY HEART

Devotions to help you maintain a Godly heart as you deal with Alzheimer's disease in your daily walk.

Paul M. Hornback

Monday: Heart of Peace

Let the peace of Christ rule in your hearts, since as members of one body you were called to peace. And be thankful. Colossians 3:15

This week we heard the terrible story of the mass shooting of twenty children and six adults at the elementary school in Connecticut by a deranged young man. Our prayers went out to the families involved in this terrible tragedy. The heroic efforts of the teachers, a principal, and a counselor who lost their lives trying to stop the gunman bring a glimmer of triumph in the midst of this terrible turmoil. Their selfless sacrifice saved the lives of other students and teachers.

As Christians we struggle with the horrendous loss of life but are reminded in today's Scripture to allow peace to rule in our hearts and to be thankful. The Apostle Paul dealt with all types of sorrow: pain, loss of liberty, hunger, beatings, and near death experiences but still allowed the peace of Christ to rule in his heart. Paul knew there would be all kinds of tragedy, sickness, heartbreak, and sorrow in our world but we are above all this because Christ paid the ultimate sacrifice. As I struggle with Alzheimer's disease, I try to remember Paul's experiences and how he rose above them so Christ would reign in his heart.

Perhaps you are struggling with the effects of Alzheimer's disease. Don't let it steal the peace Christ has placed in your heart. Talk with Him daily about what is going on in your life and ask Him to allow His peace to rule in your heart no matter what difficulties, challenges, or changes you face. Christ was surely present at the elementary school during the tragedy and He is surely present in your life today. He is your King!

Prayer: King of Kings, may Your peace reign in our hearts. Amen

Tuesday: Heart of Forgiveness

Bear with each other and forgive whatever grievances you may have against one another. Forgive as the Lord forgave you.
Colossians 3:13

Alzheimer's disease obviously creates challenges in accomplishing daily tasks but it can impact relationships with loved ones as well. After my diagnosis, I experienced problems dealing with my wife and children since I couldn't work through my frustrations. I would mentally nit-pick their comments, thought they ignored me, and questioned their love. Unfortunately, I perceived things erroneously and harbored resentment for silly things which before my illness would not have troubled me in the least.

Discussing these issues with my therapist and participating in a weekly men's group helped tremendously by providing a venue to vent my frustrations. However, the best medicine was talking with the Lord about my relational problems and reading His word to gain guidance. These two comforting acts helped me hone a heart of forgiveness. Today's short passage reinforces how vital it is to bear with each other and forgive whatever grievance has surfaced. This is really important for those who are suffering with Alzheimer's and their caregivers.

Asking the Lord daily to kindle a heart of forgiveness helps me handle grievances I experience in my relationships. Reminding myself to forgive as the Lord has forgiven me also helps me keep grievances in perspective. As you go through your daily routine, maintain a heart of forgiveness and ask God to fill you with the Holy Spirit. He will help you respond in love to any grievance committed. Then, don't forget to forgive!

Prayer: Precious Lord, fill our hearts with forgiveness, help us walk in the Spirit, and enable us to bear each other's grievances. Amen

Wednesday: A Grateful Heart Inspired by His Word

Let the word of Christ dwell in you richly as you teach and admonish one another with all wisdom, and as you sing psalms, hymns and spiritual songs with gratitude in your hearts to God.
Colossians 3:16

I've often heard the way to a man's heart is through his stomach. I remember my mother as a fantastic cook who prepared gourmet meals for my father on special occasions. These meals always put my father in a great mood and the whole family enjoyed them immensely. I suppose the rich food dwelled in him nicely and filled his heart with gratitude!

Today's passage brings a different perspective to describe how a heart filled with gratitude is developed. Paul claims if we allow the word of Christ to dwell in us richly, we will have a heart filled with gratitude. If you are dealing with Alzheimer's disease, what on earth do you have to be grateful about? As I read Christ's holy word, I am treated to a plate full of wisdom, peace, hope, joy, love, humility, faith, mercy, and understanding. For dessert, His word provides the delicacy of the promise of eternal life.

Even though I struggle with limitations, challenges, and reduced capabilities brought on by Alzheimer's disease, God's holy word assures me the fight is not my own. Christ and the Holy Spirit stand ready to protect, guide, and encourage me along the way. By trusting Him, I've found peace and developed a grateful heart. Each night before I go to sleep, I thank God for the many blessings in my life, His Son, the Holy Spirit, His word, godly friends, and a loving family. Let His word dwell in you and He will create a grateful heart within you as well!

Prayer: God, fill us with Your holy word so we might have a grateful heart that praises and thanks You every day! Amen

Thursday: Heart of Truth

Do not lie to each other, since you have taken off your old self with its practices and have put on the new self, which is being renewed in knowledge in the image of its Creator. Colossians 3:9–10

I live just outside a small town whose claim to fame is Abraham Lincoln was born nearby. His birthplace is a small one room cabin about three miles from the center of Hodgenville square where a beautiful statue of Lincoln stands. Lincoln was a man of character, integrity and truth. It has been stated in the many books written of Lincoln that he would not lie nor allow his political opponents to lie. The tenets of "right and truth" embodied the solutions of all the social and political problems Lincoln tackled. Perhaps this explains the legacy Lincoln left behind after his untimely death.

Today's passage enforces a similar doctrine we as Christians must embody as we discard the old and put on the new self. Paul reminds the early Christians of Colossae not to lie to one another as they are being remolded into the image of Christ. Perhaps, like me, you have struggled with telling the truth in all situations. Of course, these were probably not monumental lies but they marred your character. Paul deeply desired the early Christians to be beyond reproach in all their words and actions because they represented Christ. As you struggle with the debilitating effects of Alzheimer's disease, lying rather than struggling through a truthful explanation of your situation may seem easier. I encourage you, like the Apostle Paul, to be truthful in all your words, especially to your loved ones, because you remain an ambassador for Christ no matter what illness befalls you. Make it your aim to have a heart of truth so you might leave a lasting legacy others would emulate.

Prayer: Lord, instill in us a deep desire for truth in all our words and deeds. Create in us a heart of truth that nothing can change. Amen

Paul M. Hornback

Friday: Heart of Thankfulness

And whatever you do, whether in word or deed, do it all in the name of the Lord Jesus, giving thanks to God the Father through him. Colossians 3:17

Today I took some homemade cookies, brownies, fudge, candies, and treats to the faithful folks who work at the county recycling center. Most of the workers are jail inmates serving on a work release program. Many of these men have fallen on difficult times and are jailed because of non-payment of child support, petty crimes, DUI's, or other non-violent offenses. These men always greet me with a smile, kind words, and respect. When I offered up the canister of goodies they were elated. Their thankfulness was so warm and spontaneous it caught me off guard but it left me with a warm, thankful heart.

It made me think how God must feel when in the midst of our worst tragedies, we express thankfulness. Even on my worst days when Alzheimer's makes me confused, slows my conversation, causes me to misjudge things, and deters my reasoning skills, I can find something to be thankful for and express my gratitude to God. Paul reminds us in today's passage whatever we do, whether in our actions or conversations, we do it in the name of our Lord Jesus Christ while we give thanks to our heavenly Father through Him.

Last night when I prayed my prayer of thanksgiving, I thanked God even though I was having a difficult day. I was grateful for His help in enabling me to function in such a manner so as not to be a burden on my family. Even in the midst of your worldly woes, like the inmates at the recycling center, you can certainly find something to be thankful about. If so, tell God how grateful you are for His many blessings!

Prayer: Father, in all we do, give us a thankful heart. Amen

Saturday: Heart of Love

And over all these virtues put on love, which binds them all together in perfect unity. Colossians 3:14

According to the infamous line from *Love Story*, love means never having to say you are sorry. Although my wife has seen this movie, I can guarantee she does not agree with this quote! She believes true love empowers us to live our lives in such a manner we do nothing to be sorry about to the one we love. Of course, when we fall short of this goal, love demands we confess our failings, say we are sorry, and seek forgiveness. Perhaps Paul understood this which inspired Him to encourage the early Christians to clothe themselves in the Christian virtues covered with love which binds them in perfect unity.

Even as we struggle with Alzheimer's disease it is important to surround all our actions, words, and thoughts with love. Nothing is more important than love because we will fall short in relationships, adhering to daily schedules, and performing routine tasks which may cause us to lash out at loved ones. Maintaining a heart of love keeps us from thinking too highly of ourselves. If we do this then we can confess, seek forgiveness, and say we're sorry when we blow it.

Yesterday while my wife and daughter were out shopping, I fell out of a tree while attempting to cut off a branch using an old hand saw. I wasn't injured but I knew I had to "come clean" or else she'd ask how I got the bruise on my behind. So during our supper conversation, I explained the falling fiasco and lovingly apologized for being so careless. Love definitely means saying you're sorry. So, "put on love" and write a "Love Story" on the hearts of those you love!

Prayer: Lord of Love, help us put on love every morning as we get ready to start our day. Give us a heart of love. Amen

Sunday: Be Still

Be still, and know that I am God; I will be exalted among the nations, I will be exalted in the earth. The Lord Almighty is with us; the God of Jacob is our fortress. Psalms 46:10–11

The young adult Sunday school class my wife and I teach surprised us with a gracious gift at a recent social gathering. It was a beautiful white quilt trimmed in gold and brown with an embroidered tree covering the middle section. Under the tree was the beloved line from today's Scripture, "Be still and know that I am God." These young adults knew I was writing a devotional for Alzheimer's patients because I've shared it with them. However, no one in the class had any idea I'd been using this passage to close out each weeks devotions! I shouldn't be surprised because God moves in remarkably loving ways as He affirms His presence in our lives.

The gift was a great comfort because the week had been an emotional roller-coaster for my wife and me. Spending time writing about peace, forgiveness, gratitude, thankfulness, truth, and love provided some solace as I struggled with a number of deeply difficult issues. The generous gift of the quilt reminded me God not only cares for the matters of the universe, He also cares for the matters of our hearts. During one of the darkest weeks of my illness thus far, God used His special servants in the Mountain Movers Sunday School Class to reinforce the vision I had for this devotional series.

Has God ever done something like this for you? If He has, think of it often as you struggle with the daily demands of Alzheimer's disease. Now it is time to be still before God, praise Him for His agape love, and thank Him for changing your heart. He is God alone and worthy to be praised!

Prayer: Lord Almighty, thank You for shaping the matters of our hearts through the Holy Spirit and Your unfathomable love. Amen

Gabriela Insuratelu © 123RF.com

SPECIAL SECRETS

Devotions to help you find hope in the special secrets God has in store for those afflicted with Alzheimer's disease.

Paul M. Hornback

Monday: Left in the Lurch

At my first defense, no one came to my support, but everyone deserted me. May it not be held against them. But the Lord stood at my side and gave me strength, so that through me the message might be fully proclaimed and all the Gentiles might hear it. And I was delivered from the lion's mouth. 2 Timothy 4:16–17

When I was in high school, my father had to leave home for a two week training with the Bureau of Alcohol, Tobacco and Firearms. It was the middle of winter so my mom and little sister went too since the training was in Florida. I stayed home to take care of our 120 acre farm and 60 head of cattle. After they left for sunny Florida, a massive winter storm hit. 18 inches of snow fell, followed by temperatures reaching 10-15 degrees below zero. School was cancelled for nearly two weeks which was great because it took me all day to haul hay and break ice for the cattle. I felt deserted as the struggle to feed, water, and tend the cattle was a daily challenge.

In today's passage Paul's uses the Greek verb "egkataleipo," which is loosely translated as deserted. However, the Greek verb "egkataleipo" implies much more. In Paul's case, it not only meant everyone had left him but they had "left him in the lurch," or abandoned and forsaken him. This is exactly how I felt when my family left to have a working vacation in Florida! Perhaps a recent diagnosis of Alzheimer's disease has you feeling "left in the lurch." Don't you dare lose heart because God doesn't leave you in the lurch! Paul goes on to say the Lord stood by his side, giving him strength to carry on. If God could support Paul in his need, then He can surely support you in your time of need as well!

Prayer: Lord, we thank You for not leaving us in a lurch. Give us strength to carry on as Your faithful servants. Amen

Tuesday: Our Guide to the End

Walk about Zion, go around her, count her towers, consider her ramparts, view her citadels, that you may tell of them to the next generation. For this God is our God for ever and ever; he will be our guide even to the end. Psalms 48:12–14

The engineering job I had before retiring required a significant amount of travel. During my 26 years working for the Department of Defense, I visited various Army test sights, military bases, and defense contractor facilities across the United States and Europe. One of the things I especially enjoyed doing in my off time was finding a local mall and exploring its unique shops. Some of the malls were huge with three or more levels and hundreds of stores. These larger malls had kiosks with maps depicting each level's layout with the store names categorized by what they sold. However, the most helpful aspect of the kiosk map was the infamous "X" denoting "You are here." For large architecturally complex malls, there are map kiosks placed in strategic locations on each level to assist shoppers who become disoriented. Just look at the map, find the "X", and you're no longer lost!

Don't you wish there was a map kiosk or even a guide to help you navigate the Alzheimer's Mall so days of confusion wouldn't be so bad? For me, three things have been especially helpful; keeping a daily schedule, reading my Bible, and praying to my Lord. The schedule keeps me on track by enabling me to accomplish all the important tasks; Bible reading provides me wisdom, guidance, and reassurance of God's never ending mercy; and prayer provides a connection with the One who knows the intricate details of Alzheimer's disease and where you are in its complex maze. Remember, He will be your guide to the end and He is your God forever!

Prayer: Lord, be our guide through this trial to the very end. Amen

Paul M. Hornback

Wednesday: Holy Messengers

Then he reached out his hand and took the knife to slay his son. But the angel of the Lord called out to him from heaven, "Abraham! Abraham!" Here I am," he replied. Genesis 22:10–11

The faith required for Abraham to sacrifice his beloved son is unfathomable for me to understand. I can't begin to imagine sacrificing one of my sons for anything. Although we may not be called to sacrifice our children, we are called to give them the freedom to walk the path God has laid out before them. My youngest son just finished his paperwork to enlist in the Army and leaves for boot camp in five weeks. My oldest son has committed himself to the mission field and will be leaving for Belarus in May. As such, I understand how Abraham must have felt as he laid Isaac on the altar. However, even in the darkest, most demanding, and emotionally difficult task God asked of Abraham; God provided an angel to intervene at just the right moment. The Bible is filled with God's messengers intervening in the lives of His devoted servants.

Today's passage provides such an angelic intervention that forever changed the faith of Abraham and Isaac. When the angel calls out Abraham's name twice, Abraham replies "Here I am." Sometimes we are called down dark, daunting paths no one ever wants to walk. Alzheimer's disease is the most difficult path anyone could be asked to walk. However, God's holy messengers have appeared out of nowhere to help me along the way. My neurologist, clinical trial personnel, home nurse, wife, and psychologist are all messengers of God who have aided me along the way. Look around your life and you will also see God's messengers at work. If not just scream out, "Here I am Lord, send the messengers quickly!"

Prayer: Lord, thank You for Your wonderful messengers. Amen

Thursday: Chewing Solid Food

I gave you milk, not solid food, for you were not ready for it.
Indeed, you are still not ready. 1 Corinthians 3:2

My oldest son had shoulder surgery and has been recuperating at home for the past few weeks in part so his mom can wait on him hand and foot like he was a small boy again. It has been great to have him home because he always brings joy to our hearts whenever he's around. This past Sunday I attended worship at the small church he attends which is about 15 miles from our house. The service was wonderful but what I enjoyed most was the sermon. It has been a while since I've been so challenged theologically in a sermon. The message centered on suffering as described in Romans 8:18-25. The pastor's sermon lasted almost 45 minutes but I took notes making the time go by quickly. I've been chewing on the meat of this message for a few days and have yet to swallow it.

Being challenged spiritually by a sermon on suffering is what I needed since I'm struggling with Alzheimer's disease. I suppose you could say I'm suffering with Alzheimer's disease and I haven't been willing to take a spiritual look at my affliction. Perhaps you are wrestling with a similar spiritual struggle in your life. Today's passage reminds us it's time to get off the milk of easy Scripture and start chewing on the solid food Paul is referencing. If you're ready, read Romans 8:18-25 and chew on the meat of this thought-provoking Scripture for a while. Perhaps, like me, you'll come to understand your present sufferings are minimal, mere birthing pains, when you consider the future glory God has in store for those who wait patiently for their reward.

Prayer: Father, sometimes we just don't like to deal with suffering as the meat is too tough to swallow. Help us eat the solid food and mature in our faith knowing the glorious future that waits us. Amen

Friday: A Plea for Relief

All my longings lie open before you, O Lord; my sighing is not hidden from you. My heart pounds, my strength fails me; even the light has gone from my eyes. My friends and companions avoid me because of my wounds; my neighbors stay far away. Psalm 38:9–11

Today's passage was written by King David as a petition to God; a plea for relief from the Lord's rebuke. There are days I feel like David. On these days, Alzheimer's disease wears me down. I can feel my heart pound, my strength withers away, my eyes grow weary, and my brain seems dead. Like David, I feel my friends and companions are avoiding me because they don't know how to deal with my illness. It's probably difficult to carry on a conversation with me when the foggy days of Alzheimer's take their toll on my mind. On those difficult days, I desperately need the warmth, love, and companionship of friends and family.

The dark days require me to call upon the Lord and plead with Him to not forsake me like friends and family sometimes do. Of course, He is always with me and carries me through the difficult days of despair. He knows I am weak, weary, and worried so He comforts me through the Scriptures. Thankfully I don't have to speak eloquently. I can simply pray in, or through, the Holy Spirit as mere words seem to fail me on foggy days. I can lay my deepest longings before Him and He will comfort me. You see, He already knows what I truly need and is working to make it happen.

Perhaps you feel just like I do during your difficult days. Rest assured the Lord is with you always. All you need do is call on His holy name and your plea for relief is answered!

Prayer: Lord, save us from the dark days Alzheimer's brings Amen

Saturday: My God Provides Abundantly

And my God will meet all your needs according to his glorious riches in Christ Jesus. Philippians 4:19

Today we are having our house appraised to refinance at a significantly lower interest rate and consolidate two mortgages. This will save us almost twenty thousand dollars over the life of the loan. It will also keep us from having to dip into savings each month to make ends meet. Unfortunately, I had to retire at the peak of my earning potential which also corresponded to the pinnacle of my debt. We managed to put our kids through college, got them reasonably settled into life, bought them each a car, and were beginning to recoup from the financial impact when I was diagnosed with early-onset Alzheimer's disease. Over the past three years I have been trying to stabilize our finances, pay off consumer debt, sell my prized possessions, liquidate real estate, and prepare our affairs so my wife has less to manage. God has made this possible while continuing to exceed our daily needs.

Like today's passage from Philippians contends, God will meet all our needs according to His glorious riches in Christ. I know this does not exclusively mean financial needs but it most certainly does include financial concerns because it is all part of the human equation which God fully understands. My God meets my deepest spiritual needs, bountifully provides financial resources, and satisfies my fellowship and relational requirements abundantly. Even as I struggle with the daily demands brought on by Alzheimer's disease, my God continues to provide according to His riches. Perhaps you are struggling as well. If you are, my God has the resources to help if you will fully trust in Him! So, what are you worrying about?

Prayer: Lord, thank You for meeting all our needs abundantly. Amen

Sunday: Special Secrets Revealed in Stillness

Be still, and know that I am God; I will be exalted among the nations, I will be exalted in the earth. The Lord Almighty is with us; the God of Jacob is our fortress. Psalms 46:10–11

This has been an incredible week of studying God's word as we searched for the special secrets hidden within His Holy Scriptures. Now it is time to be still before the Lord, reflect on all we have studied, and know He is God. I've discovered in these times of stillness the God of Peace helps me fathom the depth of His glorious grace and never ending love. In the peaceful stillness of the morning, I can see His hand at work in my life and it helps me understand the God of Jacob:

- Provides abundantly from His glorious riches in Christ
- Knows my deepest longings and hears my pleas for relief
- Spoons out spiritual food just when I desperately need to chew on something solid
- Sends His holy messengers to glorify Him and comfort me
- Guides me gently through the seemingly difficult path stretched out before me
- Never leaves me in the lurch but always provides the strength and support I need for the task at hand.

The Lord Almighty is surely with me and in the peaceful quiet of the morning, when I am still before Him, He reminds me how much He loves me, cares for me, and desires a deep relationship with me. How about you? Do you spend quiet time with the Lord Almighty? Do you share your deepest desires with Him? If not, it's not too late to start! So, be still and know He is God Almighty, your rock and fortress.

Prayer: Lord, let us be still before You today so the special secrets from Your Scriptures might be made known to us. Amen

Matthew Gibson © 123RF.com

GOD STILL COMMUNICATES

Devotions to help you discover God still communicates in special ways when Alzheimer's disease strikes.

Paul M. Hornback

Monday: Speaking Through a Sunset

There will be no more night. They will not need the light of a lamp or the light of the sun, for the Lord God will give them light. And they will reign forever and ever. Revelations 22:5

Tonight I was feeling pretty low because I boiled soup over on the stove because I forgot I was cooking it. I felt sorry for myself and began to think about the future. I went outside to put up the chickens and began praying to God about how unfair my condition was given my young age. I wondered why he allowed this to happen and wanted a sign all would be okay. After getting the chickens in their pen, I glanced to the west to view what I thought would be a less than flamboyant sunset since there were only a few sparse clouds in the sky. To my surprise the sunset was unusually spectacular. The horizon was a tapestry of orange and yellow. The sun had dropped below the horizon but emanating from the setting sun were these long beautiful rays of pink and yellow. Between the rays the sky was a brilliant cyan blue. This particular sunset was as incredibly beautiful as it was unique.

The sunset reminded me of John's imagery of the New Jerusalem coming down from Heaven and dwelling on earth. As today's Scripture says, we won't need light because the glory of the Lord will provide the light. Needless to say, I was humbled because my heavenly Father had answered my prayer almost immediately. I was sure everything would be okay as peace flooded my spirit and anxiety was washed away. The Lord knew how to reassure, comfort, and remind me He is still in control of everything. God is amazing and still chooses to communicate to us in beautiful ways!

Prayer: Lord God, thank You for revealing glimpses of Your glory so we are assured You are surely with us and love us. Amen

Tuesday: Dreams of Encouragement

"In the breeding season I once had a dream in which I looked up and saw that the male goats mating with the flock were streaked, speckled or spotted. The angel of the God said to me in a dream, 'Jacob.' I answered, 'Here I am'. And he said, 'Look up and see that all the male goats mating with the flock are streaked, speckled or spotted, for I have seen all that Laban has been doing to you.'"
Genesis 31:10–12

One of the members of my Wednesday morning men's group shared a dream he had recently. He'd fallen asleep watching Christian television and dreamed during the night Joel Olsteen's service came on the air. He dreamed he was sitting in his living room when suddenly Olsteen popped in, sat down in the chair next to him, and started talking to him in an encouraging manner. This middle-aged man had been going through a particularly depressing period and his dream was an encouraging message from God through the comforting words of Joel Olsteen's worship service. How cool is that!

Today's passage from Genesis describes Jacob's dream concerning his stifling situation with his father-in-law Laban. In Jacob's dream, the angel of God reassured him the male goats mating with his father-in-law's flock were streaked, speckled or spotted and would produce offspring which would belong to Jacob according to his arrangement with Laban. God uses dreams to reassure us of His love and active presence in our lives. Since my diagnosis of early-onset Alzheimer's disease, my dreams have become very vivid. After reading today's passage, I'm confident God is using my dreams to reassure me of His love. If you are struggling and wondering if God cares, start paying particular attention to your dreams. God may be sending you encouragement while you sleep!

Prayer: Father, use our dreams to draw us closer to You. Amen

Paul M. Hornback

Wednesday: Devoted Servants of God

Love must be sincere. Hate what is evil; cling to what is good.
Be devoted to one another in brotherly love. Honor one another
above yourselves. Romans 12:9–10

A member of our church has been an incredible source of encouragement and strength for me. He has endured tremendous hardship in his life that initially made him bitter and tarnished during his early years as a young man, husband, and father. But through the overwhelming power of Christ, he matured into a godly man who uses his past hardships, struggles, and illnesses to demonstrate the awesome power of Christ in his life. Men like these are true treasures in the life of any congregation. They are magnificent messengers of our God who provides encouragement, strength and hope to anyone enduring the trials and struggles life dishes out.

When I was initially diagnosed with early-onset Alzheimer's disease, this man not only prayed continuously for me but also started watching out for me, monitoring my manual labor at church so I didn't overdo it, and standing up for me when others commented about my declining performance. In today's passage, Paul purports we are to be devoted to one another in brotherly love as we honor one another above ourselves. By doing this, we allow God to use us to show His love to a hurting world that desperately needs it. In my case, God used my dear friend to assist me as I continued to serve, lovingly stand up for me, and impart His love and concern for my wellbeing. As you struggle with Alzheimer's disease, rest assured God has already sent servants to assist you in your battles. They may be doctors, nurses, friends, family members, or aides. When they appear, remember they are devoted brothers and sisters in Christ who share God's love sincerely!

Prayer: Lord, thanks for the loving servants sent our way. Amen

Thursday: Biblical Words of Hope and Love

For everything that was written in the past was written to teach us, so that through endurance and the encouragement of the Scriptures we might have hope. Romans 15:4

I started reading the Bible all the way through again. I just completed reading the New Testament and started soaking up Genesis in the Old Testament. It is amazing how much I've discovered about the hope God provides in times of struggle.

Today's passage was written by the Apostle Paul to remind the Roman church to be an encouragement to others , stand unified under the gospel of Christ, and glorify God with one heart and mouth. Of course, all this is made possible by the encouragement of the Scriptures which were written under the holy inspiration of God to teach, give hope, and enable us to endure all types of trial. As I read the Old Testament, I keep Paul's words to the Romans in mind so I don't miss the encouragement God has made available for me. Often the daily demands of Alzheimer's disease can literally grind your hope away. When these days take their toll, I need a source of hope and encouragement that speaks to me personally.

My source of strength comes from His word. It amazes me anything written in 1400 BC could possibly give hope and encouragement during my battles with Alzheimer's disease. However, today's passage reinforces *everything* written in the Scriptures does provide us encouragement and hope. I miraculously find God speaking directly to me as He brings me words of love and hope. If you struggle with Alzheimer's disease, seek encouragement, hope, and love in God's holy word today. You won't be disappointed!

Prayer: Lord of Hope, speak to us individually through Your word and provide personal words of hope and encouragement. Amen

Paul M. Hornback

Friday: Words of Encouragement

Therefore, my brothers, you whom I love and long for, my joy and crown, that is how you should stand firm in the Lord, dear friends. Philippians 4:1

I absolutely love reading Philippians because it is filled with words of love, gratitude, encouragement, and praise. The Apostle Paul is so very proud of the church at Philippi and his pen overflows with praise as he writes his letter of love. I too love to write notes of encouragement to members of our congregation who are going through difficult or challenging situations. My hope is these notes will encourage them in their daily walk with Christ.

Let me share with you a little secret; I simply love receiving a note of encouragement from a Christian who understands all I am going through in my daily struggles with Alzheimer's disease as well. These words of encouragement always brighten my spirit, spur me on to continue the good fight, and remind me how much others care about my situation. In these encouraging notes, God uses people to express His deep love and concern for those struggling in life's trials.

Alzheimer's is a daily struggle for the person afflicted with the disease and the caregiver. Words of encouragement and hope enable you to press on with life. If you are struggling with this disease, don't give up hope! God's army of servants stands ready to encourage you. Pick up the Bible and read Philippians today and be encouraged. Then pick up a pen and write a note of encouragement to someone going through a tough situation. They will certainly feel better and so will you because God is lovingly using you in His service today. Hallelujah, Amen!

Prayer: Lord, enable us to encourage someone today so Your love may touch their hurting hearts and bring healing. Amen

Saturday: Godly Good from Intended Harm

But Joseph said to them, "Don't be afraid. Am I in the place of God? You intended to harm me, but God intended it for good to accomplish what is now being done, the saving of many lives. So then, don't be afraid. I will provide for you and your children." And he reassured them and spoke kindly to them. Genesis 50:19–21

When I read Genesis, I am amazed at Joseph's life and how he responded to adversity and acclaim. If you remember, Joseph was Jacob's favorite son and perhaps a little bit spoiled, at least in the eyes of his brothers. They were so jealous of his status they sold him into slavery just to get rid of him. Thus began a journey which led him into Pharaoh's service.

Today's passage occurs after Joseph's father, Jacob, passed away. He reminded his brothers he held no resentment toward them for all they did to him. What Joseph's brothers intended for harm, God used for good! Often God uses the adversity in our lives to complete something good. The key is to remain faithful, obedient, and trusting toward our Lord. Struggling with Alzheimer's disease is an adversity I wouldn't wish on anyone. But God is using this situation to accomplish good.

Since I had to retire early, I've had more time to spend with my family, to serve the church, to write this devotional, and to serve Him. I have no idea what He has in store for the future but regardless, I continue to serve Him faithfully, try to be obedient, and place my trust in Him alone. Perhaps you or a loved one are struggling with this disease as well. Don't give up hope for God is not finished yet! He will use your situation to demonstrate His love and to bring about good in some capacity. Just keep trusting Him for some godly good!

Prayer: Lord, thanks for accomplishing good in our lives. Amen

Sunday: Stillness

Be still, and know that I am God; I will be exalted among the nations, I will be exalted in the earth. The Lord Almighty is with us; the God of Jacob is our fortress. Psalms 46:10–11

This week we have focused on how God communicates His never ending love in ways that touch us deeply and personally. Now it is time to be still before the Lord and reflect on each of these examples in light of your unique situation:

- Speaking through a beautiful sunset
- Encouraging dreams
- Devoted servants ministering to your needs
- Biblical words of hope and love
- Words of encouragement
- Godly good from intended harm.

Our heavenly Father uses everything to communicate His love for us in very personal ways designed to touch us deeply. He created us, knows everything about us, and understands how to reach us personally. Be still before Him today and thank Him for His love, grace, and mercy in your life. Perhaps you feel God doesn't love you because Alzheimer's has invaded your life. Nothing could be further from the truth! God's love is unconditional and whatever you are facing, God is already there willing to help. Acknowledge His presence, ask for His help, and stand ready to receive His blessings.

God can use your dismal predicament to benefit others, bring about good, and prove His love for you as well as for others. Be still before Him today and ask for His help and guidance. Without God, Alzheimer's disease creates a bleak situation in anyone's life. However, Alzheimer's can only bow to the mighty power of the Lord if you belong to Him!

Prayer: Lord, let us be still and yield to Your mighty power as you use our unique situation for good. Amen

Lyn Watanabe © 123RF.com

GOD'S DIVINE MAJESTY

Devotions to help you find new ways to appreciate the divine majesty of God even when you struggle with the limiting impacts of Alzheimer's disease.

Monday: God's Divine Nature

*For since the creation of the world God's invisible qualities –
his eternal power and divine nature – have been clearly seen, being
understood from what has been made, so that men are without
excuse. For although they knew God, they neither glorified him as
God nor gave thanks to him, but their thinking became futile and
their foolish hearts were darkened. Romans 1:20–21*

The Apostle Paul begins his letter to the church at Rome by
addressing the righteousness and divinity of God incarnate. He
reminds them God's wrath is real and He will not force them to
worship or obey Him. Instead, if they desire to be sinful, God can
give them over to their sinful desires if they reject the salvation
provided to them through His Son. Paul explains in today's passage
God's divine nature and eternal power are evident in His creation.
There is no excuse for men to miss out on His powerful presence.
Paul postulates we are to give glory to God and remember to thank
Him for all He has done. This is absolutely essential if we are to find
peace in our lives.

As you struggle with Alzheimer's disease, it is important to
remember who God is and His absolute divine nature. This has
helped me understand the big picture of what God is doing in my life
and how He plans to use my condition to glorify Him. I know this
may sound "Pollyanna" to non-Christians but it enables me to
continue forward in the good fight knowing He is in control, His
eternal power is absolute, and His divine nature encompasses even
my illness. I will continue to glorify His name and thank Him for His
bountiful blessing in my life. Can you do that or will you be like the
Romans and ignore His holiness, eternal power, and divine nature?
So, when in Rome, do like Paul. Glorify God!

Prayer: Father, You are divine and praiseworthy. Amen

Tuesday: Divine Power

Grace and peace be yours in abundance through the knowledge of God and of Jesus our Lord. His divine power has given us everything we need for life and godliness through our knowledge of him who called us by his own glory and goodness. 2 Peter 1:2–3

I'm battling the Office of Personnel Management (OPM) regarding a retirement pay issue. My claims have been denied numerous times and I'm appealing OPM's decision to an Administrative Judge. This judge has the power to correct any wrong and overturn OPM's decision based on the merits of the appeal and law. Wielding power over individuals and situations provides an opportunity for goodness to emerge.

Today's Scripture from the pen of Peter reminds us our heavenly Father has absolute divine power and uses it to provide everything we need for life and godliness. It is the divine nature of God that defines the excellence of His being which is expressed to us in the virtue of His goodness. Our Father is indeed a loving God who meets our every need and longs for our expressions of love toward Him.

Every day I see the goodness of God revealed in His creation, the people He has called, and the gracious acts of kindness He expresses. His divine nature and eternal being demand a response from me through acts of thankfulness, praise, and worship no matter what is happening. Even though I struggle through foggy days brought on by Alzheimer's disease, today's Scripture reminds me I have everything I need to love and adore Him through the knowledge He has given. How can I do anything but praise Him? Take time today to remember He is worthy of all your praise. Then praise Him!

Prayer: Father God, let us praise, worship, and adore You today for all You do in our lives. You are God alone! Amen

Wednesday: God's Majestic Beauty

The Lord reigns, he is robed in majesty; the Lord is robed in majesty and is armed with strength. The world is firmly established; it cannot be moved. Your throne was established long ago; you are from all eternity. Psalm 93:1–2

This morning the air was cool and crisp so my wife and I decided to walk on the farm rather than in the park. The ground was frozen hard so walking in the tilled fields of the farm was relatively easy. As we strolled along we began to notice interesting ice formations that had developed on the ground adjacent to certain weed stems. The majestic beauty of these delicate ice delights against the desolate landscape of a tilled farm field was simply striking. My wife took several pictures to capture their beauty before the warmth of the sun removed all evidence of their existence.

After our walk, we "googled" 'Ice Formations' and discovered there is little written about them. They are more commonly known as frost flowers, ice flowers, or ice ribbons. As I viewed our pictures, it made me think about the majestic beauty of God in contrast to humanity's desolate landscape.

Today's passage from Psalms reminds us God is robed in majesty as He reigns over His creation. Our Father's throne was established long ago and unlike the frost flowers, He cannot be moved or destroyed by anything on earth. His majesty, kingdom, and divinity are eternal which means He is always with us no matter what circumstances surround us. Perhaps Alzheimer's disease is slowly wearing on your spirit. Take time today to remember the divine majesty of our Father and ask Him for help. He won't fade away or let you down!

Prayer: Heavenly Father, You are robed in majesty, Your power is eternal. Help us remember Your majesty as we live today. Amen

Thursday: Majesty in a Burning Bush

*There the angel of the Lord appeared to him in flames of fire
from within a bush. Moses saw that though the bush was on fire it
did not burn up. So Moses thought, "I will go over and see this
strange sight – why the bush does not burn up." When the Lord saw
that he had gone over to look, God called to him from within the
bush, "Moses! Moses!" And Moses said, "Here I am."*
Exodus 3:2–4

As a teenager, I remember all the hard work we did to improve
the appearance of my father's farm. Our first task was to clean out
the overgrown fence rows so we could put up new fencing. My
father was old school, so we used an axe and corn knife to cut down
trees, briars, weeds, and tall grass. We stacked the debris in large
brush piles and burned them down to ash. The fire was so intense
you'd singe your hair if you ventured too close to the pile of burning
brush.

Moses experienced the heat of brush fires and was therefore
perplexed at the sight of this burning bush. Moses couldn't
understand why the fire failed to consume the bush. To his surprise,
the majesty of the Lord was in the burning bush. God spoke to him
and reminded him he was on holy ground. It is amazing God's
majesty was displayed in such a remarkable manner. The glory of
God's likeness was akin to fire but it did not harm the bush. God's
majesty always surprises us since it is far greater than anything we
can imagine.

After being diagnosed with Alzheimer's disease, I've thought
about how wonderful it will be to worship God for all eternity. I will
be on holy ground, I'll probably hide my face, and I'll be speechless
as His majesty will surely overcome me. Take time today to think
about His majesty and then praise Him!

*Prayer: Father, we can only image what it will be like when we
come face to face with You and worship Your majesty. Amen*

Friday: Majestic Is His Name

O Lord, our Lord, how majestic is your name in all the earth!
You have set your glory above the heavens. Psalm 8:1–2

Sometimes you run across a song that moves your heart and soul in unexplainable ways. We sing an unbelievably moving song during our worship service entitled *Shout to the Lord*. This song always touches me deeply. When I sing the words I am overcome with humility as I lift my voice in praise. These simple words somehow remind me of the majesty of our Lord. As I sing the lyrics, my spirit is moved to worship Him. These particular words hit my spirit like a ton of bricks:

Shout to the Lord, all the earth let us sing
Power and majesty praise to the king.
Mountains bow down and the seas will roar
At the sound of your name.

Today's precious passage from Psalms reminds us just how majestic our Lord's name is in all the earth! His name is more powerful than anything we can imagine on earth. He has set His glory far above the heavens. Even though I struggle with the limiting effects of Alzheimer's disease, this song always brings comfort and reassurance the Lord is still in complete control of everything going on in my life. I can't explain why these words have such a dramatic impact on me. Perhaps the lyrics contain the power of His name and press me to praise Him! The Lord is truly my comfort, my savior, my tower of refuge, and my strength.

If you struggle with Alzheimer's disease, spend some time today praising His holy name as you shout to the Lord in song. It helps me remember how majestic He is and how important it is to worship Him. Perhaps it will help you as well!

Prayer: Lord, Let us shout Your name in praise! Amen

Saturday: His Majesty Demands Our Utmost

There is no one like the God of Jeshurun, who rides on the heavens to help you and on the clouds in his majesty.
Deuteronomy 33:26

My youngest son left today for Fort Leonard Wood, Missouri where his first round of Army training will be conducted. His Army basic combat and initial military police training will last approximately 5 months. Hopefully, we will get to see him between basic training and military police training in about 10 weeks. It was hard to say goodbye at the recruiting office and even harder to come back home to see all his belongings neatly packed up in his room. I know he is in good hands, his training will be rigorous, and he will finally begin his path toward the goals he set many years ago.

It got me to thinking about the goals I've set for my faith and if I'm on the right path. My Lord deserves much more than just a haphazard stroll down the spiritual path He's laid out for me. His divine majesty demands far more than I've given Him lately. Even though I struggle with Alzheimer's disease, His kingdom has work I can be doing now. What is holding me back? Perhaps it's the fear I'll fail, not be able to express myself eloquently, or disappoint Him because I forget to do something. These are all real issues when Alzheimer's disease is involved. But isn't His strength sufficient and His grace enough to cover my shortcomings?

Perhaps you struggle with the same questions. Don't let them stop you from doing something great for Him. His divine majesty demands the utmost of our service. Whatever you do, don't let Alzheimer's be your excuse to do nothing. His divine majesty and never ending love demand we enlist to fight the good fight with Him. So sign up today and serve Him!

Prayer: Lord, let our service be worthy of Your majesty. Amen

Paul M. Hornback

Sunday: Stillness in a Majestic Sunrise

Be still, and know that I am God; I will be exalted among the nations, I will be exalted in the earth. The Lord Almighty is with us; the God of Jacob is our fortress. Psalms 46:10–11

The sunrise this morning was ablaze with majestic color. The fiery reds, flaming oranges, and glowing ambers provided a striking display of morning light against a sea of cyan blue adrift with white clouds. The incredible beauty of the morning sunrise made me stand in awe of God's creation and His amazing power to sustain such a sunrise. I took time to be still before the Lord as the sunrise beautifully unfolded. In the fleeting moments of the morning dawn, I knew God was present and in complete control. This week we focused on the divine nature and awesome majesty of our heavenly Father. He created everything and still reigns over His creation.

In spite of all I am are going through as I struggle with Alzheimer's disease, I realize He is still God eternal and He deserves all my praise and worship. He is forever faithful, eternally excellent, everlastingly loving, and amazingly awesome. In the midst of my suffering He surrounds me with His goodness, never-ending blessings, and gifts of creation. All of these remind me He is in control. Therefore, I need not be afraid of anything for my God understands my sufferings and provides me comfort. Like an unbelievably beautiful sunrise, I begin my day by being still before the Lord and knowing He is God alone and God of all creation.

Spend time today being still before the One who created everything. Spend time praising and worshipping His holy name. His peace will fill your heart if you do!

Prayer: Lord, help us be still before You today as we soak in the majesty of the God of all creation. You are our God! Amen

Svetoslav Sokolov © 123RF.com

CONVERSATIONS WITH GOD

Devotions to help you discover the importance of maintaining daily conversations with God as you battle Alzheimer's disease in your life.

Monday: God Calling

Call to me and I will answer you and tell you great and unsearchable things you do not know." Jeremiah 33:3

When I attended my first Emmaus Walk, I received a paperback book entitled *God Calling.* I have read completely through it numerous times. The book was written by two English women who depended on the Lord for their daily needs and because they called on Him, He blessed them.

It had been over 20 years since I had even picked up this book. Today I began reading the comforting words these two women wrote from their daily conversations with the Lord. Their words provide me inspiration as I struggle more and more with the changes brought on by Alzheimer's disease. It is difficult to understand why God speaks to some while remaining silent to others; however, I continue my daily conversations with God. Often He chooses to respond in ways that don't require words. The key is to keep the dialogue going. Pour out your heart, talk with Him about anything, and hold nothing back. He understands your frustrations, longs to hear your joys, is excited about your successes, and feels your sorrows. No one else can comprehend all you are going through. Talk with Him like you would a trusted friend.

I've found my conversations help me put my struggles in perspective. Like today's passage states, when you call on Him he will answer and reveal great things. Perhaps this is what the women who wrote *God Calling* found when they called upon the Lord. Perhaps you will find the Lord waiting to converse with you as you spend some time in prayer today.

Prayer: Lord, as we call upon Your name and pour out our hearts, may You always answer us in Your marvelous way. Amen

Tuesday: Conversations of Hope

I pray also that the eyes of your heart may be enlightened in order that you may know the hope to which he has called you, the riches of his glorious inheritance in the saints, and his incomparably great power for us who believe. Ephesians 1:18–19

In the mornings, I love to go outside and walk around our farm and homestead. In the quiet of the morning, I often have heart to heart conversations with God about things on my mind. If I'm worried about one of my children, we talk about it. If I'm concerned about finances, we talk about my budget. If I'm feeling anxious about how Alzheimer's disease is affecting me, we chat about the problems plaguing me. My conversations are informal and I suppose all I'm looking for is hope. I don't necessarily expect God to immediately change things troubling me. I just want Him to know how I'm feeling and I need His reassurance He has everything under control.

Today's Scripture reminds us God has called us into His hope, the riches of His glorious inheritance, and His incomparably great power. I don't know about you, but I need to hear those words often. I forget sometimes how great our heavenly Father truly is in comparison to all my petty problems. Often during our friendly chats, He reminds me how awesome He is by simply drawing my attention to something astounding in His glorious creation. When this happens, I am filled with heavenly hope leading me to conclude He is always in control of everything including all my concerns. All I need do is trust in Him and keep the conversations flowing. So remember, He's called you into hope so call on Him today!

Prayer: Father God, You call us into hope so let us keep calling on You when we need to be reminded of Your great power. Amen

Paul M. Hornback

Wednesday: Conversations in the Garden

Seek the Lord while he may be found; call on him while he is near. Isaiah 55:6

One of my favorite hymns is *In the Garden* and it brings tears to my eyes when we sing it. There have been times during worship when I could not even speak the words because I was so overcome by His spirit as we sang. Perhaps this is because I spend so much time talking with God while working, walking, or standing in the gardens at our home. I am able to open up with Him about all my troubles, joys, concerns, and successes when I'm outside working or walking through the beauty of His creation. The words to the chorus strike at my heart:

And he walks with me
And he talks with me
And he tells me I am his own
And the joy we share as we tarry there
None other has ever known.

Somehow I feel His presence and assurance I am truly His own. I am comforted through our conversations. Even though Alzheimer's disease creeps into my day to steal my thoughts and words, I know He understands my deepest yearnings when I can't verbalize them properly. Perhaps you struggle with these same effects of Alzheimer's disease as it robs your thoughts and words. Just remember, our Lord understands all you are going through and He longs to hear about all your worries, concerns, and hopes for the future. Like today's Scripture from Isaiah says, call upon the Lord while He is near and can be found. So spend some time walking and talking with Him today. Then you will share in His joy and come to realize you are truly His own.

Prayer: Lord, as we walk and talk with You today, help us to understand how precious we are and how much You love us. Amen

398

Thursday: Conversations with a Gracious Lord

Then I called on the name of the Lord: "O Lord, save me!" The Lord is gracious and righteous; our God is full of compassion. The Lord protects the simple-hearted; when I was in great need, he saved me. Psalm 116:4–6

Last night I had the strangest dream. I was at the home of one of our beloved church members where many of our Christian friends were gathered. I was struggling with the symptoms of Alzheimer's disease. I was slow to respond, not following conversations well, forgetting people's names, and in a state of confusion. The interesting aspect of the dream was no one really paid heed to my struggles and everyone was warm and helpful. When I could not find the words to talk, they waited. When I could not remember their names, they introduced themselves. When I had trouble following the conversation, they purposely slowed it down. They all lovingly nurtured me so I felt remarkably comfortable.

I finally awoke and talked with God about my dream and how it made me feel. I asked if this was His way of bringing me hope for the future. I thanked Him for the dream as it put my fears to rest. You see, last night I attended a dinner party and struggled to follow the conversations. I was confused and somewhat anxious. Therefore, I knew the dream was purposely meant to comfort me so I'd stay socially active.

One of the difficult things with Alzheimer's disease is staying socially active. I used to be the life of the party but now I remain quiet. The dream and conversation with God reminded me not to worry. Perhaps you struggle with remaining socially active as well. If so, talk it over with God and He will fill your need.

Prayer: Gracious Lord, You save us in so many ways. Thank You for Your eternal compassion, protection, and graciousness. Amen

Paul M. Hornback

Friday: Conversations of Joy and Gladness

But may all who seek you rejoice and be glad in you; may those who love your salvation always say, "The Lord be exalted."
Psalm 40:16

Our Sunday school lesson this week dealt with one of my favorite fruits of the Spirit, goodness. The lesson, written by Stuart Briscoe, purports we must always measure goodness against the standard God set in dealing with us. Up until this lesson, I thought I was a pretty good person. After the lesson, I realized my goodness pales in comparison to God's goodness.

This particular lesson, made me think about my conversations with God. Was I being the "good" person I should be when I casually converse with God? Was I joyful and spirit filled when I came to him in prayer?

Today's Scripture reminds us to rejoice and be glad in God whenever we seek Him. If we truly love Him and appreciate the blessed salvation He has provided, then we should exalt Him at every opportunity. I realize I fall short of this standard in my dealings with God. I understand how my goodness just doesn't meet the goodness of God. Does this mean I shouldn't come to Him daily? Absolutely not! However, as I grow in the knowledge and understanding of God, my attitude should change from selfishness to gratefulness as I come before Him.

Perhaps you think this isn't possible because you struggle with Alzheimer's disease. The truth is God is still good and deserves your praise no matter what your circumstance. Converse with Him today and rejoice with gladness in your heart. Then you will begin to understand the glory and goodness of God.

Prayer: Good Father, Your gracious goodness fills our lives with joy and gladness. Thank You for all You do for us. Amen

Saturday: Gracious Conversations with God

He who loves a pure heart and whose speech is gracious will have the king for his friend." Proverbs 22:11

We received our first letter from our son in Army boot camp. I know first-hand how stressful boot camp can be but his letter was filled with the joy of doing something important, moving forward toward his career goals, and finally being challenged. Boot camp is tremendously tough as each day is filled with drill instructors barking commands, getting in your face, and never being satisfied with your efforts. Although boot camp has much to complain about, my son's letter was filled with how boot camp was moving him forward in life.

His letter made me think once again about my conversations with God concerning my own boot camp of Alzheimer's disease. I must confess my chats with God have been filled with complaints about how Alzheimer's has limited my activities, changed my daily routine, and upset my future goals. Now I realize even though these things may be true, God already knows how the disease is impacting my life. I'm sure He'd much rather hear how I'm adjusting to the changes, how His word is helping me endure, and how His daily presence is making my life easier. Perhaps I should dwell on these things in my daily conversations with God.

Are your chats with our Lord comprised of complaints or congratulations, gripes or gratitude, problems or praises? Maybe it is time to focus on how God is improving your life rather than the way Alzheimer's is limiting it. Then, like today's passage from Proverbs says, you can be gracious in your speech and the King of Kings will befriend you forever!

Prayer: Lord, give us a pure heart so our speech might be filled with the grace and knowledge of Your precious goodness. Amen

Paul M. Hornback

Sunday: Stillness Leads to Conversations

Be still, and know that I am God; I will be exalted among the nations, I will be exalted in the earth. The Lord Almighty is with us; the God of Jacob is our fortress. Psalms 46:10–11

This morning was incredible! After waking up and starting my morning coffee (an absolute necessity to get moving in the mornings), I noticed it had just started snowing. The flakes were large and beautiful as they fell through the dim light of the dawning day. The snow squall left the ground lightly covered with a beautiful white blanket glistening in the dawn's light. I began thanking God for the delightful dawn display as I finished my morning coffee. God blesses me with something unique on Sunday mornings and it always prepares my heart for worship. The snow silently reminded me to be still before God and exalt Him above all things.

These gentle reminders of God's presence in our lives propel us to carry on conversations of joy and thankfulness with Him. They enable us to set aside the frustrations of dealing with Alzheimer's disease and focus on Him. Perhaps this is why God brings something unique to our Sunday mornings. He wants us to focus on Him as we prepare our minds, hearts, and souls for worship.

What is God preparing for you today so your mind, heart, and soul will be ready to worship Him? Take time to be still before Him and discover the delightful promise of His great gifts manifested in a unique way. Remember to be thankful as you joyfully talk with Him. Then you will be able to set aside your daily frustrations with Alzheimer's disease and be still before God knowing He is Lord of All!

Prayer: Lord, thank You for Your delightful gifts of grace that warm our hearts and draw us ever closer to Your holy presence. Amen

Svetoslav Sokolov © 123RF.com

LIVING LIFE WITH ALZHEIMER'S

Devotions to help you find new ways to live a fruitful life even with Alzheimer's disease.

Monday: Living Loving Lives

"For God so loved the world that he gave his one and only Son, that whoever believes in him shall not perish but have eternal life."
John 3:16

On Sunday, my wife fixes a feast for our extended family and friends to enjoy after church. Today she fixed brownies with ice cream, chocolate sauce, and whipped cream for dessert. It is one of our favorites so there was only one large piece of brownie remaining after lunch. For supper we had a slim salad and, as a reward, we decided to have dessert. Since there was only one large brownie remaining, I jokingly asked my wife if I could divide it and give her the smaller piece. She replied by saying, "Give me as much brownie as you love me!" Wow, was I ever put in my place! You'd better believe she got the bigger piece with lots of chocolate syrup and whipped cream!

Living your life with Alzheimer's disease is much like dividing the last brownie with God. He has provided me abundant life and now I have these few precious years remaining. How will I chose to use them? Will I be generous or selfish? Will I argue with God about my unfortunate condition or will I thank Him for the good days ahead? It all comes down to this one question, "Do I love God more than myself?" If I do, I will live my life with Alzheimer's in a way pleasing to God which reflects my love for Him. Just like my wife said about the brownie, God says, "Give me as much of your life as you love me." Alzheimer's is just a condition with which some of us have to cope. It doesn't mean God no longer loves us. Like today's Scripture reveals, God loved us so much He gave up His one and only Son. As such, we can certainly live our lives in a way that shows our love for Him!

Prayer: Lord, help us live our lives showing our love for You. Amen

Tuesday: Plowing Ahead without Looking Back

Jesus replied, "No one who puts his hand to the plow and looks back is fit for service in the Kingdom of God." Luke 9:62

Growing up as a teenager on a small farm in Kentucky was a great place for my father to begin changing me from a childish boy to a mature young man. He orchestrated this change in some very subtle ways. He balanced hard work on the farm with fatherly chats under nearby shade trees. These chats centered on doing what was honorable, serving your country, helping others, standing by your word, honoring your parents, and taking pride in your work. My father was pretty shrewd in his approach because these father-to-son chats were pretty low key, intertwined with humorous stories or jokes, and always welcomed since it meant a lengthy break from our hard work.

My father taught me hard work was honorable. It was a necessary part of building character and having a sense of accomplishment in life. As I struggle with Alzheimer's disease, I try to view it as yet another hard farm chore to complete. It will take perseverance, hard work, and determination to continue living a worthy life. Just because the task is difficult doesn't mean we can sidestep the challenge.

Like today's Scripture from Luke implies, we must continue moving forward even though the task is difficult. We can't look back at how easy our life once was and decide to throw in the towel. We must continue to plow forward and honor our Lord by striving to live a life worthy of the gospel. Your hand is already on the Alzheimer's plow; what you do now says volumes about who you are in Christ!

Prayer: Father God, give us the strength, determination, and perseverance to plow the row that is ahead of us now. Amen

Paul M. Hornback

Wednesday: The Lord Goes with You

"Be strong and courageous. Do not be afraid or terrified because of them, for the Lord your God goes with you; he will never leave you nor forsake you." Deuteronomy 3:6

As a young boy growing up in Baltimore, I can remember how much I admired and respected my father who was a master sergeant in the Army. I always wanted to do things with him and couldn't wait to spend time with him on the weekends. Three years before my dad retired from the Army, he took a second job as a security guard which meant he had to work every weekend and most holidays.

One Christmas, my dad had to work but he invited me to go along with him. I was in heaven because his assignment for the day was a small manufacturing facility. When we arrived at the factory, I was amazed at the size of the building. I went with him on his first few rounds and got to use the time clock device he carried to the various stations he had to check. After making the initial rounds, Dad asked if I would like to make a round by myself. For a young boy of 11, the factory was pretty scary but I didn't want to show fear and disappoint my dad. I manned up and made the hourly rounds for the rest of his shift. However, I was unaware he followed in the shadows to make sure I didn't panic as I tackled this daunting task.

As I struggle with the daunting task of living with Alzheimer's disease, today's scripture reminds me my heavenly Father also goes with me. Even though the road ahead is difficult, scary and uncertain, I need not be afraid for my God will never leave me nor forsake me. As you struggle with your illness, keep today's Scripture in mind for God is greater than our disease. Therefore you need not fear the future!

Prayer: Lord, thank You for going with us and never leaving. Amen

Thursday: The City of the Dead

Another disciple said to him, "Lord, first let me go and bury my father." But Jesus told him, "Follow me, and let the dead bury their own dead." Matthew 8:21–22

On a recent trip to New Orleans, my wife and I took a tour of an old cemetery located in the city's historic district. The cemetery was quite unusual and contained numerous above ground crypts because the cemetery was below sea level. The cemetery was even surrounded by a wall which also contained crypts. Our guide referred to the cemetery as the "City of the Dead," a name passed on from ages ago.

In today's Scripture, Jesus is talking to one of his disciples who wants to join Him but can't until he buries his father. Jesus' reply is pretty cutting when He says, "Follow me, and let the dead bury their own dead." As I struggle with Alzheimer's disease, I'm tempted to be just like this young disciple. I want to wait to follow Jesus' after I'm cured of my disease. But Jesus says to me, "Follow me and don't worry about being cured because I'm all you need. Like the young disciple who was only offering up an excuse, I easily lean on my disease as an excuse for inaction. Why should I wait to be His disciple? In His service I experience my closest moments with Him and my dear Christian friends. If I wait around for a cure, I'll miss out on a deeper relationship with Him.

How about you? Are you using Alzheimer's disease as an excuse not to follow Him? If you are, change your thinking today and choose to follow Him. Otherwise, you are just like the disciple in today's Scripture who was waiting to become a permanent citizen of the "City of the Dead."

Prayer: Living Lord, help us forget about our disease so we can follow You wholeheartedly and live abundantly in Your care. Amen

Friday: Calming the Storm

He got up, rebuked the wind and said to the waves, "Quiet! Be still!" Then the wind died down and it was completely calm. He said to his disciples, "Why are you so afraid? Do you still have no faith?" Mark 4:39–40

Today's passage from Mark reminds us Christ's perfect power is made manifest in the height of our storms. For the disciples, His power was always with them and He could have easily calmed the storm on the Sea of Galilee at any point. Instead, he waited for the squall to reach a tempest, then commanded the waves to stop and the wind to be still.

As you struggle with Alzheimer's disease, you are in the midst of a terrible storm. Confusion and frustration cloud your days. You may feel tossed about as you wander forgetfully through your home. For me, my storm was made worse as I stressed and worried over what might happen later. I finally turned it all over to Christ and asked Him to calm the storm raging inside my brain. You see, Christ had not left me nor forsaken me. He was with me all along. All I had to do was call out to Him and He readily calmed my storm. Now I am at peace in the midst of my battle with Alzheimer's disease. It is hard to explain how Christ has comforted me in this catastrophic crisis. I no longer worry about what the future brings. Instead, I simply enjoy the pleasures of living an abundant life in Him.

In the midst of an unconscionable illness, He can bring peace and joy if you yield complete control to Him. Christ asks in today's Scripture, "Why are you afraid? Do you still have no faith?" Take firm hold of your faith and ask for His help. He will bring peace in the midst of your raging storm!

Prayer: Comforting Christ, quiet the Alzheimer's storm raging deep within and bring us Your perfect peace. Amen

Saturday: Straining Ahead

Brothers, I do not consider myself yet to have taken hold of it. But one thing I do: Forgetting what is behind and straining toward what is ahead... Philippians 3:13

Today's Scripture comes from the Apostle Paul's prison letter to his beloved church at Philippi. There is little doubt his letter was written while a prisoner under house arrest in Rome. There he was free to share the gospel in his letters and with anyone who came to visit him.

I've never been under house arrest or even imprisoned but I understand the concept of being confined. As a midshipman, I spent 72 days underwater on a submarine where the conditions were confining for an old farm boy used to roaming wide open spaces. I know firsthand how confinement can wear on an individual's sunny disposition. However, the Apostle Paul used his confinement to encourage his fellow followers of Christ and to thank them for their generous gifts. Although Paul was physically confined, he was spiritually free!

While I struggle with Alzheimer's disease, I find myself under house arrest when I don't feel comfortable leaving the boundaries of our homestead. On these days, I try to write encouraging words for my fellow Alzheimer's detainees. Like Paul, I forget about what lies behind (my diagnosis, my struggles, and my fears) and I lean forward to what lies ahead in my continuing walk with Christ (hope and peace). My joy is in Christ, not in the confines of Alzheimer's disease. Christ holds the key and I place my trust in Him. If Paul can spread joy during confinement, then why can't I do the same? Perhaps you can benefit from straining toward the cross of Christ and allow Him to frame your future!

Prayer: Lord, help us strain forward to a Christ focused future. Amen

Paul M. Hornback

Sunday: Stillness Brings Life

Be still, and know that I am God; I will be exalted among the nations, I will be exalted in the earth. The Lord Almighty is with us; the God of Jacob is our fortress. Psalms 46:10–11

It is very early in the morning and once again I've awoken long before the alarm went off. The house is quiet as Black Jack, Poco, Slayer, and Joe (my four Chihuahuas) are still curled up asleep waiting for dawn to break. Quiet mornings are a special gift for me. I can be still with God before the disruptive distractions of my daily routine unfold. I often read Scripture, meditate on the passage as I sip my morning coffee, and talk with the Lord about situations in my life. In the stillness of a quiet morning, I find it easy to know He is God.

This morning I read Psalm 46. It begins by declaring God is our refuge, our strength, and an ever-present source of help when in trouble. I find this especially comforting as I face my troubles with Alzheimer's disease. God has been my refuge, source of strength, and ever-present help as I struggle with the limitations brought on by this illness. God helps me cope by reminding me about all the things I can still do! I am truly thankful and gratitude fills my prayers daily.

As you struggle with the effects of Alzheimer's disease, find time to be still before the Lord and thank Him for all the things you can still do in your life. He is an amazing God! He wants to be the Lord of your life and your ever-present help when Alzheimer's clouds your daily routine. Be still before Him today, know He is God alone, and remember He is worthy of your praise!

Prayer: Father God, thank You for the quiet moments we spend together in the early mornings. Help us to be still before You and listen to Your words of encouragement. Amen

Fotoklok © 123RF.com

UNWANTED JOURNEYS

Devotions to help you understand that unwanted journeys are a part of life with Alzheimer's disease.

Paul M. Hornback

Monday: A Walk to Prison

When his master heard the story his wife told him, saying, "This is how your slave treated me," he burned with anger. Joseph's master took and put him in prison, the place where the king's prisoners were confined. But while Joseph was in prison, the Lord was with him; Genesis 39:19–21

We all know the story of Joseph and how he was sold into slavery. You probably remember how Potiphar's wife tried to seduce Joseph but he loved his master so much he honorably resisted her advances. Even though Joseph did the honorable thing he was still put in prison. Can you imagine how Joseph felt as he was escorted to the jail reserved for the King's prisoners? He had done nothing wrong, honored his master, made him successful, avoided the advances of an unfaithful wife, honored his father's teachings, and is locked up in prison with men of questionable character. Needless to say, the walk to prison was probably a walk Joseph didn't want to take.

I can remember a similar walk. After several visits, my neurologist recommended I have a positron emission tomography (PET) scan to determine why I was having so many problems with memory and reasoning. I remember being pretty anxious about the test and what might be revealed. After getting injected with the special dye before the process began, I remember a perfect peace came over me. I was calm for the rest of the procedure. It was weeks before I heard back from the doctor and he said we needed to talk. I can remember thinking I'd done nothing wrong in my life and was a reasonably good man. Why this? But God would use it for His good and His glory just like He did with Joseph. You see, God is with me and He is surely with you. You simply have to trust in Him!

Prayer: Lord, be with us and may Your favor shine upon us. Amen

Tuesday: A Walk in the Desert

The whole Israelite community set out from the Desert of Sin, traveling from place to place as the Lord commanded. They camped at Rephidim, but there was no water for the people to drink. So they quarreled with Moses and said, "Give us water to drink." Moses replied, "Why do you quarrel with me? Why do you put the Lord to the test?" Exodus 17:1–2

Moses must have wondered why he ever agreed to lead these people on their historic walk through the desert. All they did was complain about the food and drink! At times he even thought they'd stone him to death because they'd rather die in Egypt around pots of meat and vats of wine than live starving and thirsty in the desert! Moses did all God wanted him to do and yet God's people were still not content. This walk through the desert wasn't what the travel brochure promised, was it?

I remember my epic walk to the doctor's office after all the special tests, blood work, trips to famous clinics, and mental testing was over. I was ready for some answers and I was darn sure I didn't want any more testing! Boy, did I ever get an answer when he told me I had early-onset Alzheimer's disease. Thus began my personal walk in the desert.

Perhaps you are on your heroic walk in the Alzheimer's desert and maybe it's not all the travel brochure promised. Even though it's not the walk you envisioned taking, you won't walk it alone. Like the children of Israel, God goes graciously along on your desert trek. Hopefully you are not like those whining children, complaining all along the way even when God met all their basic needs! Walk in confidence. God is with you and is preparing the path ahead. Besides, like Moses said in today's Scripture, why would you want to test God?

Prayer: Father, walk with us on our desert journey. Amen

Wednesday: A Walk to a Furious King

Furious with rage, Nebuchadnezzar summoned Shadrach, Meshach and Abednego. So these men were brought before the king, and Nebuchadnezzar said to them, "Is it true, Shadrach, Meshach and Abednego, that you do not serve my gods or worship the image of gold I have set up?" Daniel 3:13–14

I wonder what Shadrach, Meshach and Abednego were thinking when they walked into the chambers of King Nebuchadnezzar after refusing to worship his images of gold. Were they anxious and terrified or were they confident and exuberant in their faith? All we know is they would only worship the Lord their God and not Nebuchadnezzar.

I remember the walk into my family room to tell my children I had early-onset Alzheimer's disease. Initially I was pretty confident in my ability to lay it all out but as I got started my confidence gave way as I found it difficult to talk without tears. In the back of my mind I was struggling with why this had happened to me. Had I done something terribly wrong, was it part of my gene pool, or was this just Satan's way of trying to turn my faith around? I just wanted my children to know I trusted God and believed He would help me through the rough road ahead. Like Shadrach, Meshach and Abednego, my Lord would be my salvation through this trial.

I don't know how this walk will turn out or the path God will choose for me. All I know is He will guide me through the fiery furnace awaiting me! Perhaps you are struggling with your walk right now. If you are, remember the strong faith, confidence, and conviction of Shadrach, Meshach and Abednego. Then face your fiery furnace knowing God is already there waiting to walk you through its fiery flames!

Prayer: Lord, protect us from the fiery furnaces we face. Amen

Thursday: A Walk into Uncertainty

But David thought to himself, "One of these days I will be destroyed by the hand of Saul. The best thing I can do is to escape to the land of the Philistines. Then Saul will give up searching for me anywhere in Israel, and I will slip out of his hand." 1 Samuel 27:1

I love to read the exciting exploits of David as he wrestled with his unfaltering faith in God, commitment to the anointed King, solemn oath to Jonathan, and deep love for Israel. Today's passage explains how David dealt with the continual threat of death from King Saul; he opted to leave Israel. I'm sure he desired to stay in his homeland rather than walk into a land of uncertainty. David left Israel knowing God would be with him as he sought refuge with the Philistines.

I understand the feeling of uncertainty David felt as he left his homeland. I felt it the day I walked into my first appointment to start my clinical trial for Alzheimer's disease. I was scared but knew I had to do something to help in the fight against Alzheimer's. I had no idea what I was about to embark on but I was certain God would be walking with me. He even arranged things so I got the test drug rather than the placebo. That was pretty awesome!

Perhaps you are struggling with your battle and wonder how God is moving on your behalf. Rest assured He has already prepared the way as you step out in faith to walk into your land of uncertainty. He will definitely not leave you nor will He forsake you. Like God did for David in the land of the Philistines, He will protect you and give you safe passage!

Prayer: Lord, abide with us daily in our walks of uncertainty. Amen

Friday: A Walk of Servitude

So Joseph also went up from the town of Nazareth in Galilee to Judea, to Bethlehem the town of David, because he belonged to the house and line of David. He went there to register with Mary, who was pledged to be married to him and was expecting a child.
Luke 2:4–5

I can't begin to imagine the journey Joseph and Mary took as they walked to Bethlehem to register for Caesar Augustus' census. Not only was the journey long but it really served no useful purpose for them. Unfortunately, because they lived under Roman rule, they had no choice but to comply with the government's demands. Thankfully, God had everything planned out so His precious son would be born in just the right place, time, and manner He had envisioned. The only necessity was for Joseph and Mary to follow through with their walk of servitude to Bethlehem.

Sometimes we are forced to take a walk of servitude even though we don't see any useful purpose in doing it. My walk of servitude was to our lawyer's office after I was diagnosed with early-onset Alzheimer's disease. Based on our research and our lawyer's advice, we were directed to put everything in my wife's name. My lifetime of accumulating "stuff" in my name was over. I had to rely on God, stop being selfish, and trust my wife. I knew what needed to be done and trusted God to help me in this humble walk of servitude.

Perhaps you are struggling with a similar situation. If so, remember how Joseph and Mary complied with their decree. Then follow through with what you need to do knowing God is faithfully watching out for your best interests. Just trust Him and act accordingly!

Prayer: Lord, help us faithfully follow the footsteps of Joseph as we begin our walk of servitude. Amen

Saturday: A Walk to the Garden of Decision

*Then Jesus went with his disciples to a place called
Gethsemane, and he said to them, "Sit here while I go over there
and pray." He took Peter and the two sons of Zebedee along with
him, and he began to be sorrowful and troubled. Matthew 26:36–37*

It's impossible to understand the sorrow and troubled thoughts
Jesus had while He prayed at Gethsemane prior to His arrest by the
Sanhedrin. Today's passage from Matthew lays the groundwork for
what Jesus faced. A similar passage in Mark says Jesus' "soul was
overwhelmed with sorrow to the point of death." You see, Jesus was
wrestling with His earthly desire to continue His ministry and live
versus His heavenly decree to endure the cross and die. He prayed so
earnestly about this decision Luke records His sweat was like drops
of blood.

I'm sure I've never prayed in such an intense manner about
anything. However, I do understand what it's like to be sorrowful
and troubled over a situation. Since my diagnosis of early-onset
Alzheimer's disease, I have been wrestling with my decision to
continue driving. I have limited my driving to only very familiar
places. I no longer take long road trips to just drive around viewing
the scenery. This was one of my favorite things to do but I know it is
no longer an option. Now, my wife does most of the driving and I
stay within a five mile radius of home. This makes her feel
comfortable and I admit I feel comfortable as well. Soon I'll have to
give up my driver's license but I'm prepared to do so at my family's
request.

Perhaps you are also wrestling with this issue. Like Jesus, we
must decide to put the welfare of others ahead of our own. If you're
hesitating, take a walk in a garden. It worked for Jesus.

*Prayer: Lord, help us make our tough decisions appropriately
after we've prayed earnestly with You about them. Amen*

Paul M. Hornback

Paul M. Hornback

Vlastimil Kuzel © 123RF.com

WRAPPING IT UP

Devotions to help you discern additional ways to live a faithful life with Alzheimer's disease.

Paul M. Hornback

Monday: Run the Race to Get the Prize

*Do you not know that in a race all the runners run, but only one
gets the prize? Run in such a way as to get the prize.*
1 Corinthians 9:24

As a long time runner, I appreciate the analogy Paul uses in
today's passage to the church at Corinth. I ran my "race" for three
specific reasons: to reduce the stress of a high pressure career, to
improve my health, and to maintain my fighting weight! This triad of
benefits was the precious prize for running the race successfully. The
Apostle Paul uses this analogy to inspire the Corinthians in their
spiritual race to spread the gospel in a manner worthy of Christ's
sacrifice.

After being diagnosed with Alzheimer's disease, I made a
conscious decision to continue running my spiritual race in a manner
worthy of the prize of Christ. I could have simply given up the
challenge and let Alzheimer's run its course. No one would have
blamed me for this "selfish" action because I have only a few good
years left so why spend them serving others? Instead, I opted to
press on in my spiritual race in spite of my situation. I continue to
teach, write, read, pray, serve, and give like nothing changed in my
life. You see, in a race there are often steep hills runners must endure
if they are to complete the race. I see Alzheimer's as just another
steep hill in my spiritual race. Rather than give up, I push on to the
top!

Perhaps you are struggling in your spiritual race as you deal
with Alzheimer's disease. Don't give up hope. Hold on to what Paul
penned in today's passage. Keep running but do run in a manner
worthy of Christ's calling. Run so you will get the prize waiting for
you in Heaven's winners' circle.

*Prayer: Faithful Father, help us to run our race with
endurance, strength, faith, honor, and dignity as we continue in
service. Amen*

Tuesday: Strict Training for the Race

Everyone who competes in the games goes into strict training. They do it to get a crown that will not last; but we do it to get a crown that will last forever." 1 Corinthians 9:25

Yesterday we witnessed the terrible tragedy at the Boston Marathon where terrorists exploded two Improvised Explosive Devices (IED's) causing several deaths and massive injuries. The heroic actions of bystanders, first responders, doctors, nurses, and aid workers saved many lives. This tragedy got me thinking that during a marathon there are many others who've also trained their lifetime to compete, not just the runners. In the case of the Boston Marathon, first responders, doctors, nurses, aid workers, and police have spent years training for an emergency just like the one yesterday. They don't do it to get recognition, awards, or trophies. They do it in service to their fellow countrymen.

Today's Scripture reminds us we also compete in a game requiring strict training. It's a spiritual game requiring years of reading, study, memorization, prayer, service, and worship. All these disciplines come together to create a spiritual athlete ready to face Satan's terrorists. It is not an easy competition by any definition and requires years of tough training.

My years of tough training served me well when Alzheimer's came knocking. Without this training, I would have lost and fallen out of the race. Instead, I continue my race knowing a crown awaits me if I don't give up. As you face your race remember you don't run it alone. God is with you and will continue to help you along the way. So stay in the race and perhaps you can be a spiritual first responder to someone who has felt the sting of one of Satan's IED's.

Prayer: Father, help us to continue training, running the race you've marked out for us, and maintaining our relationship with you. Amen

Paul M. Hornback

Wednesday: A Spiritual Race

Therefore, I do not run like a man running aimlessly; I do not fight like a man beating the air. 1 Corinthians 9:26

I have to admit there are days in my battle with Alzheimer's disease when I feel like I am running a race aimlessly or fighting like a man beating the air. Of course, these days correspond with my foggy days of confusion. On these days, I have to struggle to write, read, pray, and find purposeful activities to help me muddle through the confusion. I also have to rely on my faith to keep me moving forward. I have to remember I serve a Savior who wants only the best for me and promises to give me life more abundantly.

Today's passage reminds us even in our days of struggle we live for a higher purpose with a heavenly focus. We live to serve our Master and share His good news with a world hungry for truth. After being diagnosed with Alzheimer's disease, I finally understood the reason for the foggy days I had been experiencing. Like Paul, I have a thorn in the flesh reminding me my life on earth is only temporary. Therefore, I must press on to share my struggles and my hope which is Jesus Christ.

As I share my story, my race is no longer aimless nor is my fight like a man beating the air. My battle is with the spiritual forces of darkness condemning mankind and playing on the weaknesses of our flesh. If you feel like I do, remember you don't fight alone but with a risen Savior who stands by your side urging you forward. His story is your story and your story is His story. Together you press on in a spiritual battle!

Prayer: Lord, we don't fight alone for You are with us. Help us lean on You when our flesh is weak for the battle ahead. Amen

422

Thursday: Confidence in Christ

Such confidence as this is ours through Christ before God. Not that we are competent in ourselves to claim anything for ourselves, but our competence comes from God. 2 Corinthians 3:4–5

While on vacation in Savannah we ate lunch at the infamous Lady and Sons Restaurant owned by Paula Dean. Before we entered we knew the food would be fabulous because we had to make reservations a day ahead just to have lunch. We were not disappointed because the aroma from the buffet was absolutely incredible. After filling our plates and sitting at the table, we noticed there wasn't any salt or pepper. Rather than ask for it, we dove right in and to our surprise we didn't need either seasoning. The food was so delicious no additional flavoring was required. Paula was so confident in her recipes and chefs she purposely left salt and pepper off the tables!

Today's Scripture reminds us we too should be confident of our recipe in Christ. As Christians, we should need no other seasoning for our Lord's recipe is perfect. Even though I struggle with the daily difficulties of Alzheimer's disease, I still need to be confident in the Lord's recipe for my life. He is the Master Chef and nothing He has planned for me needs to be adjusted, tweaked, or modified to improve it. If my recipe for life includes Alzheimer's, then so be it. All I need do is trust the Master Chef and rely on Him alone.

Perhaps you are struggling with your life's recipe. I urge you to stop and talk with the Master. Listen to His words, be courageous, and trust He knows what is best for you. His recipes are perfect since they are seasoned with the Holy Spirit. Therefore, remain confident in Christ for He is confident in you.

Prayer: Lord, may our confidence remain in You alone. Amen

Friday: Diligence in Faith

*God is not unjust; he will not forget your work and the love you
have shown him as you helped his people and continue to help them.
We want each of you to show this same diligence to the very end, in
order to make your hope sure. We do not want you to become lazy,
but to imitate those who through faith and patience inherit what has
been promised. Hebrews 6:10–12*

As human beings we desperately desire to be the center of
attention. My niece Mary is no exception. She loves to be the center
of everything but in a good way. Whenever we gather for family
meals and talk about her various achievements, her entire face
brightens up as she gets this incredibly beautiful smile on her face.
Of course, we often talk about her just to see her bright smiling face
come to life!

If we aren't the center of attention, we feel forgotten. During
difficult times, Christians may think God has deserted them and
forgotten all they've accomplished for Him. People who struggle
with Alzheimer's are especially prone to this as they deal with the
difficulties of the disease.

Today's passage says our loving Father has not forgotten our
plight or our good works. Perhaps as you wrestle with today's
Scripture and your unique situation, you wonder if it's possible to
remain faithful, trust the Lord, and hold on to hope. I would have to
answer a resounding yes to all three. Since my diagnosis, my faith
has grown beyond measure. His angels watch over me and keep me
out of harm's way. He has met every need in my life. He is the air I
breathe and my daily bread. Therefore, remain diligent and trust in
the promises He has made for those who call Him Abba!

Prayer: Lord, help us to be diligent in our faith and hope. Amen

Saturday: A Caregiving Companion

Let us then approach the throne of grace with confidence, so that we might receive mercy and find grace to help us in our time of need. Hebrews 4:16

While enjoying my morning coffee on the front porch, two geese flew gracefully overhead. One honked encouragingly to the other one as they headed on their northward flight. At this time of year, there are normally many more geese flying in their signature "V" formation and honking like crazy. This morning I found it strange there were only two geese in the gaggle. Then I remember reading if a goose is ill, weak, or falls out of the gaggle another goose stays with it. Perhaps today's gaggle of two geese was the result of such an event.

It got me thinking about my weakened condition with Alzheimer's disease. I once soared with a large flock of humans at work, church, and play. That is no longer the case as I find it difficult to keep up with the crowd in conversation, stamina, and desire. Now, like one of the weakened geese, I travel with only one companion. She is my incredible wife of 38 years who has vowed to stay by my side. Of course, I'm absolutely confident the Lord is by my side as well.

Today's Scripture prompts us to remain confident as we approach the throne of grace so we will be mercifully blessed and discover His glorious grace. A faithful companion like a spouse, child, friend or professional caregiver, is indeed a merciful gift from God if you have Alzheimer's disease. If you are blessed with such a companion, thank the Lord for His great blessing in your life. In fact, honk out loud like geese do so God hears your wonderful expression of gratitude!

Prayer: Lord, we are blessed in so many marvelous ways by Your extended mercy. Thank You for meeting our every need. Amen

Paul M. Hornback

Sunday: Stillness in Prayer

*Be still, and know that I am God; I will be exalted among the
nations, I will be exalted in the earth. The Lord Almighty is with us;
the God of Jacob is our fortress. Psalms 46:10–11*

It has rained all weekend here on the farm making everything
green and beautiful. The grass is wet this morning and the four
Chihuahuas are extremely hesitant to venture out on the lawn to take
care of their morning duties. In fact, the dogs would have preferred
to go back to their warm beds rather than get their feet wet. This
made me think how often we hesitate to take care of our Christian
duties because we'd rather stay in our warm beds rather spend time
with the Lord in prayer and meditation.

Today's passage from Psalms prompts us to be still before the
Lord so we might exalt Him above all things. It has been almost six
years now since I started struggling with the daily demands of
Alzheimer's disease. My memory continues to decline, my
vocabulary dwindles, and my foggy days are beginning to outweigh
my days of clarity. However, I have noticed in the past few months it
is easier to be still before the Lord because I'm not thinking about
other things. I suppose this is a blessing in disguise.

When I pray, I now rely on the Holy Spirit to help when my
words and thoughts are jumbled. As a result, my prayer time is more
precious than before. Take time today to be still before the Lord in
prayer. Ask the Holy Spirit to take over if your words and thoughts
become too muddled. Perhaps you will discover a glorious peace
surpassing all understanding as you bask in the warmth of your
heavenly Father's presence.

*Prayer: Lord, let us be still before You today and come to know
You are the one true God in whom our faith and future rests. Amen*

Starry Night Publishing

Everyone has a story...

Don't spend your life trying to get published! Don't tolerate rejection! Don't do all the work and allow the publishing companies reap the rewards!

Millions of independent authors like you, are making money, publishing their stories now. Our technological know-how will take the headaches out of getting published. Let "Starry Night Publishing.Com" take care of the hard parts, so you can focus on writing. You simply send us your Word Document and we do the rest. It really is that simple!

The big companies want to publish only "celebrity authors," not the average book-writer. It's almost impossible for first-time authors to get published today. This has led many authors to go the self-publishing route. Until recently, this was considered "vanity-publishing." You spent large sums of your money, to get twenty copies of your book, to give to relatives at Christmas, just so you could see your name on the cover. Now, however, the self-publishing industry allows authors to get published in a timely fashion, retain the rights to your work, keeping up to ninety-percent of your royalties, instead of the traditional five-percent.

We've opened up the gates, allowing you inside the world of publishing. While others charge you as much as fifteen-thousand dollars for a publishing package, we charge less than five-hundred dollars to cover copyright, ISBN, and distribution costs. Do you really want to spend all your time formatting, converting, designing a cover, and then promoting your book, because no one else will?

Our editors are professionals, able to create a top-notch book that you will be proud of. Becoming a published author is supposed to be fun, not a hassle.

At Starry Night Publishing, you submit your work, we create a professional-looking cover, a table of contents, compile your text and images into the appropriate format, convert your files for eReaders, take care of copyright information, assign an ISBN, allow you to keep one-hundred-percent of your rights, distribute your story worldwide on Amazon, Barnes & Noble and many other retailers, and write you a check for your royalties. There are no other hidden fees involved! You don't pay extra for a cover, or to keep your book in print. We promise! Everything is included! You even get a free copy of your book and unlimited half-price copies.

In four short years, we've published more than fifteen-hundred books, compared to the major publishing houses which only add an average of six new titles per year. We will publish your fiction, or non-fiction books about anything, and look forward to reading your stories and sharing them with the world.

We sincerely hope that you will join the growing Starry Night Publishing family, become a published author and gain the world-wide exposure that you deserve. You deserve to succeed. Success comes to those who make opportunities happen, not those who wait for opportunities to happen. You just have to try. Thanks for joining us on our journey.

www.starrynightpublishing.com

www.facebook.com/starrynightpublishing/

Made in the USA
San Bernardino, CA
22 April 2016